STUDY GUIDE

Michael Konopaski
Trent University

John Friedlan
University of Ontario Institute of Technology

Financial Accounting
A Critical Approach

John Friedlan
University of Ontario Institute of Technology

Toronto

0-13-039243-X

Executive Acquisitions Editor: Samantha Scully
Developmental Editor: Meaghan Eley
Production Editor: Mary Ann McCutcheon
Production Coordinator: Deborah Starks

2 3 4 5 08 07 06 05 04

Printed and bound in Canada.

Table of Contents

Introduction

Welcome to introductory financial accounting. Being able to understand and interpret accounting information is essential for all business people and is important and useful for others as well. However, many students find accounting to be the most difficult, frustrating, and time-consuming course they take. Even the best students can struggle with many of the concepts and methods in accounting. In writing *Financial Accounting: A Critical Approach* I have tried to explain the concepts, ideas, and issues as clearly and as thoroughly as I could. I hope that I have been successful in achieving this goal.

That said, why is a Study Companion needed to support an already thorough textbook? I think that the textbook stands well on its own and it is possible to succeed at introductory financial accounting using only the textbook. Still, many students find that they need or want some extra assistance in working though the textbook. This is where Study Companion comes in. I wrote this Study Companion to provide that helping hand that many students want.

The biggest challenge I faced in writing the Study Companion was figuring out what should go into it. I felt that it shouldn't re-explain what was in the textbook itself since I provided the best possible discussions and explanations that I could in the textbook. If my discussions and explanations in the Study Companion were better than what is in the text itself, those discussions and explanations should be in the textbook. So what I have provided in the Study Companion for each chapter is as follows:

- A brief overview of the chapter
- Study points and study tips for the material in the chapter
- Solved study problems

The overview provides a summary of the content of the chapter. The purpose is to briefly let you know what the chapter covered and how the chapter fits in the context of the entire book. The overview will not serve as a thorough review of the chapter but it will identify the main themes and provide a framework for approaching your studying. The study points and study tips highlight important and difficult parts of the chapter and give some insight and guidance on how to think about, understand, and study the material in the chapter.

For each chapter I have selected a number of Study Problems that reflect the material that is covered in the chapter. Each Study Problem has a detailed solution and I have provided commentary where appropriate to explain the solution. Needless to say, your learning will be best served by attempting the Study Problems *before* looking at the solutions. Some of these problems will challenge you to think and apply your knowledge. Others will test your mechanics. Also, and very important, as is pointed out in the book, there is often more than one "right answer" or approach to the assignment material in the book and to the Study Problems in this Companion. Do not be discouraged if your response does not exactly reflect the solution provided. You may have followed a valid approach that differs from the one I used. If you think your approach makes sense but is different from the one provided, it may be worthwhile to discuss the situation with your instructor. It is also important to emphasize that while there is often more than one right answer to accounting problems, there are always wrong ones. The statement that there is "no one right answer" does not imply that all answers are right.

The Study Companion is not a substitute for the book itself. You can't read the Companion and expect to know what is in the book. The Study Companion is intended to support your study of the book. Don't expect to read the Study Companion just before your exam or assignment and be successful. You must use the Study Companion in conjunction with the textbook.

Your course in financial accounting will be challenging and interesting. I hope that you find my book, *Financial Accounting: A Critical Approach*, interesting and an asset to your study.

John Friedlan

Chapter 1
The Accounting Environment: What Is Accounting and Why Is It Done?

Chapter Overview

Chapter 1 of the text states that accounting is full of mystery and intrigue. Mystery and intrigue? Come on, this is accounting. Surprising as it may seem, accounting is a subject that requires judgement, analysis, interpretation, and even intuition to make the most of it. Numbers in financial statements cannot simply be taken at face value. *Financial Accounting: A Critical Approach* was written to introduce you to some of the mystery and intrigue of accounting and help you learn to use accounting information effectively. Chapter 1 starts the journey by introducing some of the context of accounting. To understand accounting information it is necessary to understand the factors that influence how accounting is done in any given situation—factors such as who will be using the information, who is preparing it and why, and the overall environment that entities operate in. Chapter 1 also explains the nature of accounting and accounting information.

Summary of Key Points

- Accounting is a system for producing information about an entity and communicating that information to people who want or need the information for making decisions. Effective decision making requires information, and accounting is a crucial source of information. The numbers in an accounting report tell a story but the numbers cannot be taken at face value. Using, preparing, and understanding accounting information requires a set of high-level cognitive skills, including judgment, analysis, synthesis, evaluation, problem solving, critical thinking, and creativity.

  Preparers of accounting information often have considerable leeway and choice in how they will do their accounting. The existence of choices makes it necessary for users to exercise a great deal of care to ensure they are aware of the choices that the preparer made and of how those choices affect their decisions.

  Financial accounting is the field of accounting that provides information to people who are external to an entity—people who do not have direct access to an entity's information. Managerial accounting is the field of accounting that provides information to the managers of the entity and other decision makers who work for the entity to assist them in making decisions related to operating the entity.

- Accounting does not operate in a vacuum. You cannot sensibly use or provide accounting information without considering the accounting environment, which includes the social, political, legal, cultural, and economic environment of a society, the types of entities that are of interest to stakeholders and the characteristics of those entities, the different stakeholders that may have an interest in an entity, and the constraints that limit the accounting choices an entity can make. The diversity of the accounting environment makes it impossible for a single accounting report to be appropriate for all situations. Accounting reports must be tailored to suit the circumstances of an entity's accounting environment.

- The stakeholders in an entity who require accounting information for their decision making rely on the entity to provide the information. The preparers are not neutral. When preparing accounting reports preparers may be influenced by their own personal interests, and these interests may conflict with those of the stakeholders.

- The most valuable use of the information produced by accounting systems is that it allows stakeholders to measure different attributes of an entity. Two characteristics of accounting information make it especially useful for measuring the attributes of an entity. First, accounting information is quantitative; second, accounting information is presented in terms a single unit of measure, usually money. These characteristics make it possible for the data entered into an accounting system to be organized, processed, and converted into information that is useful to stakeholders.

- GAAP are the principles, conventions, practices, procedures, and rules that define acceptable accounting practices and guide the preparation of financial statements in certain situations. A set of rules for preparing accounting information can help reduce the cost and difficulty of communication between entities and users. Canadian GAAP describe four qualitative characteristics that financial statement information must have in order to be useful to users: understandability, relevance, reliability and comparability. GAAP do not provide solutions to all accounting problems. GAAP are not universal, not every entity needs or is required to follow GAAP, and GAAP are flexible.

Study Points and Study Tips

What is Accounting?

- Accounting is a system for producing information about an entity and communicating that information to people who want or need it for making decisions.
  - Crucial in this definition is communication. If accounting does not effectively communicate with the people using the information it is not serving a useful purpose.

- Accounting systems accumulate data about an entity's economic activities and convert them so that they can be useful for making decisions. There are a number of complexities involved in this process:
  - First, there are many people with different interests and different decisions to make about an entity. It is not likely that the same information will be best for all these different people.
  - Second, it is not always obvious how an entity's various economic activities should be accounted for. Economic activity can be very complex and summarizing it in an accounting system can require judgement and interpretation by the people who prepare the accounting information.
  - Third, the people who manage an entity and who are responsible for preparing the accounting information can be affected economically by the information. As a result, these people are not likely neutral in how they approach the preparation of the information. This is not to say that these people are dishonest or unethical. Rather, like most people, their personal interests affect their choices. These interests can include such things as the amount of compensation they receive, their personal wealth, and the amount of tax they pay.
  - These three factors help explain why accounting is full of mystery and intrigue and why it can take detective work to fully make sense of accounting information. At this early stage these points may be confusing or unclear. This is understandable since we haven't even begun to look at actual accounting information. However, these points are important and they are repeated throughout the book because they are so fundamental to being able to understand and use accounting information.

Why do People Need and Want Information?

- People need and want information so that they can make better decisions. Without information a "decision" is nothing more than a guess.
- Not all information is equivalent. Information will vary in quality depending on its source and appropriateness for the decision at hand. Information that is relevant for one decision may not be relevant for another.
  - This general point about the usefulness of any particular piece of information depending on the intended use is very important for accounting. Accounting information, for example the information contained in financial statements, will not be equally useful for all decisions and all decision makers.
- Accounting is an important source of information for decision makers. However, accounting is not the only source of information. There are many different sources and types of information that can provide valuable input into a decision. Some examples of other sources of information include newspapers, press releases by an entity, and information about the economy can be important sources of information.
- There are limits to the amount of information that people will gather.
  - Information will only be gathered if the benefit exceeds the cost. If the cost of gathering information is greater than the benefit, the decision maker will actually be worse off by having gathered the information. In economic terms this cost benefit tradeoff means that information will be acquired until the marginal cost of the information equals the marginal benefit.
  - There are also limits to the amount of information a decision maker can process and manage. Too much information, or information overload, can impair a decision maker's ability to make decisions.

The Two Fields of Accounting: Financial and Managerial Accounting

- Accounting is usually divided into two fields, financial and managerial.
  - Financial accounting refers to the field of accounting that provides information to people who are external to an entity. These external users include investors, lenders, taxation authorities (Canada Customs and Revenue Agency), competitors, and many more. Usually users of financial accounting information do not have direct access to information about the entity and must rely on the entity to provide information to them.
  - Managerial accounting refers to the field of accounting that provides information to the managers of the entity and other decision makers who work for the entity. This information assists them in making decisions related to operating the entity, including setting the price of products, deciding whether the company should expand, determining which products are successful and which are not, figuring out how much should be produced, and so on. Managerial accounting information is often much more detailed than financial accounting information, and its content and organization is more flexible.
  - While these two fields of accounting are described separately and are usually taught as separate courses, they are not independent. Entities usually collect and organize information in a single accounting system, so that even though the information is presented differently for the two fields, "financial" and "managerial" accounting information usually comes from the same pool of data.

The Accounting Environment

- The preparation of accounting information does not take place in a vacuum. The accounting environment affects what and how information is presented to stakeholders. The accounting environment represents the context in which accounting operates. Figure 1-1 in the text provides a framework for the approach used in the book. The figure emphasizes a number of important factors:
  - The nature of a society—its political, cultural, economic, competitive, regulatory, and legal institutions and traditions—will significantly impact its accounting. The society's accounting evolves from these institutions and traditions and differences among different societies help explain why accounting is different in different countries.
  - An entity is an economic unit of some kind. An entity can be an individual, a business, part of a business, a charity, a school, a government, a club, or an industry, and so on. Whether an entity will provide information to a decision maker depends on the characteristics of the entity and the relationship the decision maker has with the entity.
    - There are three types of business entities:
      - Corporations—Corporations are separate legal entities created under the corporation laws of Canada or of a province, or of some other jurisdiction in the world. A corporation has many of the rights and responsibilities that an individual has (they must file tax returns, can be sued, and can enter into contracts). Corporations provide limited liability to their shareholders. It is relatively easy to transfer ownership of a corporation from one shareholder to another. The shares of public corporations can be purchased by anyone who is interested in owning a piece of the entity and has the money to buy the shares. The shares of public corporations can usually be purchased or sold on a stock exchange. A private corporation is one whose shares and other securities are not available for purchase without agreement by the private corporation or its shareholders.
      - Proprietorships—A proprietorship is an unincorporated business that has one owner.
      - Partnerships—A partnership is an unincorporated business owned by two or more individuals called partners.
    - Non-business entities include not-for-profit organizations, governments, and individuals.
  - Stakeholders are groups or individuals that have an interest or a "stake" in an entity. The interests of the various stakeholders are different and they have different decisions to make. Different stakeholders may require different information to make their decisions. Examples of stakeholders include owners, lenders, suppliers, governments, taxation authorities, and consumers (see Figure 1-1 for more stakeholders).
  - Characteristics of entities—Each entity has a set of characteristics that make it unique. An entity's characteristics may influence the accounting choices its managers make. Characteristics include size, industry, ownership, risk, and stage in the life cycle (see Figure 1-1 for more characteristics).
  - Constraints—How an entity does its accounting and what information it reports are not entirely up to the people who prepare the information. Often, the choices available are constrained by contracts, laws, accounting rules, and the information needs and demands of powerful users of accounting information.

- Stakeholders versus preparers
  - The preparers of accounting information are the people responsible for deciding what, how, and when information is going to be presented in an entity's financial statements and other accounting reports. The preparers (or managers) are not likely to be neutral in how they approach preparing financial statements.
  - This perspective may be surprising to people new to the study of accounting. The reality of accounting is that there can often be more than one way to report an entity's economic activity. This does not mean that there is fraud or misrepresentation occurring (although this does happen). There are often legitimate alternative ways of accounting. The textbook devotes considerable space to exploring the existence and implications of these alternatives.
  - There are two main explanations for why preparers of accounting information are not neutral:
    - Entities usually have many stakeholders with different information needs. It is usually not possible or practical to provide separate information to each stakeholder. Therefore, the preparers must choose among the competing interests of the different stakeholders.
    - Preparers have their own interests. An entity's financial statements can have economic consequences for the entity's managers and these consequences may influence how they choose to account. These economic consequences probably explain many of the corporate scandals that have occurred in recent years.
  - The implication of this imperfect relationship between stakeholders and preparers is that the accounting information that a stakeholder receives from an entity may not be fully appropriate for the decision that stakeholder has to make. This means that stakeholders must be able to critically evaluate the information in financial statements and other accounting reports so that they can assess its appropriateness.

Accounting is for Measurement

- Accounting systems are designed to allow measurement of various attributes of an entity. Attributes that accounting information can help measure include performance of an entity and its managers, the amount of tax an entity should pay, and the value of the entity.
- Two characteristics of accounting information make it useful for measuring the attributes of an entity.
  - Accounting information is quantitative.
  - The accounting information that is produced by an accounting system is presented in terms of a single unit of measure, usually money.
- There are often many ways to measure the same "thing." For example, a car can be measured in terms of its cost, what it would cost to replace, what it could be sold for, and the amount for which it should be insured. These measures are stated in terms of dollars. There are many other measurements one could make for a car. Examples include its fuel efficiency, how fast it can go, its cargo capacity, and the number of people it can seat.
  - The measurements a decision maker needs will depend on the decision being made. This point is important. Accounting information that is presented by an entity may not necessarily provide appropriate measurements for every stakeholder. Stakeholders usually do not have the right to obtain or demand the exact information they require so it

is important for them to understand the usefulness and limitations of the information they receive.

The Rules of the Game

- Accounting is a tool that has been developed by people as a means of providing information for decision making. Unlike gravity, accounting has no natural laws that define how it should be done. As a result, it is necessary to establish rules of the game. If there were no rules it would be much more costly and difficult to make sense of the information contained in accounting reports because it would be necessary to learn and understand the rules that each entity was using.
- The rules in accounting are known as generally accepted accounting principles or GAAP. GAAP are the principles, conventions, practices, procedures, and rules that define acceptable accounting practices and guide the preparation of financial statements in certain situations. In other words, GAAP provide a structure for preparing financial statements.
- There are a few limitations worth noting about GAAP:
  - GAAP are not universal. GAAP in each country differs.
  - Not every entity follows GAAP or has to follow GAAP.
  - GAAP are flexible. Preparers often have many choices that can affect the information contained in financial statements.
- The *CICA Handbook*, which lays out the conceptual groundwork for Canadian GAAP and is the source of some specific GAAP, describes four qualitative characteristics that financial statement information must have if it is to be useful to users. The four characteristics are:
  - Understandability: Users must be able to understand information if it is to be useful to them.
  - Relevance: The information provided to users must be relevant or useful for the decisions they have to make.
  - Reliability: The information provided to users must be a reasonable measure of what it is intended to measure. In other words, the information must be precise and unbiased.
  - Comparability: Users should be able to compare the accounting information provided by different entities and the information of a particular entity from period to period.
- In practice these characteristics often conflict so that trade-offs are often made in setting GAAP. Because of these trade-offs the information available under GAAP will not satisfy all users in all situations.
- It is essential for any user or preparer of accounting information to know and understand GAAP. No user or preparer of accounting information can afford not to have an understanding of the concepts, principles, and rules that underlie GAAP. However, every user, preparer, and accountant must also understand that GAAP have significant problems and limitations. GAAP are not applicable to every user and every decision in every situation. Sophisticated users of financial statements will know when not to rely on GAAP-based statements, when to adjust the GAAP statements, and when to look elsewhere for information. Sophisticated users will also understand the flexibility that preparers of financial statements have even under GAAP and understand that this flexibility can have a significant effect on the appearance of the statements. We will explore these issues as we progress through the book.

♦ GAAP are discussed in depth in Chapter 5.

Study Problems

Study Problem 1 (Reasons for organizing a business as a corporation) You have agreed to invest $100,000 in a business opportunity being started by some acquaintances. Your cash will be used to help start the business. In return for your investment you will own 20% of the business. You will not be involved in managing the business. Explain why organizing this business as a corporation would probably be most appropriate from your point of view.

Study Problem 2 (Identifying stakeholders and explaining their stake) Identify the stakeholders in the government of Canada and explain what their stake is.

Study Problem 3 (Alternative measurements) Professional sports teams are an important part of many communities. Teams such as the Montreal Canadiens, Toronto Raptors, Saskatchewan RoughRiders, and Vancouver Canucks bring entertainment and excitement to their fans. The success of these teams is important to fans, owners, and other stakeholders. Identify different ways to measure the success of a professional sports team and explain which stakeholders each measure would be of interest to. Don't limit your evaluation to financial measurements.

Study Problem 4 (Classify and organize information so that it is useful for decision making) Carlos recently graduated from his university business program and is about to begin his first job. He has also just moved into his own apartment after living at home while attending university. Carlos is a bit unsure about what managing his finances will be like so he decides to keep a detailed record of his spending. During the month Carlos received $2,120 in wages from his employer and a $500 gift from his parents. For his first month Carlos records the following:

Date	Amount	Purpose	Date	Amount	Purpose
Jul. 1	$825	Rent for apartment	Jul. 23	$9	Lunch
Jul. 2	57	Groceries	Jul. 23	31	Evening out with friends
Jul. 2	78	Purchase of household items	Jul. 24	175	Clothes
Jul. 5	45	Dinner and movie with Nicole	Jul. 24	26	Dinner
Jul. 6	12	Beer for Sam's party	Jul. 25	51	Groceries
Jul. 9	17	Gift for Aiden's birthday	Jul. 26	5	Lunch
Jul. 12	110	Car insurance	Jul. 27	18	Gas for car
Jul. 15	22	Cable TV	Jul. 27	3	Donuts and coffee
Jul. 16	21	Gas for car	Jul. 27	14	Subscription
Jul. 17	18	Dinner	Jul. 27	55	Evening out with Nicole
Jul. 17	15	Fitness club membership	Jul. 29	11	Lunch
Jul. 18	5	Beers after baseball	Jul. 30	79	Home furnishings
Jul. 19	12	Books	Jul. 31	39	Phone bill
Jul. 20	10	Internet service	Jul. 31	31	Groceries
Jul. 22	8	Lunch	Jul. 31	6	Lunch

Required: Prepare a statement that organizes Carlos' spending information in a useful way. Explain why you organized the information the way that you did. How could you use the information if you were Carlos?

Solutions to Study Problems

(Note that comments that appear in the solutions in *italics* are intended to provide explanations and clarifications to help you understand the material. These comments are not required as part of a complete solution)

Solution to Study Problem 1

A key benefit to organizing as a corporation in this situation is limited liability. You are investing in a business opportunity but you will have little say in day-to-day operations, and with only a 20% ownership interest you may not have much to say about the policy and strategic decisions that are made. As a result you are especially vulnerable to bad decisions and choices made by the people actually operating the business. By setting the business up as a corporation the most you can lose is your $100,000 investment (not a small amount but at least there is a maximum amount of loss). With a corporation your loss is limited to the amount invested. If this business were organized as a partnership you could be responsible to pay more than the $100,000 investment if, for example, the business was unable to repay a loan or lost a lawsuit.

Solution to Study Problem 2

Stakeholder	Explanation of stake
Taxpayers/citizens	The government of Canada manages the country on behalf of its citizens. Citizens will have a stake since the decisions the government makes can have significant social and economic consequences. Taxpayers will be concerned about how the government is spending the taxes it collects and will want to evaluate the government's spending priorities.
Lenders/prospective lenders	The government of Canada has borrowed large amounts of money from lenders in Canada and around the world. These lenders will be interested in government policy to assess the risk associated with their loans. Prospective lenders will want to evaluate the attractiveness of lending to the government of Canada.
Politicians/potential politicians	Politicians are the elected representatives of the people of Canada. Politicians in government or opposition will have in interest in the laws the government passes and the actions it takes. Politicians also have an interest in their own careers and government actions and politicians responses to those actions will affect their career paths.
Allies/enemies	Foreign governments will have an interest in the policies and positions taken by the government of Canada because these policies and decisions may influence some actions taken by these foreign governments.
Provinces	The provinces receive a lot of money from the government of Canada. The ability and willingness of the federal government to make these payments has a significant impact on the budgets of the provinces. In poor economic times or in times of large federal budgetary deficits the federal government might be inclined to reduce these transfers to the provinces.
Interest groups	There are many groups, companies, organizations, and individuals that rely on the federal government for

	financial and other types of assistance. For example, farmers will turn to the government in times of serious drought. These interest groups have a significant stake in the actions and policies of the government of Canada because they will want to know that the government will continue to support them

Comment: This list is not a comprehensive one. You may have been able to identify other stakeholders. What is important to recognize from this problem is that an entity can have many stakeholders and that these stakeholders will often be interested in different things.

Solution to Study Problem 3
There are many possible ways to measure the success of professional sports teams. Some are identified and discussed below.

Measure of performance	Explanation
Number of championships won/performance on the field	Many stakeholders have an interest in this measure of performance. Fans of course. Owners will as well because success on the field can also be correlated with profitability. Sponsors will be interested because it may be more effective for their marketing programs if they are associated with a successful team.
Attendance	The number of fans who attend games will be important to owners since more fans means more revenue. It can also be interpreted as an indicator of how the team is received in the community. Broadcasters often comment negatively about teams that don't "draw well at the gate."
Television ratings	High television ratings are an indication of the popularity of a team. The higher the ratings the more the team can charge broadcasters for the rights to broadcast the team's games. Higher ratings also means that broadcasters can charge advertisers higher rates. Thus, television ratings are indicators of success for broadcasters, advertisers, and owners.
Sales of team merchandise	An important source of revenue for teams and leagues is the sale of team merchandise. Thus these sales will be a measure of success for owners. Sales of team merchandise will also be a measure of success for retailers, which will view teams whose merchandise is popular as successful.
Market value of the team	This measure will be of interest to the owners of the team, especially if they are interested in selling it. Also, the professional sports league might be interested as an indicator of the amount that new franchises in the league might be sold for.
Profitability	Profitability, of course, is of interest to owners since it is a measure of how much money the team is making. Profitability will be of interest to taxation authorities because taxes are based on an entity's income. Players and their unions will be interested in the profitability of the teams in a league because players salaries can be related to profitability.

Comment: It's easy to limit our thinking of the measurements of success of a professional sports team to success on the field. However, this is a narrow view. Success on the field is of interest to fans, but other measurements will be relevant to other stakeholders. The purpose of this question is to highlight that there can be many ways to measure of an attribute such as success and the relevance of each will depend on the stakeholder. The list above is not comprehensive. You may have been able to identify other reasonable indicators of success.

Solution to Study Problem 4

Comment: There are many ways that Carlos could organize the information that he recorded. The key is knowing the decisions that he wants to make. In assessing your response to this question you must evaluate whether the statement will answer his questions.

Statement of Cash Inflows and Outflows for July		
Cash inflows:		
Salary	$2,120	
Gift	500	$2,620
Cash outflows		
Rent	825	
Groceries	139	
Car expenses	149	
Entertainment	151	
Meals away from home	83	
Other (fitness club, subscription, books)	41	
Clothes	175	
Utilities (phone, cable, internet)	71	
Household items and furnishings	157	
Miscellaneous (Aiden's gift)	17	1,808
		$812

This statement breakdowns Carlos' spending by type of spending. It tells Carlos how he spent his money in terms of broad categories, but it does not give many specifics (type of entertainment, type of groceries). With the information in the statement Carlos can get an idea of how he spends his money. Since he has money left over at the end of the month he can look forward and think about perhaps increasing the amount he spends on entertainment or dining out, or he could start making contributions to an RRSP or save for a vacation. Because this is the first month it is unwise to draw too many conclusions. However, after a few months some patterns should begin to emerge that will allow Carlos to assess his position. It is important for Carlos to recognize that while he spent $812 less than he took in, $500 of the cash inflows was a gift that is not likely to occur every month. So Carlos should not plan to spend that money each month. That is why the gift from his parents is shown separately in the statement. If it weren't, Carlos might think the amount of cash he can expect to receive each month will be greater than it will actually be.

Comment: There are other approaches that could be used. For example discretionary and non-discretionary spending. In that scenario rent, groceries, and car expenses would, for the most part be non-discretionary (assuming Carlos needed his car). Most dining out and entertainment could be considered discretionary because, presumably, he could live with out spending that money. Whatever approach is used, the summary aspect of the statement is important. For example, the three expenditures on groceries are summarized on a single line—there is little benefit to recording each of these separately. It would also be possible to partition the shown statement differently. For example, entertainment with friends might be separated from entertainment with Nicole. There are endless possibilities. They key is assessing what the statement is going to be used for. It is crucial to recognize that there is no one right way to prepare this statement. It must be tailored to Carlos' situation

Chapter 2
Financial Statements: A Window on an Entity

Chapter Overview

Chapter 1 described the nature of accounting and introduced the accounting environment, the context in which accounting operates. Chapter 2 introduces the financial statements. While accounting systems can produce a wide range of different types of information and reports, the most commonly seen outputs of an accounting system are the financial statements, which comprise the balance sheet, income statement, statement of retained earnings, cash flow statement, and the notes to the financial statements. The financial statements provide important information about the financial position of an entity and its economic activity for a period. It is important to understand what the information that is provided in the financial statements represents. Remember from Chapter 1 there is often more than one way to measure the same thing. In Chapter 2 we begin to explore what goes in to the numbers reported in the financial statements and what they represent. The Chapter also introduces some of the mechanics of accounting, a topic that will be explored in depth in Chapter 3. At this stage of studying accounting it is easy to get lost in the mechanics. Avoid doing so. While it is important to have an understanding of the mechanics it is necessary at each step of the way to keep in mind the lessons of Chapter1—the importance of context and the accounting environment.

Study Points and Study Tips

General Purpose Financial Statements

- General purpose financial statements are intended for use by many different stakeholders and for many different purposes, and are not necessarily tailored to the needs of any or all stakeholders or purposes. In other words, general purpose financial statements are intended for no one in particular and for everyone in general.
  - Because they are designed for general use rather than a specific purpose, general purpose financial statements may not meet the needs of stakeholders who have specific information needs.
  - In most circumstances a stakeholder will receive the general purpose financial statements, even if he or she is also able to obtain special purpose information. As a result it is important to understand the basis upon which the general purpose statements are prepared and their strengths and limitations.
  - An entity can only prepare one set of general purpose financial statements. This is one of the reasons why they can't be tailored to the specific needs of each stakeholder.
  - The general purpose financial statements of public companies are available to any stakeholders who want them. The general purpose financial statements of private companies are not widely available. The general purpose statements of private companies will be available to stakeholders who must received them (e.g. CCRA) or who the owners or managers choose to give them to (e.g. lenders, prospective investors).
  - General purpose financial statements are usually prepared according to GAAP.
- Special purpose reports can be prepared as required by the entity. There is no limit on the number of special purpose reports an entity can prepare. Special purpose reports will be prepared to meet the needs of specific stakeholders that need additional information. However, special purpose reports will not be prepared for any stakeholders that request them.

The entity must be willing to supply them. Also, any special purpose reports that an entity prepares will not be available to other stakeholders.

The Balance Sheet

- The balance sheet provides information about the financial position of an entity at a specific point in time. In a balance sheet, financial position means information about assets, liabilities, and owners' equity.
- Balance sheets conform to the **accounting equation,** which is the conceptual foundation of accounting. The accounting equation is:

  Assets = Liabilities + Owners' Equity

- A balance sheet is like a photograph—it captures the scene at the moment the photo is taken. The situation could be dramatically different the moment before or after the picture is taken.
- Assets are economic resources that provide future benefits to an entity for carrying out its business activities.
  - Current assets are assets that will be used up, sold, or converted to cash within one year or one operating cycle. Examples of current assets are cash, inventory, accounts receivable (though some receivables can be non-current), and prepaid assets.
  - Non-current assets are assets that will not be used up, sold, or converted to cash within one year or one operating cycle. Examples of non-current assets include capital assets such as land, buildings, computers, patents, and copyrights.
  - According to GAAP an asset must meet the following criteria:
    - an asset must be the result of a transaction with another entity
    - the cost of an asset can be determined (GAAP requires that an asset be valued at the amount paid for it—that is, its cost—whether the payment was in cash or some other form
    - an asset must provide a future benefit to the entity and the benefit must be reasonably measurable (if you are not sure what the benefit is, the amount of the benefit, or that there will be a benefit, you cannot call an item an asset)
  - These criteria result in resources that we might intuitively consider to be assets not being reported as assets on GAAP-based financial statements (e.g. research, advertising, investment in education).
  - GAAP are not the only way to account for assets. There are many different ways that assets and other financial statement components can be defined and measured.
- Liabilities are the obligations of an entity, such as to pay debts or provide goods or services to customers.
  - Current liabilities will be paid or satisfied within one year or one operating cycle.
  - Non-current liabilities will be paid or satisfied in more than one year or one operating cycle.
  - Liquidity is the entity's ability to pay its obligations as they come due.
- Owners' equity is the investment the owners have made in the entity. In terms of the accounting equation owners' equity represents the assets of an entity that have been financed by owners (as opposed to creditors).

- For corporations, the shareholders' equity section of the balance sheet has two components:
  - Direct investments by shareholders are reported in the Capital Stock account. **Capital stock** represents the amount of money (or other assets) that shareholders have contributed to the corporation in exchange for shares in the corporation.
  - Reinvested net incomes are accumulated in the Retained Earnings account. **Retained earnings** is the sum of all the net incomes a corporation has earned since it began operations, less the dividends paid to shareholders. (**Dividends** are payments of a corporation's assets (usually cash) to its shareholders.) Dividends represent distributions of the corporation's net income to the shareholders.
- In addition to corresponding with the structure of the balance sheet, the accounting equation is also the basis for recording data in most accounting systems. All of an entity's transactions and economic events can be summarized in terms of their effect on the accounting equation. While accounting systems break down assets, liabilities, and equity into many subcategories, the essence of any transaction or economic event can be tied to some combination of the three basic components. Also, the equality between assets and liabilities and equities must always be maintained.

The Income Statement

- The income statement is a "how did we do?" statement, reporting the economic performance of the entity over a period of time such as a year. The format of the income statement is:

  Revenues - Expenses = Net income

- Net income is a measure of how an entity performed and how the owners' wealth changed over a period of time.
- Revenues are economic benefits earned by providing goods or services to customers. Revenue results in an increase in owners' equity or the wealth of the owners of the entity. Revenue represents an increase in owners' equity because the revenue is associated with an increase in assets or a decrease in liabilities.
- Expenses are economic sacrifices or costs incurred to earn revenue. Sacrifices result from using up an asset or by incurring a liability. Expenses decrease owners' equity because they represent what an entity must give up to earn the revenue.
  - Entities often have assets that contribute to earning revenue over many years. Examples of these types of assets include building, machines, and furniture. Because these types of assets contribute to earning revenue over many years their cost has to be expensed over many years. The process of expensing the cost of an asset over time is called amortization.
- The form of the income statement can be incorporated into the accounting equation. Net income is actually a component of owners' equity. Revenues represent increases in the owners' wealth and expenses represent decreases. The accounting equation can be rewritten as:

Assets = Liabilities + Owners' Equity at the beginning of the period + Revenue – Expenses – Dividends

or

Assets = Liabilities + Owners' Equity at the beginning of the period + Net income – Dividends

and

Owners' Equity at the end of the period = Owners' Equity at the beginning of the period + Net income – Dividends

- As can be seen from the equation, revenue increases owners' equity and expenses decrease it.

- There are different ways performance can be measured. The two most commonly used methods in accounting are the cash basis of accounting and accrual accounting:
  - The cash basis of accounting reports the cash flowing into and out of the entity. Under this method, economic performance is the change in cash over the period.
  - Accrual accounting measures the economic impact of transactions and economic events rather than cash flows. Accrual accounting attempts to measure economic changes rather than simply changes in cash.
  - For general purpose reporting in Canada accrual accounting is by far the most common method used.
- Dividends are not reported as an expense on the income statement. Dividends are a distribution of wealth to shareholders, not a cost of earning revenue.

The Statement of Retained Earnings

- The statement of retained earnings summarizes the changes to retained earnings during a period and serves as the bridge between the balance sheet and the income statement.
- Retained earnings represents the accumulation of an entity's net incomes over its life, less the dividends paid to the shareholders over the entity's life.
  - Another way of thinking about retained earnings is that it is the amount of net income that shareholders have re-invested in the entity. The portion not re-invested is paid to shareholders as dividends.
  - Retained earnings represents a source of an entity's assets. In the context of the accounting equation assets are financed from two sources, liabilities (debt) and investment by owners. Investment by owners can be direct, through the purchase of shares from the entity (capital stock), or indirect, through the re-investment of earnings.
  - Remember, though, that net income and retained earnings are not the same as cash. An entity can have high retained earnings but little or no cash.
- In equation form the statement of retained earnings can be expressed as:

  Retained earnings at the end of the year = Retained earnings at the beginning of the year + Net income for the year - Dividends declared during the year

- If an entity has a net loss for a period (i.e. its net income is negative) retained earnings is reduced by the amount of the loss.
  - An entity that has a loss in a period can still pay dividends. As long as the entity has enough cash it can pay dividends to shareholders.
- Net income and dividends are not the only events that affect retained earnings, but they are the most common. Other transactions and economic events that affect retained earnings will be mentioned in Chapter 11.

The Cash Flow Statement

- The cash flow statement shows how an entity obtained and used cash during a period
- The cash flow statement is broken down into three components:

  - Cash from operations—the cash an entity generates from or uses in its regular business activities.
  - Investing activities—the cash an entity spends buying capital and other long-term assets and the cash received from selling those types of assets.
  - Financing activities—the cash an entity raises and pays to equity investors and lenders.

Notes to the Financial Statements

- The notes to an entity's financial statements provide additional details and explanations about the numbers reported in the financial statements as well as providing additional information about the entity's circumstances.
- It is essential to read the notes to fully understand the financial statements.
- The note that describes an entity's "significant accounting policies" (usually one of the first notes) is especially important. There are often alternative ways for accounting for certain transactions and economic events and the significant accounting policies note describes the choices the entity made.

Users of MWW's Financial Statements

- When Mark's Work Wearhouse was a public company there were many stakeholders that had access to its financial statements and that would have likely found useful information in them. These stakeholders included:
  - Shareholders
  - Creditors
  - Franchise owners
  - Potential investors
  - Competitors
  - Canadian Customs and Revenue Agency (CCRA)
  - Now that MWW is privately owned, far fewer stakeholders will have access to the financial statements. The stakeholders that would be able to obtain MWW's financial statements include shareholders (there is only one now, Canadian Tire), creditors, and CCRA.

Format of General Purpose Financial Statements

- There is no one right way to organize a set of financial statements. Even under GAAP there are no requirements for how financial statements should be presented. The *CICA Handbook* requires that certain information be included in the financial statements, but the preparer decides how that information is presented.
- Some entities provide considerable detail in their financial statements while others provide only the minimum required.
- It is important to understand that many different formats and levels of detail are possible in financial statements. One should not be surprised or "put-off" by a format that has never been seen before. An unfamiliar format will require some thought and the application of basic principles to understand.

Additional comments

- Obtaining and examining financial statements are often only the first steps in evaluating an entity. Financial statement numbers can be analyzed to obtain additional insights. Financial ratios and measurements introduced in this chapter:
  - Working capital—Working capital is an indication of an entity's liquidity. The more working capital an entity has, the better able it is to meet its current obligations as they come due.

$$\text{Working Capital} = \text{Current Assets} - \text{Current Liabilities}$$

  - Current ratio—The current ratio is used as a measure of an entity's liquidity. The higher the current ratio the more current assets that are available to satisfy current liabilities and the better able the entity is to meet its current obligations.

$$\text{Current ratio} = \frac{\text{Current assets}}{\text{Current liabilities}}$$

  - Debt-to-equity ratio— The debt-to-equity ratio is a measure of how an entity is financed. The higher the ratio, the more debt an entity is using relative to equity. The debt-to-equity ratio is a measure of risk. The more debt an entity has the riskier it is because debt has a fixed cost, called interest, associated with it. Interest is the cost of borrowing money.

$$\text{Debt-to-equity ratio} = \frac{\text{Liabilities}}{\text{Shareholder's equity}}$$

  - Gross margin percentage—The gross margin percentage indicates the percentage of each dollar of sales that is available to cover costs other than the cost of the goods sold and return a profit to the entity's owners. Gross margin percentage is defined as:

$$\text{Gross Margin Percentage} = \frac{\text{Gross margin}}{\text{Sales}} = \frac{\text{Sales} - \text{Cost of sales}}{\text{Sales}}$$

Study Problems

Study Problem 1 (Determine the missing information) For each of the following independent situations, replace the missing information (indicated by a question mark) with the appropriate amount.

a)

Assets	=	$1,750,000
Owners' equity	=	1,125,000
Liabilities	=	?

b)

Expenses	=	$5,844,000
Net income	=	985,000
Revenues	=	?

c)

Revenue	=	$555,000
Gross margin	=	115,000
Cost of sales	=	?

d)

Retained earnings at the end of the year	=	$925,000
Retained earnings at the beginning of the year	=	760,000
Net income	=	310,000
Dividends declared during the year	=	?

e)

Net income	=	$50,000
Gross margin	=	450,000
Cost of sales	=	550,000
Revenue	=	?
Expenses	=	?

Study Problem 2 (Record the effect of transactions on the accounting equation) Show the effect that each transaction described below has on the elements of the accounting equation. Also, specify the type of asset, liability or owners' equity account that would be affected.

Transaction	Assets	=	Liabilities	+	Shareholders' Equity
Example: Shareholders purchase shares for $10,000	$10,000+ Cash +				$10,000+ Capital stock +
a) $5,000 of inventory is purchased on credit by a retail store. The store will pay for the inventory in 30 days.					
b) Inventory that was purchased by a retail store 30 days ago is paid for when a cheque for $3,000 is mailed to the supplier.					
c) Repairs on a store's delivery truck are made. The store pays the mechanic $500 in cash for the repairs.					
d) A store sells inventory that cost $1,000 to customers for $1,500. The customers promise to pay for the merchandise in 20 days.					
e) A store collects $1,500 from customers for merchandise previously purchased.					
f) A piece of land that is recorded on an entity's balance sheet at $100,000 is sold for $100,000 cash.					

Study Problem 3 (Classify the effect of economic events on income on the cash and accrual bases) Indicate whether each of the following events would be included in a calculation of net income on the cash basis, the accrual basis, or both:

Economic Event	Net income on the cash basis	Net income on the accrual basis
a) An entity purchases an insurance policy for cash that provides coverage beginning in the next fiscal period.		
b) An entity collects cash from a customer that purchased merchandise in a previous period.		
c) An entity repairs equipment and pays the repair company in cash.		
d) An entity provides services to customers for cash.		
e) An entity operates its business out of space in a downtown office building. The business paid its rent for the current period last year.		

Study Problem 4 (Prepare an income statement and balance sheet from a list of accounts) You have been provided with the following alphabetical list of accounts for Cheapside Ltd. (Cheapside) for 2004. Use the information to prepare an income statement for the year ended December 31, 2004 and balance sheet as of December 31, 2004. Use the information from your financial statements to calculate Cheapside's working capital, current ratio, and debt-to-equity ratio.

Accounts payable and accrued liabilities	$56,000	Intangible assets	$72,000
Accounts receivable	75,000	Interest expense	40,000
Accumulated amortization	110,000	Loans from shareholders	65,000
Amortization expense	38,000	Long-term debt	152,000
Amounts owing from employees	30,000	Miscellaneous expenses	44,000
Bank loan (short-term)	31,000	Prepaids	9,000
Capital assets	359,000	Promotion expense	17,000
Capital stock	155,000	Retained earnings at the beginning of the year	107,000
Cash	46,000	Revenue	576,000
Common shares of other companies owned	145,000	Salaries and wages expense	110,000
Current portion of long-term debt	35,000	Salaries and wages payable	12,000
Dividends declared and paid	25,000	Selling and administrative expense	82,000
Income tax expense	71,000	Supplies expense	91,000
Income taxes payable	23,000	Supplies inventory	68,000

Study Problem 5 (Cash versus accrual accounting) Dunstaffnage Corp. (Dunstaffnage) is a very small business that sells housewares door to door. Wendy LeTour, the sole shareholder of Dunstaffnage, visits the homes of her neighbours to show them her catalogue and samples of the products she sells. If a customer is interested in purchasing any of the products Wendy orders the merchandise from the distributor and delivers it to the customer. Time from order to delivery is usually about 30 days. Most customers pay for their merchandise when Wendy takes their orders.

Wendy's sister works for Dunstaffnage when help is needed. Her sister is paid $8 per hour. You are provided with the following information about Dunstaffnage for the three months ended March 31, 2006:

- $6,250 was collected from customers. Of this amount $1,100 pertained to merchandise that would not be delivered until April.
- In January Wendy delivered $1,500 of merchandise that was ordered and paid for in December.
- The cost of the merchandise delivered to customers during the period cost Dunstaffnage $3,975.
- Dunstaffnage paid its supplier $4,450.
- Wendy's sister was paid $375 during the period.
- During the period Wendy's sister worked 52 hours.
- During the period Dunstaffnage incurred other costs of $610, all of which were paid in cash.

Required:

a) Prepare income statements on the cash basis and on the accrual basis for the two months ended December 31, 2006. Assume that for accrual accounting purposes a sale is recorded when merchandise is delivered to the customer.
b) Explain the reasons the two statements are different. Be specific.
c) Which statement gives a better indication of how Dunstaffnage has performed? Explain.

Study Problem 6 (Classification of cash flows) Classify each transaction as an operating, financing, or investing cash flow. Explain your thinking in each case.

i) Cash paid by a computer retailer for 20 top-of-the-line computers for sale in the store.
ii) Cash paid by a large candy company for 20 top-of-the-line computers for use by its employees.
iii) Wages paid to employees.
iv) An entity purchases some of its common shares back from its shareholders.
v) A clothing store sells clothes to customers.
vi) A manufacturing company sells land at a profit.

Solutions to Study Problems

(Note that comments that appear in the solutions in *italics* are intended to provide explanations and clarifications to help you understand the material. These comments are not required as part of a complete solution)

Solution to Study Problem 1
(Amounts that had to be calculated are shaded)

a) Assets	=	Liabilities	+	Owners' equity
$1,750,000	=	$625,000	+	$1,125,000
b) Revenues	-	Expenses	=	Net income
$6,829,000		$5,844,000		$985,000
c) Revenue	-	Cost of sales	=	Gross margin
$555,000	-	$440,000	=	$115,000

d) Retained earnings at the end of the year	=	Retained earnings at the beginning of the year	+	Net income	-	Dividends declared during the year
$925,000	=	$760,000	+	$310,000	-	$145,000

e) Revenue	-	Cost of sales	=	Gross margin	-	Expenses	=	Net income
$1,000,000	-	$550,000	=	$450,000	-	$400,000	=	$50,000

Comment: This question required that you organize the data and then solve for the missing information. The purpose is to show the basic relationships that exist among the elements of the various financial statements. People sometimes say that accounting is a mathematical discipline. In fact, accounting does not require sophisticated math skills. For the most part it involves addition and subtraction with some multiplication and division. It is important to understand the relationships among the various parts of the financial statements so that meaning can be drawn from them.

Solution to Study Problem 2

Transaction	Assets	=	Liabilities	+	Shareholders' Equity
Example: Shareholders purchase shares for $10,000	$10,000+ Cash +				$10,000+ Capital stock +
a) $5,000 of inventory is purchased on credit by a retail store. The store will pay for the inventory in 30 days.	$5,000 + Inventory +		$5,000 + Accounts payable +		

Comment: Assets increase by $5,000 because inventory was purchased. Inventory is an asset because it can be sold to customers. The store did not pay cash for the inventory, instead it promised to pay later. The promise to pay a supplier, which is called accounts payable, is a liability because it represents an obligation to pay.

Transaction	Assets	=	Liabilities	+	Shareholders' Equity
b) Inventory that was purchased by a retail store 30 days ago is paid for when a cheque for $3,000 is mailed to the supplier.	$3,000 - Cash -		$3,000 - Accounts payable -		

Comment: When the inventory was purchased on credit the store recorded a liability called accounts payable. By mailing a cheque to the supplier the liability is being paid so liabilities decrease. To satisfy the liability the store gives up cash, which is an asset, so cash decreases.

Transaction	Assets	=	Liabilities	+	Shareholders' Equity
c) Repairs on a store's delivery truck are made. The store pays the mechanic $500 in cash for the repairs.	$500 - Cash -				$500 - Repairs expense -

Comment: Repairs are a cost of keeping the delivery truck operating, so it is an expense, which reduces shareholders' equity. The repairs are paid for in cash, so the asset cash decreases. Note that as a result of the payment the repairs expense increases (there is more repairs expense), but shareholders' equity decreases. This format will be developed further in Chapter 3.

d) A store sells inventory that cost $1,000 to customers for $1,500. The customers promise to pay for the merchandise in 20 days.	$1,500 + Accounts receivable +	$1,500 + Revenue +
	$1,000 - Inventory -	$1,000 - Cost of sales -

Comment: This situation has two components—the sale of merchandise to customers and the cost of the merchandise sold. The sale increases assets because the customers have promised to pay $1,500 for the merchandise they purchased. The promise is an asset. The $1,500 also represents an increase in the wealth of the shareholders. Since the asset side of the accounting equation has increased, something on the liabilities and owners' equity side must also increase. Since no liabilities were incurred, owners' equity must increase to keep the accounting equation in balance.

The second component recognizes that to make the sale the store had to give up assets costing $1,000. The asset "inventory" decreases by $1,000 because the customers received the inventory (so the store no longer has it and inventory and assets decrease). Shareholders' equity also decreases by $1,000 because the store sacrificed inventory costing that amount to make the sale. By giving up the inventory the owners' wealth decreased. Note that as a result of the payment cost of sales increases (there is more cost of sales), but shareholders' equity decreases. This format will be developed further in Chapter 3.

Note that taken together shareholders' equity increased by $500 ($1,500 - $1,000), so overall the wealth of the owners and their investment in the entity increased by $500.

e) A store collects $1,500 from customers for merchandise previously purchased.	$1,500 + Cash +	
	$1,500 + Accounts receivable -	

Comment: This is a conversion of one asset into another. Accounts receivable, the amount that customers promised to pay, has been satisfied because the customers paid the $1,500 owing. As a result, the asset "cash" increases but accounts receivable decrease. Overall, total assets remain the same but the composition of the assets has changed.

f) A piece of land that is recorded on the balance sheet at $100,000 is sold for $100,000 cash.	$100,000 + Cash +	
	$100,000 - Land -	

Comment: Land is an asset because it has future benefits for an entity (it can be built upon, it can be sold). Since the land was sold the asset "land" must decrease by $100,000, the amount recorded on the balance sheet. The land was exchanged for another asset, cash, As a result, cash increases by $100,000. Overall, the total amount of assets did not change but the nature of the assets change (land was exchanged for cash).

Solution to Study Problem 3

Economic Event	Net income on the cash basis	Net income on the accrual basis
a) An entity purchases an insurance policy for cash that provides coverage beginning in the next fiscal period.	Yes	No

Comment: Cash was paid for the insurance coverage so the amount is deducted in the calculation of net income on the cash basis. The amount is not included in accrual net income because the coverage is for a future period. The amount paid for the insurance would be reported as a prepaid insurance asset until the coverage was used.

b) An entity collects cash from a customer that purchased merchandise in a previous period.	Yes	No

Comment: Cash was collected from customers so the amount is included in the calculation of cash basis net income. The amount is not included in accrual net income because the merchandise was sold in a previous period and so the sale would have been recognized in that previous period.

c) An entity repairs equipment and pays the repair company in cash.	Yes	Yes

Comment: The repairs would be deducted in the calculation of net income using both cash and accrual accounting. The amount would be deducted under the cash basis because cash was expended for the repairs. The amount would be expensed under accrual accounting because it is a cost relating to the current period—a cost incurred to ensure the vehicle operates properly.

d) An entity provides services to customers for cash.	Yes	Yes

Comment: The transaction would be included as revenue in the calculation of net income using both cash and accrual accounting. Cash was received from the customer so it is included in the cash basis income statement. The services were provided to the customer in exchange for cash so the transaction represents revenue under accrual accounting.

e) An entity operates its business out of space in a downtown office building. The business paid its rent for the current period last year.	No	Yes

Comment: No cash was spent during the current period for rent so there is no effect on the cash basis income statement. There is an effect on the accrual statement because the space was used during the period. Under accrual accounting an expense is recorded when an economic resource is consumed. In this case the payment made last year was recorded as prepaid rent. In the current period when the space pertaining to the payment was used the amount is expensed.

Solution to Study Problem 4

Cheapside Ltd.
Balance Sheet
As of December 31, 2004

Assets		**Liabilities and Owner's Equity**	
Cash	$46,000	Bank loan	$31,000
Accounts receivable	75,000	Accounts payable and accrued liabilities	56,000
Amounts owing from employees	30,000	Salaries and wages payable	12,000
Supplies inventory	68,000	Income taxes payable	23,000
Prepaids	9,000	Current portion of long-term debt	35,000
		Loans from shareholders	65,000
Total current assets	$228,000	Total current liabilities	222,000
Capital assets	359,000	Long-term debt	152,000
Accumulated amortization	(110,000)	Total liabilities	374,000
Intangible assets	72,000	Capital stock	155,000
Commons shares of other companies	145,000	Retained earnings	165,000
Total assets	$694,000	Total liabilities and shareholders' equity	$694,000

Cheapside Ltd.
Income Statement
For the year ended December 31, 2004

Revenue	$576,000
Salaries and wages expense	110,000
Supplies expense	91,000
Selling and administrative expense	82,000
Amortization expense	38,000
Promotion expense	17,000
Interest expense	40,000
Miscellaneous expense	44,000
Income tax expense	71,000
Net income	$ 83,000
Retained earnings at the beginning of the year	107,000
Dividends declared and paid	25,000
Retained earnings at the end of the year	$165,000

Working capital = Current assets - Current liabilities
= $228,000 - $222,000
= $6,000

$$\text{Current ratio} = \frac{\text{Current assets}}{\text{Current liabilities}}$$

$$= \frac{\$228,000}{\$222,000}$$

$$= 1.027$$

Debt-to-equity ratio $= \dfrac{\text{Liabilities}}{\text{Shareholders equity}}$

$= \dfrac{\$374{,}000}{\$320{,}000}$

$= 1.169$

Comment: This question is fairly straightforward. Most of the accounts identified in the question can be found in the chapter or figured out. However, the following are in need of some additional explanation:

> *Amounts owing from employees—This account represents a receivable from employees. Cheapside loaned money to some employees and it is expected that the employees will repay the loan within one year.*
>
> *Intangible assets—Intangible assets are resources that meet the definition of an asset but do not have physical substance. Examples of intangible assets are patents, copyrights, and development costs. MWW shows a significant amount of goodwill on its balance sheet. Goodwill is another intangible asset. The clue for how to classify this item when answering the questions was the term asset. That indicated that these were assets and should be included on the balance sheet.*
>
> *Common shares of other companies—This was a difficult one. Cheapside owns some shares of other companies. In the same way that an individual can invest in shares of corporations, so can other corporations. If shares in other corporations are owned by an individual or another corporation, the investments represent assets. The investments will meet the definition of assets because they presumably were acquired in an exchange with an other entity (exchanged for cash, for example), the cost is known (presumably Cheapside knows what it paid for the shares), and the shares have future benefit (Cheapside will be able to earn dividends or see the price increase over time).*
>
> *Loans from shareholders—Cheapside's shareholders loaned the company money. Even though the loans came from shareholders they are legitimate liabilities that would appear in the liabilities section of the balance sheet.*

Solution to Study Problem 5

a)

Dunstaffnage Corp.
Income Statement
for the three months ended March 31, 2006
(Prepared using the cash basis)

Revenue (cash collected)	$6,250
Less: Expenses (cash spent)	
For merchandise sold	(4,450)
For employee	(375)
For other costs	(610)
Net income (cash flow)	$815

Dunstaffnage Corp.
Income Statement
for the three months ended March 31, 2006
(Prepared using the accrual basis)

Revenue ($5,150 of merchandise ordered and delivered during the period ($6,250 - $1,100) plus $1,500 of merchandise delivered in January but paid for in December.)	$6,650
Less: Expenses	
Cost of merchandise delivered to customers	(3,975)
Earned by Wendy's sister (52 hours x $8)	(416)
Other costs	(610)
Net income	$1,649

b) The two statements are different because cash inflows and outflows are not the same as accrual revenue and expenses. On the cash flow statement revenues are simply cash inflows—amounts collected from customers—regardless of when the revenue was earned by Dunstaffnage. Similarly, expenses are simply cash outflows, actual amounts paid to suppliers, employees, and so on. In contrast, the accrual income statement is based on economic flows, not cash flows. Revenue is recorded when merchandise is delivered to customers, even though cash is collected when Wendy takes the order. The expense for merchandise sold represents the cost of the merchandise delivered to customers, not the amount paid to suppliers. The wage expense to Wendy's sister is the cost of the work actually done during the period, not the amount she was paid. The idea is to match the economic costs (expenses) of generating economic benefits (revenue).

c) This is a difficult question. The answer really depends on what is meant by performance. If performance means net cash flows, then the cash flow statement gives a better indication. If performance is intended to have a broader economic meaning—a measure of the change in the wealth of the entity—then the accrual statement may give a better indication. The key point is that you cannot usually say that one accounting approach will always be best or better. Most of the time the best approach will depend on the specific situation—who the users are and what decisions they have to make.

Solution to Study Problem 6

i)	Cash paid by a computer retailer for 20 top-of-the-line computers for sale in the store.	Operations. The computer store's business is to sell computers. The computers are the store's inventory. Therefore, the cash spent on the inventory is an operating activity.
ii)	Cash paid by a large candy-making company for 20 top-of-the-line computers for use by its employees.	Investing activity. These computers are not part of the regular business activity of a candy maker. The computers will contribute to the earning of revenue indirectly by helping manage the company.
iii)	Wages are paid to employees.	Operations. Wages are operating activities because employee costs are part of the day-to-day operation of an entity.
iv)	An entity purchases some of its common shares back from its shareholders for cash.	Financing activity. Transactions involving shares are financing activities. The fact that the transaction generated a cash outflow does not affect the classification.
v)	A clothing store sells clothes to customers for cash.	Operations. A clothing stores business is to sell clothes. Therefore sales to customers is an operating activity
vi)	A manufacturing company sells land for cash.	Investing activity. The sale of land is not part of the day-to-day operations of a manufacturing company. The sale of land is incidental to the operation of the company.

Chapter 3
The Accounting Cycle

Chapter Overview

Chapter 2 introduced the set of financial statements. Financial statements represent the output of an accounting system. Chapter 3 takes a step back and shows how data from transactions and economic events that affect an entity are captured by an accounting system and organized, summarized, and classified into information that is useful to stakeholders. In other words, Chapter 3 provides the procedures or mechanics of accounting. The process by which data about economic events are entered into an accounting system, processed, organized, and used to produce information is known as the accounting cycle. Chapter 3 also provides more discussion of the accrual accounting method that was introduced in Chapter 2. As was discussed in Chapter 2 accrual accounting is system of accounting that measures the economic impact of transactions and economic events rather than cash flows. Chapter 3 discusses an important requirement of accrual accounting, adjusting journal entries.

Summary of Key Points

- The key to producing accounting information is having an accounting system that captures raw data and organizes, summarizes, and classifies the data into a form that is useful for decision making. The information provided by an accounting system is limited by the data that are entered into it.

  The accounting cycle is the process by which data about economic events are entered into an accounting system, processed, organized, and used to produce information, such as financial statements. An accounting system is very important because if data were not processed and organized it would be very difficult for anyone to understand and use it.

- The accounting equation spreadsheet is a device that is used to record transactions and economic events in a way that allows the information to be conveniently collected and organized, and then presented in financial statements. The accounting equation spreadsheet has columns for each account in the entity's records. Each transaction or economic event is recorded on a separate line in the spreadsheet. Each entry to the spreadsheet must maintain the accounting equation of Assets = Liabilities + Owners' (Shareholders') Equity. The ending balance in each column of the spreadsheet represents the ending balance in that account at a point in time and can be used to prepare balance sheets, income statements, and statements of retained earnings.

- The journal entry is the method used in practice to enter information about economic events into the accounting system. Whenever an economic event or transaction occurs that is to be entered into the accounting system, a journal entry is made. Journal entries provide compact and concise summaries of economic events in a way that makes it easy to see and understand the effect the event has on the financial statements. Debits and credits are the notations used to record the effects of an economic event on the accounts. Debits represent increases in assets and expenses and decreases in liabilities, owners' (shareholders') equity, and revenue. Credits represent decreases in assets and expenses and increases in liabilities, owners' (shareholders') equity, and revenue.

- Devices such as accounting equation spreadsheets and journal entries are only means to an end. These devices give us the ability to record and organize, summarize, and classify data into information that is useful for decision making. Accounting methods such as accrual accounting and GAAP often provide preparers of accounting information with choices for how to record and report transactions and economic events. When managers have choices for how to account for transactions and other economic events, their decisions will affect the accounting numbers that are reported, which in turn may affect how the numbers are interpreted and the decisions stakeholders make. That is why it is always necessary to look behind the numbers.

- Accrual accounting attempts to measure the economic activity and economic changes of an entity. An entry into an accrual accounting system is usually triggered by a transaction—an exchange between the entity and a party external to the entity. Sometimes, however, economic changes occur that affect the wealth of the entity but that are not triggered by transactions. These changes must be recorded in the accounting system. Entries to the accounting system that are not triggered by exchanges with outside entities are called adjusting entries.

  There are four types of adjusting entries:

  1. Deferred expense/prepaid expense where cash is paid before the expense is recognized;
  2. Deferred revenue where cash is received before revenue is recognized;
  3. Accrued liability where the expense is recognized before cash is paid; and
  4. Accrued asset where revenue is recognized before cash is received.

- Income statement accounts are sub-accounts of an entity's owners' equity accounts (retained earnings account in the case of a corporation). Separate income statement accounts are maintained so that information about revenues and expenses can be collected. At the end of each period the balances in the income statement, or temporary accounts, must be set to zero and the balances in those accounts transferred to their permanent place in the owners' equity section of the balance sheet. The balances in the income statement accounts are set to zero so that they can accumulate information about transactions and economic events that pertain only to the next period. The setting of temporary accounts to zero and the transferring of the balances in those accounts to owners' equity is achieved by a closing journal entry.

Study Points and Study Tips

Double-Entry Bookkeeping

- An accounting system is a mechanism for capturing raw data, processing it, and producing financial statements and other financial information. Accounting systems can be simple or complex, depending on the entity and the information needs of its managers and stakeholders.

- Accounting systems do not capture all economic events that affect an entity. An accounting system will only capture economic events that the managers of the entity believe will be necessary for their own decision making, for decision-making of the entity's stakeholders, and are required to meet legal and contractual obligations. As a result, information produced by an accounting system cannot give a complete picture of an entity. For example, under Canadian GAAP assets are recorded at their cost—the amount actually paid for them.

- The accounting systems of most entities are based on the accounting equation. The accounting equation states that

$$\text{Assets} = \text{Liabilities} + \text{Owners' Equity}$$

Transactions and economic events simply result in changes to the elements of the equation. The accounting equation is not limited to GAAP. Any set of accounting principles can be applied using the accounting equation. There are exceptions to the use of the accounting equation. For example, a chequebook, which is a simple accounting system, is not based on the accounting equation.

The Accounting Cycle

- The accounting cycle is the term that is used to describe the process by which data about economic events are entered into an accounting system, processed (organized, summarized, classified), and used to produce information, such as financial statements. The accounting cycle includes the following steps (the full accounting cycle is discussed in the Appendix to Chapter 3): (a) prepare the journal entry; (b) post the journal entry to the general ledger; (c) prepare and post adjusting journal entries; (d) prepare the trial balance; (e) prepare the financial statements; (f) prepare and post closing journal entries.

Devices For Doing Accounting

- The accounting equation spreadsheet is a device used to show how transactions and economic events are recorded in an accounting system and how those data are then organized, summarized, and classified to produce financial statements. The full accounting cycle is demonstrated in an accounting equation spreadsheet.

- The accounting equation spreadsheet is arranged according to the accounting equation. A sample accounting equation spreadsheet is shown in Figure 3-1. The very top line of the spreadsheet states the accounting equation. Assets, liabilities, and shareholders' (owners') equity are divided into separate categories called accounts to represent the entity's different assets, liabilities, equities, revenues, and expenses. (Remember that revenues and expenses are part of equity.)
    - Each column of the spreadsheet represents an asset, liability, equity, revenue, or expense account. In Figure 1 the accounts are identified generically as asset, liability, revenue, and expense accounts. In an actual example these generic names would be replaced with appropriate account names such as cash, inventory, accounts payable, retained earnings, etc.

Figure 3-1 Sample of an Accounting Equation Spreadsheet

	Assets			=	Liabilities			+	Shareholders' Equity					
Transaction	Asset account	Asset account	Asset account		Liability account	Liability account	Liability account		Capital Stock	Retained Earnings	Revenue account	Expense account	Expense account	Expense account
Beginning balance														
Transaction/ Economic event														
Transaction/ Economic event														
Transaction/ Economic event														
Transaction/ Economic event														
Ending balance														

- Amounts from the entity's balance sheet at the beginning of the period are recorded on the row on the spreadsheet called "Beginning balance." This row represents the amount or balance in each account at the beginning of the period. Income statement accounts are always equal to zero on this row (see closing journal entries).

- The next group of rows on the spreadsheet are for the transactions and economic events that are recorded in the accounting system during the period (the shaded rows in Figure 3-1). Each row represents a separate transaction or economic event.
  - When a transaction or economic event affects an account, the dollar amount of the affect is recorded in that account's column. Transactions and economic events that increase the balance in the account are added and transactions and economic events that decrease the balance are subtracted.
  - The entries made on each row of the spreadsheet must maintain the accounting equation. That is, assets must equal liabilities plus owners' equity after an entry is made.
  - Note that in the textbook expenses are recorded as negative numbers.
  - If you use a computer program such as Microsoft Excel to prepare your accounting equation spreadsheet you can create a column at the end of the spreadsheet that checks whether the accounting equation holds for each transaction or economic event that is recorded. This check column should add across the row (transaction) to test whether the sum of the entries to the asset accounts equal the sum of the entries to the liability and equity accounts.
  - Transactions and economic events recorded in the spreadsheet can be transactional, adjusting, or closing entries.
- At the end of the reporting period each column in the spreadsheet is totaled. The totals are recorded in the row called "Ending balance." The total of each column is the amount that appears on the financial statements. Balance sheet totals are reported on the balance sheet and income statement totals are reported on the income statement.
- Remember that at the end of the period the income statement accounts must be closed to retained earnings to complete the accounting cycle. If the income statement accounts are not closed to retained earnings the amount in the retained earnings account will not be correct and the balance sheet will not balance (closing entries are discussed later in this section).
- If the accounting equation does not hold after an entry is made you have made an error. However, just because the accounting equation holds after an entry is recorded does not mean that an error has not been made. For example, part of an entry could be recorded in the wrong accounts (column). For example, an entity might purchase inventory for $10,000 but record the purchase as an expense or a capital asset instead of inventory. In either case the accounting equation would hold but the financial statements would not be correct.
- There are few rules on the number, type, and names of accounts that an entity can use. Management will determine the accounts for its accounting system based on the entity's reporting requirement and the information needs of its stakeholders and management.
- Journal entries are used in practice as the method of initially entering a transaction or economic event into the accounting system. Journal entries are also a compact way of summarizing the effect of a transaction or economic event on the financial statements. The format of a journal entry is:

Debit	Account name	$$$	
Credit	Account name		$$$

- A journal entry provides the following information:
  a) the accounts that are affected by the transaction or economic event—this is shown by the account name in the journal entry.

b) whether the balance in each account increases or decreases—this is indicated by whether the account is "debited" or "credited."

c) the amount by which each account is affected—this is indicated by the dollar amount

- Debits and credits are terms used to describe whether the balance in an account increases or decreases as a result of a transaction or economic event. The effect of debits and credits on the different types of accounts is summarized in the following list:

Debit	Credit
Increase assets	Decrease assets
Decrease liabilities	Increase liabilities
Decrease owners' equity	Increase owners' equity
Decrease revenues	Increase revenues
Increase expenses	Decrease expenses

- It is important to be comfortable with debits and credits. Some students struggle with the debit/credit convention but it's easier to remember than you might think. The key is remembering the accounting equation. A journal entry must maintain the accounting equation (which is why the debits in a journal entry must equal the credits). Therefore, if you know that debits increase assets, you automatically know that credits increase liabilities, owners' equity, and revenue, and that debits increase expenses. If this were not true the accounting equation would be violated.

- In a journal entry the debits must equal the credits. If they don't, the accounting equation will not hold.

- Regardless of whether an accounting equation spreadsheet or journal entries are used to reflect an entity's economic activity, it is necessary to determine the following:
  1. Which elements of the accounting equation are affected—assets, liabilities, and/or owners' equity, including revenues and expenses?
  2. Which specific asset, liability, owners' equity, revenue, and expense accounts have been affected?
  3. How are the accounts affected—that is, does the amount in each account increase or decrease?
  4. By how much has each specific asset, liability, owners' equity, revenue, and expense account increased or decreased?

- When analyzing a transaction or economic event it is helpful to stick to basics. Don't get carried away and try to be a full-fledged accountant right from the start. Instead, stick to common language and associate the parts of the transaction or economic event to the five components of the accounting equation: assets, liabilities, equities, revenues, and expenses. In other words, ask yourself "what has happened here?" and answer by thinking about the effects on the accounting equation components.
  - For example, suppose you were asked to prepare the journal entry or make the entry to the accounting equation spreadsheet for the following transaction: An entity purchases goods for $10,000 that it plans to sell to customers. The entity agrees to pay the supplier within 30 days.
    - In assessing the situation it is necessary to think about what has happened. The entity purchased some goods. The goods presumably have a future benefit because the entity can to sell them to customers. Therefore, these goods can be considered an

asset, an asset we call Inventory. As a result the Inventory account will increase by $10,000, the cost of the inventory.

- That takes care of half the transaction, but to maintain the accounting equation the entry must have at least one more part. The entity did not pay cash for the inventory but promised that it would pay within 30 days. This promise is a liability because it represents an obligation to pay money to the supplier. Therefore, liabilities will increase by $10,000, the amount the entity has promised to pay. This liability is called accounts payable.

➢ At this early stage don't get too concerned about getting the account names "right." This will come with time and experience. Right now make sure you can describe the nature of the assets, liabilities, equities, revenues, or expenses that are being affected by the transaction or economic event.

➢ The big challenge in this type of exercise is figuring out whether the transaction or economic event affects asset, liability, equity, revenue, or expense accounts. Take the time to think carefully about the transaction or economic event and the definition of the components of the accounting equation.

Accrual Accounting

♦ Accrual accounting attempts to measure an entity's economic activity rather than just its cash flows. Under an accrual accounting system revenues and expenses can be recorded before, after, or at the same time as the related cash flow. In contrast, with cash accounting revenue is recognized when cash is received and expenses are recognized when cash is paid.

♦ A key concept under accrual accounting is matching. Once an entity recognizes revenue the costs incurred to earn that revenue are expensed at the same time, regardless of when those expenses were paid. The idea is that the cost of earning revenue should be "matched" (expensed) to the revenue those costs helped earn. By matching expenses to revenues, the income statement provides a measure of performance—economic benefits minus economic costs—which is an objective of accrual accounting.

  ➢ For purposes of measuring the performance of an entity matching is an attractive concept. However, there are practical limitations to our ability to apply matching. For example, it is often difficult if not impossible to quantify the contribution a machine, a building, or a senior executive makes to earning revenue in a period. It is also difficult to determine the amount of accounts receivable that won't be collected (bad debts) or the merchandise that customers might return.

♦ Adjusting journal entries are entries to an accrual accounting system that are not triggered by exchanges with outside entities. Most entries to an accrual accounting system are triggered by transactions—exchanges with other entities. However, not all of an entity's economic changes are triggered by transactions. As a result, at the end of each reporting period it is necessary for the managers to identify any economic changes that have occurred during the period but have not been captured in the accounting system and make any adjustments (adjusting entries) that are necessary.

♦ Adjusting entries are not required in a cash accounting system because recording is triggered only by the exchange of cash, which must involve an outside entity. Entries triggered by exchanges with outside entities are called transactional entries.

♦ Five general points about adjusting entries to keep in mind are:

1. The situations that give rise to adjusting entries revolve around the timing of the cash flow versus the timing of revenue or expense recognition—revenue and expense recognition can happen at a different time than the cash flows.
2. Adjusting entries always include at least one balance sheet account and one income statement account.
3. Each adjusting entry is associated with a transaction that is recorded before or after the adjusting entry.
4. Adjusting entries are required only when financial statements are prepared.
5. Adjusting entries never involve cash. If cash is part of the entry, it is not an adjusting entry.

- There are four types of adjusting entries.

Type	Situation	Example
Deferred expense/prepaid expense	Cash is paid before the expense is recognized	Insurance Rent Capital assets
Deferred revenue	Cash is received before revenue is recognized	Deposits Subscriptions Advances Gift certificates
Accrued liability	Expense is recognized before cash is paid	Wages Utilities Interest expense
Accrued asset	Revenue is recognized before cash is received	Interest earned

- Deferred expense/prepaid expense adjusting entries recognize the consumption of assets that provide benefits to an entity for more than one period. Entities often have assets that provide benefits for more than one period, including insurance policies, equipment, buildings, and patents. To achieve the matching of expenses to revenues, a portion of the cost of an asset that contributes to earning revenue for more than one period must be expensed each period. These adjusting entries reduce the amount of the asset that is reported on the balance sheet and recognize an expense for the portion of the asset that has been consumed.

- A deferred revenue adjusting entry arises when a customer pays in advance for goods or services that will be delivered sometime in the future. The entity receives the cash but does not recognize revenue at that time. When the payment is received, the entity records a liability. The liability represents the obligation to provide the good or service that the customer has paid for. The adjusting entry is necessary when the revenue is recognized (the good or service is provided) and the obligation is fulfilled.

- The accrued liability type of adjusting entry is recorded when an entity has incurred an expense, but the recording of the expense and related liability have not been triggered by an external event. Recognition of the expense gives rise to a liability to pay for the resource that was consumed. The entry is necessary to ensure that all resources consumed in a period are expensed in that period—in other words, to ensure that expenses are matched to revenues. The adjusting entry recording an accrued liability is made before the transactional entry is made.

- The accrued asset type of adjusting entry is required when an entity has earned revenue but no transaction with another entity has triggered the recording of the revenue. Recognizing the revenue gives rise to a receivable that reflects that payment is forthcoming. The adjusting entry recording an accrued asset is made before the transactional entry is made. This is not the same as recording an account receivable that is recorded as a result of a sale to a customer, which is a transaction.

Closing Journal Entries

- Income statement accounts are also known as temporary accounts. They are temporary because at the end of each period they are reset to zero so that accumulation of revenues and expenses can begin anew in the next period. A closing journal entry is necessary at the end of the accounting cycle to reset the temporary accounts to zero. This is accomplished by making an entry to each revenue and expense account that is equal to but opposite in amount to the ending balance in the account. The other side of the entry goes to retained earnings. The closing entry has the effect of transferring the amounts in the temporary income statement accounts to retained earnings.

Additional comments

- Accounting equation spreadsheets and journal entries are devices for doing accounting and for demonstrating how the accounting process works. Learning how the process works takes practice and it can be quite challenging. The process can be useful to know and understand, especially if you are considering pursuing a career in accounting. However, it is important to understand that there is a lot more to accounting than the mechanics. In fact, the mechanics are just a small part of accounting.

- The bigger challenge in your study of accounting is figuring out and understanding how transactions and economic events are accounted for. Chapter 3 of the text gives some examples of where it is necessary for managers to make decisions about how to account. For example, in the case of Strawberries Inc. management had to decide the period over which to amortize the renovations, equipment, and furniture. It is rarely obvious what the exact useful life of an asset is, so it is up to management to make a reasonable estimate. But different "reasonable estimates" are possible. Different estimates result in different numbers in the financial statements.

- It is important to recognize that the accounting for transactions and economic events doesn't happen automatically. The managers of the entity must decide how to account. Once management has decided how to account for a particular type of transaction or economic event the actual recording is fairly routine and the recording can be done each time by bookkeepers, clerks, or junior accountants. However, for situations that are not routine senior managers will be involved in the decision on how to account and they often have to exercise judgement in making the decision. The exercise of judgement means that the managers have to choose from among reasonable acceptable alternative ways of accounting.

- Many accounting students try to seek comfort in rules for how to account for particular situations. The reality is, as is discussed throughout the text, detailed rules that a preparer (or accounting student) can fall back on often do not exist, or the rules may be ambiguous or provide for more than one alternative. This is certainly true for GAAP. It is important for users of accounting to understand the choices that managers have available to them when preparing financial statements and that these accounting choices can have a significant effect on the numbers reported in the financial statements.

- The fact that managers can choose from among alternative accounting treatments when preparing financial statements does not imply fraud or misrepresentation. The existence of alternatives is the result of a number of factors including, tradition, uncertainty about the future, and the need to provide flexibility to deal with a variety of economic circumstances and conditions. As is discussed throughout the textbook, the motivations or self-interest of managers plays a role in the accounting choices managers make.

- Financial ratios introduced in this chapter:
  - Return on equity: a measure of the profitability of an entity and its effectiveness in using the assets provided by the owners of the entity to generate net income.

$$\text{Return on equity} = \frac{\text{Net income}}{\text{Owners' (Shareholders') equity}}$$

  - Profit mar gin ratio: a measure of how effective the entity is at controlling expenses and reflects the amount of income earned for each dollar of sales.

$$\text{Profit margin ratio} = \frac{\text{Net income}}{\text{Sales}}$$

Study Problems

Study Problem 1 (Debits and credits) For each of the following state whether the event described would give rise to a debit or a credit.

a. Cash increases
b. Accounts payable decreases
c. Cost of sales increases
d. Bank loans increase
e. Capital stock increases
f. Interest revenue increases
g. Capital assets increases
h. Retained earnings decreases
i. Rent expense increases
j. Inventory decreases
k. Long-term debt increases
l. Prepaid insurance decreases

Study Problem 2 (Recording entries in an accounting equation spreadsheet/recording journal entries) Set up an accounting equation spreadsheet and enter each of the following independent economic events into the spreadsheet for Falkland Ltd. (Falkland). Also, prepare the journal entry for each of the events. Falkland has an October 31 year end.

a. On November 1 Falkland repays a $25,000 bank loan and $1,000 of interest that is owed. The interest expense was accrued in the previous period.
b. On November 10 Falkland pays $12,000 to employees. The employees earned $3,000 in October (the previous fiscal year) and the remainder in November.
c. On December 4 Falkland sells merchandise to a customer for $5,000. The customer agrees to pay within 10 days.
d. On December 11 Falkland collects $5,000 owing from a customer.
e. On February 15 Falkland purchases $100,000 of inventory on credit. Payment will be made in 30 days.
f. On March 12 Falkland pays $100,000 owed to a supplier for inventory purchased in February.
g. On May 10 Falkland receives $25,000 from a customer. The $25,000 is an advance for merchandise that Falkland will deliver to the customer in September.
h. On September 12 Falkland delivers merchandise to a customer that had paid $25,000 in May for the merchandise.
i. On September 30 Falkland pays $1,000 cash for repairs to office equipment.

j. On October 15 Falkland sells shares to investors for $100,000 cash.
k. On October 31 Falkland purchases new computers for $10,000. Falkland pays $6,000 in cash and agrees to pay the remainder in November.

Study Problem 3 (Making adjusting entries) For each of the following situations prepare the required adjusting entries for Nenagh Ltd. (Nenagh) for the year ended December 31, 2004. Also show the related transactional entries, the date the entries would be made, and state the type of adjusting entry each is. This question can be done using an accounting equation spreadsheet or journal entries.

a. On January 3, 2004 Nenagh purchased a three-year fire insurance policy for $7,200. The policy covers the three-year period beginning February 1, 2004 and runs until January 31, 2007.
b. On April 1, 2004 Nenagh signed a licensing agreement that allows another company to use some of Nenagh's proprietary materials. The company agreed to pay Nenagh $120,000 per year, payable on March 31 of each year.
c. On October 1, 2004 Nenagh received from a customer $20,000 for services that were to be delivered over the next few months. As of December 31, 2004 30% of the services had been provided to the customer.
d. On September 1, 2004 Nenagh borrowed $100,000 from a local bank. The loan carries an interest rate of 9% per year and the interest must be paid on August 31 of each year.

Study Problem 4 (Preparing closing entries) The income statement for Ascension Inc. (Ascension) for the year ended December 31, 2005 is shown below. Assume that the balance in Ascension's retained earnings account on January 1, 2005 was $195,000 and that there were no transactions or economic events during the year that affected retained earnings.

Ascension Inc.
Income Statement for the year ended December 31, 2005

Revenue		$275,800
Expenses		
Wages and salaries	$97,500	
General and administrative	59,250	
Advertising and promotion	49,500	
Amortization	18,950	
Interest	8,900	
Miscellaneous	15,900	
Income taxes	5,160	255,160
Net income		$20,640

Required:

a. Use the following spreadsheet to make the closing entry for Ascension for the year ended December 31, 2005.
b. Prepare the journal entry necessary to close the temporary accounts.
c. Why are closing entries necessary and what would be the implication if the closing entry were not made?

	Assets	=	Liabilities	+	Shareholders' Equity									
Transaction	Assets		Liabilities		Capital Stock	Retained Earnings	Revenue	Wages and salaries	General and Administration	Advertising and promotion	Amortization	Interest	Misc.	Income taxes
Balance on December 31, 2005 before the closing entry is made														
Closing entry														
Balance on December 31, 2005 after the closing entry is made														

Study Problem 5 (Explaining journal entries) Provide a description of the event represented by each of the following journal entries.

a.	Dr.	Bank loan	100,000	
	Cr.	Cash		100,000
b.	Dr.	Delivery vehicle	55,000	
	Cr.	Cash		55,000
c.	Dr.	Inventory	15,000	
	Cr.	Accounts payable		15,000
d.	Dr.	Retained earnings	25,000	
	Cr.	Dividends payable		25,000
e.	Dr.	Revenue	1,000	
	Cr.	Accounts receivable		1,000
f.	Dr.	Amortization expense	5,500	
	Cr.	Accumulated amortization		5,500
g.	Dr.	Prepaid wages	750	
	Cr.	Cash		750
h.	Dr.	Cash120,000		
	Cr.	Accounts receivable		90,000
	Cr.	Revenue		30,000

Study Problem 6 (Using the accounting equation spreadsheet to record transactions and prepare financial statements—comprehensive problem) Clear Refreshment Inc. (Clear) bottles and distributes spring water to thirsty customers in Canada and the United States. When Clear started in business, it purchased the right to draw water from a pristine spring, which is its sole source of the water it bottles. Clear pumps water from the spring and puts it into bottles of various sizes. The water is sold to distributors who are responsible for distribution to retailers and end customers. Water is shipped to distributors as soon as it is bottled. Clear purchases the bottles from a supplier.

Clear is owned by a group of investors who thought that bottled water had huge potential because of the shortage of high-quality water in many places. None of the investors are involved in the management of the company. The investors receive regular status reports from Clear's management. Clear has been, in the eyes of its owners, quite successful since it began operations in 2002 and it is looking to expand into more markets.

Clear's balance sheet as of December 31, 2004, the company's year end is shown below. Clear uses its financial statements for tax purposes, to show the holders of the long-term notes, and to provide information to the shareholders.

Clear Refreshment Inc.
Balance Sheet
As of December 31, 2004

Assets		**Liabilities and Shareholders' Equity**	
Cash	$325,000	Accounts payable	$160,580
Accounts receivable	521,500	Taxes payable	55,000
Inventory	220,000	Wages payable	68,000
Prepaid insurance	18,000	Interest payable	87,500
Total current assets	$1,084,500	Total current liabilities	$371,080
Capital assets	2,046,000	Long-term notes payable	875,000
Accumulated amortization	(901,000)		
Rights (net of amortization accumulated to date)	175,000	Capital stock	850,000
		Retained earnings	308,420
Total Assets	$2,404,500	Total Liabilities and Shareholders' Equity	$2,404,500

It is now January 2006. Clear needs to prepare its financial statements for the year ended December 31, 2005. The following information has been obtained about the fiscal year just ended:

1. Clear sold $5,768,000 of water to distributors during 2005. All sales were on credit and distributors are required to pay within 45 days of receiving the water from Clear.
2. Clear purchased bottles for $2,334,000 during 2005. All bottle purchases were on credit. Bottles are recorded as inventory on the balance sheet. During the year, bottles costing $2,269,000 were used.
3. Clear paid $35,000 in maintenance costs on its pumping and bottling equipment during 2005. In addition, at the end of 2005 Clear estimated that it owed the company that does its maintenance $8,000 for work that it had not yet been billed for.
4. Clear paid salaries to employees of $975,000. On December 31, 2005 Clear owed employees $147,500.
5. Clear collected $4,925,000 from its distributors in 2005.
6. Clear paid its bottle supplier $2,150,000 during 2005.
7. During 2005, Clear paid the income taxes it owed at the end of 2004. It also paid $43,000 in installments on its 2005 income taxes. As of December 31, 2005 management estimates that Clear owes an additional $32,000 in income taxes for 2005.
8. Clear paid $250,000 in 2002 for the right to draw water from the spring for 10 years. The right must be renegotiated in 2012. The right to draw water is referred to as "Rights" on the balance sheet.
9. During 2005 Clear purchased new equipment for $98,000 in cash.

10. The capital assets represent Clear's pumping and bottling equipment. Amortization expense for 2005 is $348,000, including amortization of the new equipment that was purchased.
11. Prepaid insurance pertains to insurance on Clear's equipment and pumping facility, as well as liability insurance. During 2005 it used $15,000 of insurance that was recorded as prepaid on December 31, 2004. In late 2005, Clear purchased and paid $28,000 for insurance for 2006.
12. During the year Clear paid $87,500 in interest to the holders of the long-term notes. Interest is paid annually on January 1. On January 1, 2005, Clear paid $100,000 to reduce the balance owed on the long-term notes. The interest rate on the notes is 10%.
13. Clear paid $410,000 in cash for other expenses related to operating the business in fiscal 2005.
14. Clear incurred $1,250,000 in advertising and promotion costs during 2005. As of December 31, 2005, all amounts owing to suppliers for advertising and promotion costs had been paid.

Required:

a. Enter each of the transactions onto an accounting equation spreadsheet. Create a separate column on the spreadsheet for each account. Make sure to enter all adjusting entries and the closing entry on the spreadsheet. Indicate whether each entry is a transactional entry, an adjusting entry, or a closing entry.
b. Provide explanations for each of your entries. You should explain why you have treated the economic events as you have (that is, why you have recorded an asset, liability, etc.).
c. Use your spreadsheet to prepare a balance sheet as of December 31, 2005 and an income statement for the year ended December 31, 2005.
d. Do you think Clear has been successful? Explain why. Would you be prepared to lend Clear $500,000 to expand? Why or why not? Also, list five questions you might ask Clear's management that would help you use the financial statements more effectively.

Solutions to Study Problems

(Note that comments that appear in the solutions in *italics* are intended to provide explanations and clarifications to help you understand the material. These comments are not required as part of a complete solution)

Solution to Study Problem 1

Comment: The purpose of this question is to provide practice learning the meaning of debits and credits. In each case it was necessary to determine the type of account that is stated and then indicate whether the change in that account (increase or decrease) is a debit or a credit.

a.	Cash increases	Debit (increase in an asset)
b.	Accounts payable decreases	Debit (decrease in a liability)
c.	Cost of sales increases	Debit (increase in an expense)
d.	Bank loans increase	Credit (increase in a liability)
e.	Capital stock increases	Credit (increase in equity)
f.	Interest revenue increases	Credit (increase in revenue)
g.	Capital assets increases	Debit (increase in an asset)
h.	Retained earnings decreases	Debit (decrease in equity)
i.	Rent expense increases	Debit (increase in an expense)
j.	Inventory decreases	Credit (decrease in an asset)
k.	Long-term debt increases	Credit (increase in a liability)
l.	Prepaid insurance decreases	Credit (decrease in an asset)

Solution to Study Problem 2—see spreadsheet on the next page.

Journal entries

		Dr.	Cr.
a)	Dr. Bank loan (liability -)	25,000	
	Dr. Interest payable (liability -)	1,000	
	Cr. Cash (asset -)		26,000
	To record repayment of a bank loan and interest.		
b)	Dr. Wages payable (liability -)	3,000	
	Dr. Wage expense (expenses +, shareholders equity -)	9,000	
	Cr. Cash (asset -)		12,000
	To record payment of wages and wages payable.		
c)	Dr. Accounts receivable (assets +)	5,000	
	Cr. Revenue (revenue +, shareholders' equity +)		5,000
	To record a sale made on credit.		
d)	Dr. Cash (assets +)	5,000	
	Cr. Accounts receivable (assets -)		5,000
	To record collection of accounts receivable.		
e)	Dr. Inventory (assets +)	100,000	
	Cr. Accounts payable (liabilities +)		100,000
	To record the purchase of inventory on credit.		
f)	Dr. Accounts payable (liabilities -)	100,000	
	Cr. Cash (assets -)		100,000
	To record payment of accounts payable.		
g)	Dr. Cash (assets +)	25,000	
	Cr. Unearned revenue (liabilities +)		25,000
	To record receipt of cash for merchandise to be delivered in the future.		
h)	Dr. Unearned revenue (liabilities -)	25,000	
	Cr. Revenue (revenue +, shareholders' equity +)		25,000
	To record recognition of revenue for merchandise paid for in advance.		
i)	Dr. Repairs expense (expenses +, shareholders equity -)	1,000	
	Cr. Cash (assets -)		1,000
	To record repairs expense.		
j)	Dr. Cash (assets +)	100,000	
	Cr. Capital stock (shareholders' equity +)		100,000
	To record the sale of capital stock for cash.		

Solution for Study Problem 2

		Assets				=	Liabilities					+	Shareholders' equity				
		Cash	Accounts receivable	Inventory	Equipment		Bank loan	Accounts payable	Interest payable	Wages payable	Unearned revenue		Capital stock	Retained earnings	Revenue	Wage expense	Repairs expense
a)	Nov. 1	(26,000)					(25,000)		(1,000)								
b)	Nov. 10	(12,000)								(3,000)						(9,000)	
c)	Dec. 4		5,000												5,000		
d)	Dec. 11	5,000	(5,000)														
e)	Feb. 15			100,000				100,000									
f)	Mar. 12	(100,000)						(100,000)									
g)	May 10	25,000									25,000						
h)	Sept. 12										(25,000)				25,000		
i)	Sept.30	(1,000)															(1,000)
j)	Oct. 15	100,000											100,000				
k)	Oct. 31	(6,000)			10,000			4,000									

k)	Dr. Equipment (assets +)	10,000	
	Cr. Cash (assets -)		6,000
	Cr. Accounts payable (liabilities +)		4,000

To record the purchase of equipment.

Comments: Explanations to spreadsheet and journal entries. Note that these explanations are intended to help you understand the entries. They were not required to answer the study question.

a. Falkland repaid a $25,000 bank loan and paid $1,000 in interest owing to the bank. In total Falkland paid $26,000, so Cash decreases by $26,000. Of the $26,000 paid $25,000 is repayment of the bank loan. This means that the Bank Loan account, which is a liability because it represents money owed to the bank, decreases by $25,000. The remaining $1,000 is interest on the borrowed money. Interest expense and Interest Payable were accrued (recorded) in the previous year when the financial statements were prepared. Now (November 1) when the interest is paid the Interest Payable liability is reduced because Falkland is fulfilling its obligation to pay interest to the bank.

b. Falkland paid employees $12,000 on November 10, so Cash decreases by $12,000. Of the $12,000, $3,000 was earned in the previous year and $9,000 was earned in the current year. The $9,000 earned in the current year represents a current expense, so Wage Expense increases (is debited) by $9,000. The $3,000 earned in the previous year would have been accrued (recorded) in that year (to match the cost of employees to revenues earned). This means that Falkland would have made an adjusting entry to accrue a Wage Expense and a Wages Payable liability for $3,000. When the employees were paid on November 10 the $3,000 Wages Payable liability was fulfilled, so the Wages Payable liability decreases by $3,000.

c. Falkland sold merchandise to a customer so it can record Revenue of $5,000. The customer promised to pay Falkland the $5,000 (Falkland did not received cash when the sale occurred) within 10 days so Falkland records an asset to reflect that cash will be paid soon. This asset is called Accounts Receivable. Accrual accounting is being used here because the sale was recorded even though cash was not collected at the time.

d. When Falkland collected $5,000 from the customer on December 11 its Cash increased by $5,000. Accounts Receivable decreased by $5,000 because the customer fulfilled its promise to pay. Falkland has converted one asset, Accounts Receivable, into another asset, Cash.

e. Falkland purchased $100,000 of Inventory, which is an asset because it has future benefit (Falkland can sell or use the inventory to earn revenue). Falkland didn't pay cash for the inventory but instead promised to pay the amount owing in 30 days. The promise to pay is a liability called Accounts Payable. The liability is the obligation to pay the supplier $100,000.

f. When Falkland pays the supplier the $100,000 it owes, Accounts Payable (liability) and Cash decrease by $100,000. Falkland has fulfilled its obligation to the supplier, which is why Accounts Payable decreases.

g. The $25,000 received from the customer increases Cash. Falkland also records a $25,000 liability called Unearned Revenue. The liability is recorded because Falkland received cash but did not deliver any merchandise. As a result it has an obligation to *deliver $25,000 of merchandise to the customer. In this case the obligation is to deliver merchandise, not to pay cash. Revenue is not recorded at this point because the revenue has not yet been earned.*

h. *By delivering merchandise previously paid for Falkland is fulfilling its obligation. As a result, the Unearned Revenue liability decreases by $25,000. Falkland also recognizes $25,000 of Revenue because by delivering the merchandise to the customer Falkland has earned the revenue. This entry is an adjusting entry.*

i. *The payment reduces Cash by $1,000. The payment represents an expense because it is a cost of operating the business during the year.*

j. *Falkland's cash increased by $100,000 because shareholders have paid $100,000 for the shares. The shares that the shareholders received in exchange for the cash represent an ownership interest in Falkland so the Capital Stock account increases by $100,000.*

k. *The computers represent an asset because they will provide Falkland with benefits in the future, likely over several years. In the spreadsheet and journal entry the Equipment account was increased by $10,000, the amount that Falkland will pay for the computers. Falkland paid $6,000 in cash for the computers so Cash decreases by $6,000. Falkland also promised to pay the remaining $4,000 in November, so it records a current liability, Accounts Payable, for that amount. Notice that the full cost of the computers is recorded ($10,000) even though only $6,000 was paid in cash.*

Solution to Study Problem 3—see spreadsheet on the next page.

a) Transactional entry on January 3, 2004

Dr.	Prepaid insurance (asset +)	7,200	
Cr.	Cash (asset -)		7,200

To record the purchase of a three-year fire insurance policy.

Adjusting entry on December 31, 2004

Dr.	Insurance expense (expense +, shareholders' equity -)	2,200	
Cr.	Prepaid insurance (asset -)		2,200

To record the insurance expense for 2004.

*Comment: This is the deferred expense/prepaid expense type of adjusting entry. The adjusting entry reflects the amount of insurance that was used up during 2004. The policy was in effect for 11 months (February to December) and therefore 11/36 of the cost of the policy should be expensed during the year (11/36 * $7,200 = $2,200).*

b) Adjusting entry on December 31, 2004

Dr.	Accounts receivable (asset +)	90,000	
Cr.	Revenue (revenue +, shareholders' equity +)	90,000	

To accrue revenue from licensing arrangement.

Transactional entry on March 31, 2005 (when payment is receive by Nenagh)

Dr.	Cash (asset +)	120,000	
Cr.	Accounts receivable (asset -)		90,000
Cr.	Revenue (revenue +, shareholders' equity +)	30,000	

To record receipt of payment pertaining to licensing arrangement.

Solution for Study Problem 3

		Cash	Accounts receivable	Inventory	Equipment	Bank loan	Accounts payable	Interest payable	Wages payble	Unearned revenue	Capital stock	Retained earnings	Sales		Wage expense	Repairs expense
l)	Nov. 1	(26,000)				(25,000)		(1,000)								
m)	Nov. 10	(12,000)							(3,000)						(9,000)	
n)	Dec. 4		5,000										5,000			
o)	Dec. 11	5,000	(5,000)													
p)	Feb. 15			100,000			100,000									
q)	Mar. 12	(100,000)					(100,000)									
r)	May 10	25,000								25,000						
s)	Sept. 12									(25,000)			25,000			
t)	Sept.30	(1,000)														(1,000)
u)	Oct. 15	100,000									100,000					
v)	Oct. 31	(6,000)			10,000		4,000									

Comment: This is the accrued asset type of adjusting entry. On December 31, 2004 it is necessary to accrue the revenue earned by Nenagh even though payment has not yet been received. Nenagh has earned the revenue because the other company has had the right to use Nenagh's proprietary materials for nine months. This is an adjusting entry because the recording is not triggered by an interaction with an outside party. The transactional entry on March 31, 2005 records the receipt of $120,000 in cash and collection of the $90,000 account receivable that was accrued on December 31, 2004. Nenagh has also earned revenue from the licensing arrangement from January through March 2005, which is why the transactional entry includes $30,000 of revenue.

c) Transactional entry on October 1, 2004

		Dr.	Cr.
Dr.	Cash (asset +)	20,000	
Cr.	Unearned revenue (liability +)		20,000

To record advance payment received from a customer for future services.

Adjusting entry on December 31, 2004

		Dr.	Cr.
Dr.	Unearned revenue (liability -)	6,000	
Cr.	Revenue (revenue +, shareholders' equity +)		6,000

To record revenue earned.

*Comment: This is the deferred revenue type of adjusting entry. On October 31, 2004 when Nenagh received the payment from the customer the credit was made to unearned revenue because Nenagh had not yet provided the services to the customer and had therefore not earned the revenue. On October 31, 2004 it has an obligation to provide services in the future. As of December 31, 2004 Nenagh had provided 30% of the services that were to be provided so it would recognize $6,000 of revenue in 2004 ($20,000 * 30%).*

d) Transactional entry on September 1, 2004

		Dr.	Cr.
Dr.	Cash (asset +)	100,000	
Cr.	Bank loan (liability +)		100,000

To record the borrowing of $10,000 from the bank

Adjusting entry on December 31, 2004

		Dr.	Cr.
Dr.	Interest expense (expense +, shareholders' equity -)	3,000	
Cr.	Interest payable (liability +)		3,000

To accrue interest expense for 2004.

Transactional entry on August 31, 2005

		Dr.	Cr.
Dr.	Interest payable (liability -)	3,000	
Dr.	Interest expense (expense +, shareholders' equity -)	6,000	
Cr.	Cash (asset -)		9,000

To record payment to the bank for interest on loan.

*Comment: This is the accrued liability type of adjusting entry. The adjusting entry on December 31, 2004 is necessary to accrue the cost of the bank loan for September through December (9% * 3/12 * $10,000). The expense needs to be recorded even though the interest payment is not made until 2005 so the cost of borrowing money in 2004 is recorded in that period. The transactional entry on August 31, 2005 records the $9,000 payment to the bank. $3,000 of the payment* *represents fulfillment of the liability that was accrued on December 31, 2004 and $6,000 represents the cost of the loan for January through August 2005.*

Solution to Study Problem 4

a. Spreadsheet

Transaction	Assets	Liabilities	Capital Stock	Retained Earnings	Revenue	Wages and salaries	General and Administration	Advertising and promotion	Amortization	Interest	Misc.	Income taxes
Balance on December 31, 2005 before the closing entry is made												
Closing entry				20,640	(275,800)	97,500	59,250	49,500	18,950	8,900	15,900	5,160
Balance on December 31, 2005 after the closing entry is made												

Comment: Note that this is a partial spreadsheet. The specific asset and liability accounts are left out and no amounts for assets and liabilities are included. The focus in this Study Problem is on the shareholders' equity accounts, in particular, the temporary (income statement) accounts and retained earnings.

b. Closing journal entry

		Dr.	Cr.
Dr.	Revenue	275,800	
Cr.	Wages and salaries		97,500
Cr.	General and administrative		59,250
Cr.	Advertising and promotion		49,500
Cr.	Amortization		18,950
Cr.	Interest		8,900
Cr.	Miscellaneous		15,900
Cr.	Income taxes		5,160
Cr.	Retained earnings		20,640

c. Closing journal entries are necessary so that the temporary accounts have zero balances at the beginning of the next period. Closing journal entries are also necessary so that Retained Earnings/Owners' Equity at the end of the period includes the activities recorded in the temporary accounts during the period.

Solution to Study Problem 5

a. Repayment of a $100,000 bank loan (liability).
b. Purchase of a delivery vehicle (asset) for $55,000 cash.
c. Purchase of $15,000 of inventory (asset) on credit (liability).
d. Declaration of a dividend. On the date of the entry the dividend is owing to shareholders and is therefore classified as a liability. When the dividend is paid the liability will be removed from the accounting records.
e. A customer returned $1,000 of merchandise. As a result the revenue and account receivable (asset) that were recorded are removed from the accounting records since, as a result of the return the customer does not owe any money and there has not been a sale.
f. An adjusting entry to record a $5,500 amortization expense for the period. Accumulated amortization is a contra-asset account.

g. Recording of an advance paid to an employee. Prepaid wages is an asset and when the employee does work the prepaid wage account will be reduced and a wage expense recorded.
h. The entity received a $120,000 payment from a customer. $90,000 of the payment was for revenue recognized (accrued) in a previous period and $30,000 was for revenue earned in the current period.

Solution to Study Problem 6—see the spreadsheet on the next two pages for part a.

a. See spreadsheet

Note: T = transactional entry
A = adjusting entry
C = closing entry

b.

Explanation

1. Clear sold water to customers on credit. Therefore it can recognize revenue in the amount of the sales ($5,768,000) and record an asset representing the amount of money the customers promised to pay. Note that in practice sales for an entire period would not be recorded in a single entry. Entries for sales would be made transaction by transaction or daily or some variation on that. The single entry is used in the example to show how revenue is recorded but to avoid having you record large numbers of repetitive transactions. Notice that the accounting equation holds because shareholders equity (revenue) and assets (accounts receivable) increase by the same amount.

2. When bottles are purchased they become part of inventory. The bottles are an asset because they are available to put water in—they are necessary to sell Clear's product. The bottles are expensed when they are used—that is, when water in the bottles is sold to customers. When Clear purchased the bottles it did not pay cash. It promised to pay for them later. Therefore Clear records an obligation or a liability for $2,334,000. This type of liability is known as accounts payable. As was in the case in item 1., in practice inventory purchases for an entire period would not be recorded in a single entry (unless the bottles were all purchased at the same time).

   During the period Clear used $2,250,000 worth of the bottles that it had on hand. Because these bottles have been used, they are no longer assets and must be expensed. An expense represents a cost incurred by the entity—in this case the cost of the bottles used. This event is recorded by reducing the amount of inventory on hand (which makes sense since the bottles have been sold along with the water) and the amount used up is a cost of earning the revenue from selling the water (an expense).

Clear Refreshment Inc.
Spreadsheet
For the year ended December 31, 2005

	Cash	Accounts Receivable	Inventory	Prepaids	Capital assets	Accumulated amortization	Rights	Accounts payable	Income taxes payable	Salaries payable	Interest payable	Long-term notes payable	Capital stock	Retained earnings
	325,000	521,500	220,000	18,000	2,046,000	(901,000)	175,000	160,580	55,000	68,000	87,500	875,000	850,000	308,420
1 T		5,768,000												
2 T			2,334,000					2,334,000						
2 T/A			(2,269,000)											
3 T	(35,000)													
3 A								8,000						
4 T	(68,000)									(68,000)				
4 T	(907,000)													
4 A										147,500				
5 T	4,925,000	(4,925,000)												
6 T	(2,150,000)							(2,150,000)						
7 T	(55,000)								(55,000)					
7 T	(43,000)													
7 A									32,000					
8 A							(25,000)							
9 T	(98,000)				98,000									
10 A						(348,000)								
11 A				(15,000)										
11 T	(28,000)			28,000										
12 T	(87,500)										(87,500)			
12 T	(100,000)											(100,000)		
12 A											77,500			
13 T	(410,000)													
14 T	(1,250,000)													
	18,500	1,364,500	285,000	31,000	2,144,000	(1,249,000)	150,000	352,580	32,000	147,500	77,500	775,000	850,000	308,420
C														201,000
	18,500	1,364,500	285,000	31,000	2,144,000	(1,249,000)	150,000	352,580	32,000	147,500	77,500	775,000	850,000	509,420

Clear Refreshment Inc.
Spreadsheet
For the year ended December 31, 2005

	Revenue	Bottle cost	Salaries expense	Interest expense	Other expense	Maintenance expense	Amortization expense	Advertising and promotion expense	Insurance expense	Income tax expense
1 T	5,768,000									
2 T										
2 T/A		(2,269,000)								
3 T						(35,000)				
3 A						(8,000)				
4 T										
4 T			(907,000)							
4 A			(147,500)							
5 T										
6 T										
7 T										
7 T										(43,000)
7 A										(32,000)
8 A							(25,000)			
9 T										
10 A							(348,000)			
11 A									(15,000)	
11 T										
12 T										
12 T										
12 A				(77,500)						
13 T					(410,000)					
14 T								(1,250,000)		
	5,768,000	(2,269,000)	(1,054,500)	(77,500)	(410,000)	(43,000)	(373,000)	(1,250,000)	(15,000)	(75,000)
C	(5,768,000)	2,269,000	1,054,500	77,500	410,000	43,000	373,000	1,250,000	15,000	75,000
	0	0	0	0	0	0	0	0	0	0

3. There are a couple of aspects to think about here. First, is the maintenance cost an asset or an expense? In most cases maintenance and repairs are treated as expenses. The rationale is that maintenance and repairs make things work as intended. They don't make the related assets better. However, the question is sometimes a gray area, depending on the nature of the maintenance cost. In the spreadsheet I have assumed that these costs are expensed as incurred.

   The second aspect is the two parts of the cost. The $35,000 is clearly a transactional entry. The $8,000 requires an adjusting entry because there has been no interaction with the supplier to trigger recording.

   The total maintenance expense for the year is $43,000. $35,000 of that amount was paid in cash. (This is a bit of an assumption because Clear could have recorded a payable that was paid by year end, but absent any information, I have made the simplest assumption that during the year amounts were paid in cash. Recording the amount first as a payable and then as a cash payment would also be OK and would not alter the year end financial statement. This assumption does not apply to the $8,000 owing at year end though.) The $8,000 that is owed as of the end of the year is an accrued liability (it is included in accounts payable, which is often done in practice.)

4. During 2005 Clear paid salaries of $975,000. Of that amount, $68,000 was to pay salaries that were owed at the end of the previous year ($68,000 is Salaries Payable on the December 31, 2004 balance sheet). This means that $907,000 ($975,000 - $68,000) of the cash payments to employees were expenses in 2005 (the money employees received in 2005 they worked for in 2005). We are also told that Clear owed its employees $147,500 at the end of 2005. As a result an adjusting entry is required to record an additional $147,500 of Salaries Expense and the same amount of Salaries Payable (liability to pay salaries). Notice that we are not specifically told the amount of Salaries Expense that Clear incurred in 2005. The amount can be determined from the Salaries Expense column of the spreadsheet. It can also be calculated in the following way:

Amount paid to employees	$ 975,000
- Amount owed to employees at the beginning of the year	68,000
+ Amount owed to employees at the end of the year.	147,500
= Salaries Expense	$1,054,500

5. Collection from customers results in a reduction of Accounts Receivable and an increase in Cash. One asset, Accounts Receivable, has been converted into another asset, Cash. Presumably, some of the cash collected is for Accounts Receivable that were outstanding at the beginning of the year.

6. Clear satisfied its Accounts Payable to bottle suppliers by paying them cash. Therefore, assets (Cash) and liabilities (Accounts Payable) decrease. Presumably, some of the amount paid was to settle Accounts Payable that were outstanding at the beginning of the year.

7. There are three components to this item. First, Clear paid income taxes that were payable at the beginning of the year. For this component Cash decreased by $55,000 (the amount of income taxes payable at the beginning of the year—see the December 31, 2004 balance sheet) and Income Taxes Payable decreased by $55,000. Notice that this component has no income statement effect. The reason is that these income taxes were expensed last year.

Second, Clear made payments of $43,000 to government for income taxes in the current year. This amount is an expense in the current year so Income Tax Expense increases by $43,000. Since the amount was paid in cash, Cash decreases by $43,000.

Third, as of the year end Clear hadn't paid all of the income taxes it was supposed to pay. As a result, Clear accrued the estimated amount of income tax owing for 2005—$32,000. The accrual increases the Income Tax Expense for 2005 by $32,000 and increases Income Taxes Payable by $32,000. This is an adjusting entry because it is not triggered by an interaction with an outside party.

8. This item implies the need to record an amortization expense for the right to draw water from the spring. Clear paid $250,000 for the right to draw water for 10 years. There are different ways this cost could be amortized (these will be discussed in Chapter 9 of the book). I will assume that the cost is amortized evenly over the 10 years or $25,000 per year ($250,000/10 years). The asset "rights" on the balance sheet is reduced directly by $25,000. It would also have been appropriate to have a separate contra-asset account called "accumulated amortization." The contra-asset approach is used for amortization of capital assets in this question.

9. The new equipment purchased during the year are assets because they will help earn revenue in the future. Since the purchase was for cash Capital Assets increase by $25,000 and Cash decreases by $25,000.

10. The cost of Capital Assets that is being matched to revenue in 2005 is $348,000. This is the Amortization Expense for capital assets. The entry increases the Amortization Expense by $348,000 and increases the contra-asset account "Accumulated Amortization" by $348,000. Remember that a contra-asset account accumulates decreases in a related asset account, so the effect of an increase in the contra-asset account is a net decrease in the related asset account. Therefore, the accounting equation holds because assets decrease and shareholders' equity decreases (expenses increase).

11. There are two events to deal with here. The first is to expense the Prepaid Insurance that was used up in 2005. We're told that Clear used $15,000 of the Prepaid Insurance that was reported on the December 31, 2004 balance sheet. Since this insurance has been used, it is no longer an asset. Therefore, the Prepaid Insurance account is reduced by $15,000 and a $15,000 Insurance Expense is recorded.

    The second is to record as an asset the $28,000 of insurance that Clear purchased in late 2005. This insurance provides coverage for 2006, so at the end of 2005 the $28,000 is an asset because it represents insurance coverage for the future. The purchase of this insurance decreases Cash by $28,000 and increases Prepaid Insurance by $28,000.

12. There are three events that have to be dealt with here. First, on January 1, 2005 Clear paid the $87,500 that it owed to holders of its long-term notes. This payment decreases Cash and Interest Payable by $87,500. There is no income statement effect here because the expense was accrued at the end of 2004. That is, Clear recognized the cost of borrowing money during the period that it had use of the money.

    Also on January 1, 2005, Clear made a payment to reduce the amount of long-term notes. In other words, Clear reduced its Long-term Notes Payable liability by $100,000 and reduced its Cash by $100,000.

The third item we have to address is the Interest Expense for 2005. Clear had $775,000 of long-term notes outstanding for all of 2005 ($885,000 - $100,000). The interest rate on the notes is 10% so the cost of borrowing is $77,500 ($775,000 x 10%). This expense has to be accrued at the end of 2005 because the interest does not have to be paid until January 1, 2006. However, the $77,500 is the cost of borrowing for 2005 and the cost should be expensed in 2005 regardless of when the cash is paid (under an accrual accounting system).

13. The $410,000 of operating expenses were paid in cash so Cash decreases by $410,000 and Other Expenses increase by $410,000.

14. Advertising and promotion are almost always expensed as incurred. Clear expended $1,250,000 in cash for advertising and promotion in 2005 so Cash decreases by $1,250,000 and the Advertising and Promotion Expense increases by $1,250,000

The closing entry reduces each of the revenue and expense accounts to zero and moves those amounts to the retained earnings account.

c. Financial statements

Clear Refreshment Inc.
Balance Sheet
As of December 31,

	2005	2004		2005	2004
Assets			**Liabilities and Shareholders' Equity**		
Cash	$18,500	$325,000	Accounts payable	$352,580	$160,580
Accounts receivable	1,364,500	521,500	Taxes payable	32,000	55,000
Inventory	285,000	220,000	Salaries payable	147,500	68,000
Prepaid insurance	31,000	18,000	Interest payable	77,500	87,500
Total current assets	$1,699,000	$1,084,500	Total current liabilities	$609,580	$371,080
Capital assets	2,144,000	2,046,000	Long-term notes payable	775,000	875,000
Accumulated amortization	(1,249,000)	(901,000)			
Rights (net of amortization accumulated to date)	150,000	175,000	Capital stock	850,000	850,000
			Retained earnings	509,420	308,420
Total Assets	$2,744,000	$2,404,500	Total Liabilities and Shareholders' Equity	$2,744,000	$2,404,500

Clear Refreshment Inc.
Income Statement
For the year ended December 31, 2005

Revenue		$5,768,000
Expenses		
Bottle cost	$2,269,000	
Salaries	1,054,500	
Interest	77,500	
Other	410,000	
Maintenance	43,000	
Amortization	373,000	
Advertising and promotion	1,250,000	
Insurance	15,000	5,492,000
Income before income taxes		276,000
Income taxes		75,000
Net Income		$201,000

d. Evaluating whether Clear is successful is difficult because of the absence of comparative information, either from its previous years' operations or for other water bottling companies. Clear earned a profit in 2005, which is better than a loss, but that is pretty much all that one can infer without comparative information. Clear's profit margin is 3.6%, which is low for some industries and high for others. Again comparative data is required.

We have comparative information on the balance sheet, which allows for some analysis. Clear's cash position has deteriorated significantly since last year. On December 31, 2005 Clear has only $18,500, which isn't very much. It is not clear whether Clear has a line-of-credit available from the bank that would provide it with cash in the event it requires it. Clear's current ratio has declined slightly since last year but is still very high, indicating that it has adequate liquid assets available to meet its obligations. However, there are some worrying signs. Accounts receivable have more than doubled. What is the cause of the increase? Is it that sales have increased dramatically as well, or has collection of receivables become a problem? Also, accounts payable have also more than doubled, while inventory has increased only slightly. Is clear having trouble paying its bills on time and is delaying payment because of a shortage of cash? Or is there some other reason that payables have increased so much?

I would probably not lend Clear $500,000. The company's cash situation has deteriorated significantly and its operating cash flow was negative for the year ($108,500). If the negative cash flow continues, the company will consume the $500,000 very quickly. Before agreeing to lend the money I would want additional information regarding how the cash would be used and indications of how the company would rectify its negative cash flow information. Are there specific areas where the cash flows can be improved? Cash flow forecasts would probably be useful in assessing whether Clear would be able to pay the debt.

There are many questions that could be asked in this situation. Some examples are:

- What will the money be used for?
- What type of collateral or security is available?
- When are the long-term notes scheduled to be paid back?
- Are the long-term notes secured against any of the company's assets? Which ones?
- What cash flow is expected in future periods?
- Why have accounts receivable increased by so much over the last year?
- Why have accounts payable increased so significantly over the last year?

Chapter 4
Income Measurement and the Objectives of Financial Reporting

Chapter Overview

Chapter 3 examined "how" accounting works. The mechanics of accounting are important because ultimately, if you are going to "do" accounting it is necessary to know how accounting systems work. In the context of this book, knowing how accounting works is important for understanding the relationship between how transactions and economic events are recorded in an accounting system and the way the economic activity appears in the financial statements.

In Chapter 4 we turn our attention to "why." Two vital but very different themes are introduced in Chapter 4. The first part of the Chapter is devoted to revenue and expense recognition—when sales and expenses are reported on an entity's income statement. This is an important and sometimes complex accounting issue that has significant implications on the numbers that are reported in the financial statements. Revenue and expense recognition is the first in-depth examination we undertake of an accounting issue for which managers have flexibility to choose how to do the accounting. In the chapter we will see why managers have flexibility and the implications of that flexibility.

Chapter 4 also examines the objectives of financial reporting. The objectives of financial reporting are reasons why financial accounting information is provided to stakeholders. Managers must decide what and how to communicate with stakeholders in the financial statements. The objectives of financial reporting provide part of the framework that needs to be understood to understand why a manager would choose one acceptable and reasonable alternative over another.

Summary of Key Points

- To recognize revenue in a logical and rational matter we need some criteria to guide the choice. Under GAAP the following four criteria are used:
    1. The revenue has been earned.
    2. The amount of revenue can be reasonably measured.
    3. The costs required to earn the revenue can be reasonably measured.
    4. Collection of payment is reasonably assured.

  These criteria provide guidance to preparers, but they are open to interpretation and judgment. An additional, overriding criterion requires that the revenue recognition point selected provides a reasonable and fair representation of the entity's activities, given the needs of the people who are using the accounting information.

- Conceptually, earning revenue is a continuous process. Each activity an entity undertakes that increases the value of a good or service represents an economic gain or benefit to the entity. As a practical matter it can be very difficult for accountants to determine when and how much revenue should be recognized along the series of actions leading to a sale to a customer. Accountants have devised two approaches for recognizing revenue: the critical-event approach and the gradual approach.

  Under the critical-event approach, an entity chooses an instant in the earnings process that it considers an appropriate time to recognize revenue. That instant is called the critical event. When the critical event occurs, 100% of the revenue is recognized.

Under the gradual approach, revenue is recognized gradually over a period of time. The gradual approach, which is often used when an entity has long-term contracts, provides useful and timely information to stakeholders about long-term contracts.

- There are different ways and times that revenues and expenses can be recognized, and the methods chosen can affect the amount of revenue, expense, and income that an entity reports. Different revenue and expense recognition methods also affect many accounting and financial ratios. Even though the income statement will be affected by different revenue and expense recognition methods, the underlying economic activity of the entity is the same regardless of the methods chosen.

- The percentage-of-completion method is a gradual approach method that allocates revenues and related expenses over more than one reporting period, based on a measure of the effort completed in each period.

  If the revenues or expenses of a long-term project cannot be reasonably estimated, or if it is difficult to estimate the portion of the project that has been completed, then the completed-contract method is used. The completed-contract method is a critical-event approach to revenue recognition that recognizes revenue in full when a contract is completed.

- Accrual accounting requires that all costs be matched to revenue in the same period as that in which the revenue that those expenses helped earn is recognized—whether the cash is expended before, at the same time as, or after the revenue is recognized. Not all costs are easy to match to revenue. Costs that are expensed in the period that they are incurred are called period costs. Costs that can be matched to specific revenues (for example, the cost of MWW pants that are sold) are called product costs. Product costs are expensed when the revenue they help generate is recognized.

- Preparers of accounting information can often choose from a number of reasonable accounting treatments for transactions and other economic events, even under GAAP. Some of the reasons for, implications of, and limitations to flexible accounting rules are:

  - The economic circumstances surrounding a transaction or economic event can sometimes make it difficult to identify one best way to account. As a result there is often more than one reasonable way to account for a transaction or economic event. The people who prepare the financial statements must exercise judgment.
  - The choices made by the people preparing the financial statements can be influenced by two broad factors: the information needs of stakeholders and the self-interest of preparers.
  - Entities are allowed to prepare only one set of general purpose financial statements (but many additional special purpose reports).
  - There is often a variety of stakeholders with different decisions to make and different information needs. A single general purpose report may not be useful or appropriate for all stakeholders.
  - There are many different objectives of financial reporting. Different objectives of financial reporting can result in very different financial statements. It is the preparer who gets to choose which objective or objectives the financial statements will serve.
  - It can be very difficult for a user to determine what the preparer's objectives are.
  - There are limitations to the choices that preparers can make. The constraints include GAAP, securities laws, tax laws, corporations laws, the terms of contracts, and others. Constraints may reduce or eliminate choice in some circumstances. However, it is rarely possible to eliminate by law or by contract all accounting choices.

- The existence of alternative accounting treatments makes it necessary to decide which accounting alternative to choose. Choosing among accounting alternatives requires consideration of the relevant constraints, facts, and objectives, and application of a problem-solving approach that incorporates the following steps:
    1. Assess the entity and its environment.
    2. Create a framework for analyzing the accounting issues.
    3. Identify the accounting problems.
    4. Rank the problems in order of importance and emphasize the more important problems in the analysis.
    5. Analyze the accounting problems.
    6. Make a recommendation and explain why the recommendation is consistent with the framework for analysis that you initially set up.

Study Points and Study Tips

Revenue Recognition

- Revenue recognition refers to when an entity records revenue in the accounting system and when revenue or sales are reported on the income statement.
    - Under accrual accounting revenue represents economic benefits gained by the entity. Revenue does not have to be recognized when cash is received. Because revenue represents economic benefits and not simply cash inflows, "when" revenue should be recognized is not always obvious and may require that the preparers exercise judgement.
    - Revenue recognition drives the information in the income statement. How and when revenue is recognized not only affects the amount and timing of revenue but also of expenses because the timing of many expenses depends on when revenue is recognized.
- The journal entry to record revenue is:

Dr. Cash (asset +) or Accounts Receivables (asset +) or Unearned Revenue (liabilities -)	xxx	
Cr. Revenue (revenue +, owners' equity +)		xxx
To record revenue.		

- Under GAAP four criteria have been established to guide the choice of when revenue should be recognized. The four criteria along with brief explanations are:
    - The revenue has been earned.
        - To recognize revenue, the entity must have fulfilled most of what it had to do to receive the benefits associated with the effort being provided. The *CICA Handbook* states that revenue is earned when the significant rights and risks of ownership have been transferred from the seller to the buyer.
    - The amount of revenue can be reasonably measured.
        - The amount of revenue that will be earned is known.
    - The costs required to earn the revenue can be reasonably measured.
        - It is necessary to know or estimate the costs that were/will be incurred to earn the revenue, including costs that will be incurred after the revenue is recognized. This criterion is necessary if expenses are going to be matched to revenue.
    - Collection of payment is reasonably assured.
        - There must be a reasonable expectation that payment will be received.

- An additional, overriding criterion requires that the method of revenue recognition must provide a reasonable and fair representation of the entity's activities, given the needs of the people who are using the accounting information.
- While these criteria provide guidance to preparers, they are open to interpretation and judgement. For example, the criteria do not explicitly stated when revenue is earned. As a result there are many situations where arguments can be made for more than one revenue recognition point. It is also not exactly clear when revenue and costs can be reasonably measured and when collection is reasonably assured.
  - The revenue recognition policies of some companies, particularly public companies came under close scrutiny in the early 2000s. Securities regulators, particularly in the U.S., took steps to tighten the rules so that managers had less flexibility.
- Broadly, accountants have devised two approaches for recognizing revenue.
  - Critical-event approach: Under the critical-event approach, an entity chooses an instant in the earnings process as the revenue recognition point. That instant is called the critical event. When the critical event occurs, 100% of the revenue is recognized. Examples of critical events include delivery of goods or services to customers, completion of production of the product, and collection of cash.
  - Gradual approach: With the gradual approach revenue is recognized gradually over a period of time. The gradual approach is used for long-term construction contracts (dams, buildings) where the earnings process continues over more than one accounting period. It is also used in situations where the earning process is continuous, such as earnings interest on a bond or bank account.
    - The percentage-of-completion method is a gradual approach method in which revenue is recognized based on the proportion of the project that has been completed. One method of estimating the proportion of the project completed is to determine the percentage current period costs are of total estimated costs for the project. The calculation of the amount of revenue to recognize in a period is:

$$\text{Revenue for the period} = \frac{\text{Cost incurred during the period}}{\text{Total estimated costs for the project}} \times \text{Estimated revenue for the project}$$

    - If it is expected that a long-term contract will lose money, the full amount of the loss must be recognized immediately. A loss is not spread over the life of the contract.
    - If it is not possible to use a gradual approach such as the percentage-of-completion method for a long-term contract, a critical event method called the completed contract method is used. It might not be possible to use the percentage-of-completion method if the percentage of the project that has been completed cannot be reasonably estimated or if total costs are too difficult to estimate.
- The critical event and gradual approaches are not substitutes for one another. Each is appropriate in different circumstances.
- The timing and approach to recognizing revenue can have a dramatic effect on an entity's financial statements. Many of the numbers reported in the financial statements will be affected, as will various financial ratios that are used in the analysis of an entity. It is important to remember that even though the numbers may be different, the underlying economic activity that those numbers represent is the same. Different accounting treatments simply lead to different representations of that economic activity.

Gains And Losses

- A gain or loss arises when an entity sells an asset that it does not usually sell in the ordinary course of its business for an amount that is different from the asset's net book value (NBV). A gain or loss is calculated as follows:

  Gain/(Loss) = Selling price of asset - NBV

  When the selling price is greater than the NBV a gain occurs. When the selling price is less than the NBV there is a loss.
- A gain is a credit to the income statement because an asset is being sold for more than its book value so net assets and owners' equity increase. A loss is a debit to the income statement because an asset is being sold for less than its book value so net assets and owners' equity decrease.
- When a gain or loss is reported, the amount is shown net. That is, when incidental assets such as capital assets are sold, the selling price minus the NBV are reported as a single number on the income statement. In contrast, when an entity sells its inventory or provides its services as part of its normal business activities, revenue and costs are reported separately.
- Gains and losses are typically not included in revenue on the income statement. Instead they are usually shown separately somewhere below gross margin. If gains and losses are included in revenue, the revenue number is more difficult to interpret because it includes amounts that are not part of the ordinary revenue generating activities of the entity.
- The amount of a gain or loss is affected by how an asset is accounted for. Different accounting choices lead to different NBVs which lead to different amounts of gains and losses.
- In this chapter and in Study Problem 5 that follows, land is used as the basis for the examples. The reason is that land is not amortized. Gains and losses on assets that are amortized is discussed in Chapter 9.

Expense Recognition

- In accrual accounting expenses are the costs of earning revenue and are matched to revenue. This means that first revenue is recognized and then the costs incurred to earn the revenue are expensed in the same period as the revenue is recognized.
  - The direction of this process is important. Expenses are matched to revenues, not the other way around.
  - In accrual accounting expenses are recognized regardless of whether the cash expenditure associated with the expense occurs before, after, or at the same time the expense is recognized.
- Matching is an attractive concept because it associates economic costs with economic benefits. This association between costs and benefits makes accounting income (in principle, at least) a measure of performance of an entity and a measure of the increase in wealth of the owners.
- While matching is desirable in accrual accounting it is not practical for many costs. Many costs are difficult to associate with specific revenues or to the revenues earned in a particular period.
  - The direct costs of producing a product—costs such as direct labour and materials can logically be matched to the revenue that is recognized when the product is sold.

  - Costs that can be matched to the revenues they help earn are called product costs.

- In contrast, salaries of senior executives, amortization of buildings, and advertising and promotion are difficult to match to any particular revenues, although it is clear that these costs contribute to earning revenue. It's just difficult to say which revenues, when, and how much.
  - Costs that are expensed in the period they are incurred are called period costs.
- The classification of costs as period or product costs is not uniform from entity to entity. The costs that one entity treats as a product cost another might classify as a period cost. These differences reduce the comparability of entities' financial statements.
- Because it is not possible to perfectly match all costs to revenue, the relationship between economic costs and benefits is impaired and there are limits to the usefulness of income as a measure of performance and as an indicator of future performance.
  - For example, Canadian GAAP requires all costs an entity incurs for research to be expensed when incurred. By expensing research costs when incurred, a major cost of certain goods and services that will be sold in the future will not be matched to the revenues those products earn. This problem is especially acute in the high technology and pharmaceuticals industries.

- Matching is not attractive for all users and uses of accounting information. If the preparers are interested in minimizing income taxes they will want to recognize expenses as early as possible and delay revenue recognition, even if matching is not achieved.

The Objectives of Financial Reporting

- The objectives of financial reporting define how preparers approach their entities' financial reporting and why stakeholders want financial statement and other accounting information.
  - An entity's general purpose financial statements cannot be equally useful to all stakeholders and for all decisions. Since an entity can only prepare a single set of general purpose financial statements, managers must make choices about how to approach their financial reporting.
  - Financial reporting is like any other form of communication. The communicator will try to tailor the message so that it most effectively communicates with the intended audience. For example, an advertiser will not use the same approach to market a product to different age groups.
- Managers approach to financial reporting of the entity is motivated by two factors:
  - the information needs of stakeholders
  - the self-interests of the managers
  - Ideally, managers should focus on the information needs of stakeholders. However, even if self-interest is not an issue, managers must choose among the information needs of the different stakeholders.
- Because financial statements and other accounting information are prepared by an entity's management, the managers get to decide what the objectives of reporting are. The needs of stakeholders will influence the choices of management, but the choice belongs to management.

- The objectives of financial reporting are summarized below. These objectives are discussed in depth in the textbook.

Objective	Brief description
Tax minimization	Pay as little tax as is legally possible.
Stewardship	Provide the owners of assets with information about how those responsible for looking after the assets and the interests of others have carried out their responsibilities.
Management evaluation	Assess the performance of an entity's management.
Performance evaluation	Assess the performance of an entity.
Cash flow prediction	Predict future cash flows.
Monitoring contract compliance	Determine whether the terms of contracts have been complied with.
Earnings management	
Managing earnings to reduce income	Making accounting choices that tend to reduce earnings.
Managing earnings to increase income	Making accounting choices that tend to increase earnings.
Managing earnings to smooth income	Making accounting choices that tend to smooth earnings.
Minimum compliance	Provide the minimum amount of information necessary to comply with reporting requirements

- It is crucial to understand that different accounting choices (motivated by different objectives of financial reporting) can result in the same underlying economic activity being presented very differently in the financial statements. However, the different choices do not affect the underlying economic activity of the entity. Only how that economic activity is reported is affected.

- The idea that there can be different ways to account can be troubling to some people. A possible explanation why some people are troubled is the misconception that accounting is strictly mathematical. That is, accounting is simply a matter of adding and subtracting—and we know there is little ambiguity in arithmetic.
  - In reality, accounting is as much an art as it is a science. There are a lot of ambiguities and uncertainties in accounting and deciding how to reflect complex economic activity in financial statements is challenging and requires judgement. Because of the ambiguities and uncertainties there can often be multiple approaches to financial reporting that can be sensible, reasonable, and appropriate—there is not necessarily "one right answer" to accounting problems.
  - Absent any clear-cut "right answer" managers must choose from the alternatives. The objectives of financial reporting are the basis of making the choice.

- Consider an example. Most entities would want to pay as little tax as legally possible. However, suppose a company has shareholders who are not involved in managing the company and who rely on the general purpose financial statements for information about the performance of the entity. An entity can prepare only one set of general purpose financial statements and it is required for both tax purposes and by the shareholders so there is a conflict. Should the managers make accounting choices that reduce taxes or that provide information that is useful to the shareholders?

- When preparers manage their earnings, or make any accounting choices, they are usually operating within the rules. For entities that follow GAAP this means that the accounting choices the managers make will be consistent with GAAP.
- The impact of different accounting choices is not necessarily transparent. Finding accounting differences among entities can require a lot of careful reading and analysis. Some differences may not even be detectable. For example, it is not necessary for entities to disclose the amount and basis of many of the estimates that are required to prepare financial statements.
  - Entities are required to disclose the accounting policies they use, but it may be difficult to determine what the accounting numbers would have been had some alternative policy been used.

Can Preparers Do Whatever They Want?

- Preparers are not free to do whatever it takes to achieve their objectives. As shown in Figure 4-1 in the text there are a number of factors that can limit or restrict the choices available to preparers.
  - The choices available can be limited by contracts (e.g. lending agreements), laws (e.g. tax, securities, and corporations laws), accounting rules (e.g. GAAP), and the information needs and demands of powerful users of accounting information (e.g. bankers, large shareholders).
- Accounting choice is also limited by the economic circumstances surrounding a transaction or economic event. The accounting method used must be reasonable and supportable given the circumstances. Preparers cannot choose an accounting method that is contrary to the facts just because it suits their objectives.
- Recent accounting controversies that have called into question the reliability of financial statement information have arisen because there is flexibility in financial reporting.
  - It is attractive, even seductive, to suggest that GAAP should eliminate choice and flexibility. However attractive such a proposal may seem there are practical limitations. Economic activity is too complex and ever changing to make it possible to define comprehensive rules that apply to all situations.
  - That said, tightening accounting rules where possible and sensible would to help increase the confidence that users of financial statements have in the information.
  - Perhaps more important is the need for integrity and ethical behaviour by managers and auditors in their involvement with financial statements.
- The existence of accounting choice is a double-edged sword. If there were a comprehensive set of rules that all entities had to follow there would be no question of how each entity did its accounting. However, simply because all entities use the same accounting methods does not mean that the accounting is sensible in all cases. Different economic circumstances make

different accounting treatments appropriate. Forcing all entities to use the same treatments could make financial statements misleading.

- On the other hand, the availability of alternatives from which preparers can choose provides flexibility that the preparers can use to pursue their self-interests.

Solving Accounting Choice Problems

- Perhaps the most challenging aspect of this book is applying the themes discussed in this chapter. Chapter 4 introduced two important themes:
  - First, an accounting issue, revenue recognition, was introduced that sometimes provides legitimate and reasonable alternative ways of accounting. In such a situation preparers have to exercise judgement in deciding how to account for revenue.
  - Second, the objectives of financial reporting were introduced. These objectives provide reasons why a manager might choose one accounting alternative over another.
- Chapter 4 introduces a problem solving process that links these two themes. The problem solving process places you in the roles of users and prepares so that you can understand the process that managers might follow in making their accounting choices and the implications of accounting choices on users.
- The following factors must be considered when making accounting choices:
  - Constraints—formal external limitations on the choices available to preparers, such as GAAP, legal requirements, and contract terms.
  - Facts—the circumstances surrounding and related to the transaction or economic event being accounted for.
  - Objectives—the objectives of financial reporting.
- If the constraints and the facts still provide more than one possible reasonable and legitimate accounting choice, the preparer can then appeal to the objectives. That means that from the remaining alternatives a manager can choose the alternative that best suits his or her objectives. However, remember that:
  - The objectives are the last consideration, not the first. If the constraints and/or facts point to an accounting treatment that is not consistent with the objectives, that is the treatment that must be used.
  - Alternatives available after considering the constraints and the facts are legitimate alternatives. Each alternative remaining after considering the facts and constraints must be supportable by the facts and constraints.
- The problem solving approach described in the chapter focuses on the preparer's perspective. Preparers must decide how to prepare their entities' financial statements. They must consider the users and uses of the financial statements and the needs of the entity, determine and rank the reporting objectives and use the ranking as the framework for preparing the financial statements. (In practice preparers might not follow this process formally, but there can be little doubt that the objectives of financial reporting come into play.)
  - Some readers might wonder why problems with a preparer perspective get such heavy emphasis in a book whose focus is understanding financial statements and other accounting information. The reason is that viewing the world from a preparer's perspective should provide insight into preparers' financial reporting decisions. Understanding how a preparer must deal with the competing objectives of various

stakeholders and the role of the preparer's self-interest will make users more aware of the nature, risks, and limitations associated with accounting information and allow users to use accounting information more effectively.

- The user's perspective is simpler. A user must only consider his or her own objectives and information needs. The objectives of other stakeholders are not relevant. What is important to the user is to assess the appropriateness, usefulness, and reasonableness of the information provided by the entity for the user's purpose. A user who disagrees with particular accounting choices would provide his or her interpretation of the facts to make a case for his or her preference. Like the preparer, a user must be able to support the preferred accounting choice. A choice is not acceptable simply because it is preferred.
- When analyzing cases and other certain types of accounting problems remember:
  - Understand and play your role.
  - It is never possible, in textbooks or in the real world, to have all information. The cases in the book are more limited than the real world, but it is ultimately always necessary to make *reasonable* assumptions to fill in the missing information.
  - There can be more than one reasonable approach to analyzing cases. Different rankings of objectives, interpretations of the facts, and so on can lead to different recommendations. The key to success in these types of cases is the process of getting to the conclusion, not necessarily the conclusion itself. However, while there may be more than one acceptable or reasonable approach, there are also many poor or unreasonable approaches.
- CAUTION! The discussion in this section of the book can be an ethical minefield, both in practice and in studying accounting. In reading the discussion in this section it is easy to come to the conclusion that preparers of accounting information are always scheming and manipulating to the disadvantage of the users of the information. The accounting scandals of the early 2000s can certainly reinforce this belief.
  - The reality of accounting is that managers often have choices to make and those choices sometimes are made to serve the interests of those managers rather than the interests of stakeholders. One of the objectives of *Financial Accounting: A Critical Approach* is to make you aware the nature of accounting so that you can understand these controversies and be aware of the impact of this characteristic of the discipline.
  - There clearly are problems with accounting. A higher standard of ethical behaviour by managers, accountants, auditors, financial analysts, and others would go a long way to adding credibility and confidence to accounting information.
  - Recognize that accounting is not unique in being influenced by self-interest. Some physicians have been accused of recommending more costly medical procedures because they result in more income for the physician. Politicians are routinely seen to allocate money to projects and regions that will improve their likelihood of they and their party being re-elected. Advertisers promote products by emphasizing positive attributes and minimizing negative ones. There are many more examples.

Study Problems

Study Problem 1 (Determining when to recognize revenue) For each of the following situations explain when revenue should be recognized. Consider the constraints, facts, and objectives in your response and identify possible alternative revenue recognition points.

a. A small retail clothing store operated by the owner and sole shareholder sells a suit to a customer. A customer pays for the suit using his MasterCard. The suit cannot be returned but the store promises to make any minor alterations as long as the customer owns the suit.

b. A manufacturer receives a custom order from a customer. The customer requests that the manufacturer hold the order for several months until the goods are needed by the customer. At this stage the customer is not sure when the goods will be needed but has made the order now to ensure availability as required. The goods have been stored in a secure area of the manufacturer's warehouse. Because of the custom nature of the order the goods cannot be sold to other customers.

Study Problem 2 (Determining the objectives of financial reporting) Explain what the primary objective financial reporting of each of the following stakeholders might be:

a. The owner-manager (sole shareholder) of a small incorporated business.
b. Shareholder of a large, publicly traded corporation.
c. A prospective lender considering whether to give a small business a large loan.
d. Managers of a privately owned business (the owners are not involved in day-to-day management) who are compensated in part on the basis of the business' performance.

Study Problem 3 (Accounting for gains and losses) Part A: For each of the following land sales, prepare the journal entry that would be recorded and indicate the amount of the gain or loss that would be reported. Assume that in each case, the sale of land is not a main business activity of the entity.

a. Land costing $550,000 is sold for $857,000.
b. Land costing $925,000 is sold for $925,000.
c. Land costing $1,750,000 is sold for $1,100,000.

Part B: Calculate the missing amounts (indicated by a question mark) using the information provided:

	NBV of land	Gain (loss) on sale of land	Selling price of land
a.	115,000	27,000	?
b.	?	(85,000)	610,000
c.	?	0	250,000
d.	47,000	(15,000)	?
e.	?	122,000	380,000

Study Problem 4 (Determining the effect of different revenue recognition methods on accounting information) On, April 15, 2004 Seabright Dry Dock Ltd. (Seabright) signed a contract to refit a super tanker. The tanker required extensive work on its hull and engine. Seabright has provided you with the following information about the contract:

i. Seabright expects the refitting to take just under two years to complete.
ii. Seabright will receive $23,500,000 for the renovations. Seabright will receive payments on the following schedule:

- $2,500,000 when the contract is signed
- $8,000,000 on October 15, 2005
- $13,000,000 on May 15, 2006, the expected completion date of the refitting

iii. The total cost of the renovations is expected to be $16,000,000. Seabright will incur costs on the following schedule:
- 2004: $0
- 2005: $9,075,000
- 2006: $7,425,000

iv. Other costs associated with the contract are $1,200,000 in each of 2005 and 2006. These costs should be treated as period costs in the calculation of income.

v. Seabright's year end is April 30.

Required:

a. Calculate revenue, expenses, gross margin, and net income for each year using the following revenue-recognition methods:
   i. Percentage-of-completion
   ii. Completed-contract
   iii. Cash collection (Hint: use the cash basis to record expenses.)

b. Calculate the gross margin percentage and the profit margin percentage for each year.

c. Does it matter how Seabright accounts for its revenue from the renovation contract? To whom does it matter and why?

d. Which method should Seabright use to recognize revenue on the tanker contract? Be sure to consider constraints, facts, and objectives in your response.

Study Problem 5 (Application problem) Graphite Discount Building Supplies Limited (Graphite) is a chain of large building supply stores. Graphite sells building supplies to individuals and small contractors and builders. Until recently Graphite was a division of another company, but the previous owner decided to sell Graphite because it was not in its core business. Graphite had been profitable, but the profits were small and it was consuming too much of senior managements' time. A group of 25 business people purchased Graphite. None of the new owners will be involved in the day to day management of Graphite, but some of them will sit on the board of directors. The new owners paid cash for Graphite. The new owners also agreed to pay the previous owner each year an amount equal to 10% of Graphite's net income for each of the next three years (including 2004) as reported in Graphite's audited general purpose financial statements. The board of directors hired a new management team to operate Graphite. The managers will receive performance-based bonuses, in part based on net income as reported in the general purpose financial statements.

It is now mid-January 2005. Graphite is preparing its financial statements for its fiscal year ended December 31, 2004. The chair of the board of directors of Graphite has asked you to provide advice on a number of outstanding accounting issues. After the Board has discussed your recommendations, they will be given to Graphite's management team for implementation. The following are the issues you have been asked to address.

a. Graphite implemented a new policy that requires customers to pay an annual membership fee to shop at its stores. The annual fee is payable when the customer "joins" and on each anniversary of joining. The fee gives a customer the right to shop at Graphite's stores and benefit from the discounts it offers. A customer has the right to cancel the membership at any time and receive a full refund of the membership fee. The fee is refundable in full at any time during the year, regardless of whether the customer has purchased anything in the store. If a customer requests a refund he or she is not allowed to rejoin for one year. Management estimates that about 40% of its customers will request refunds each year.

b. Graphite's business with most customers is transacted in cash or on credit cards. Graphite offers credit terms to builders and contractors, allowing them up to 90 days to pay. Graphite has made special credit arrangements with a small number of struggling builders of homes. Graphite has extended credit terms to these struggling builders even though sales of the homes they are building have been slower than expected. In these cases, Graphite has agreed to accept payment each time a builder sells one of its homes.
c. During the year Graphite launched a major advertising campaign to increase awareness of its stores and products. Management wanted to raise the profile of the Graphite chain in the minds of customers and potential customers so that people would think of Graphite when they needed hardware and building supplies. Costs of the campaign included television, radio, and newspaper advertising and sponsorship of community events.

Required:

Prepare the report requested by Graphite's board of directors. Your report should:

i) Identify the likely users of the financial statements and describe the uses they will have for the statements.
ii) Identify and explain the possible objectives of financial reporting and rank the objectives. (You should respond from the perspective of an advisor to Graphite's board of directors. Recognize that different stakeholders could have different objectives. For example, the objectives of the managers may not be the same as the board.
iii) Are there any constraints that limit the accounting choices that Graphite can make?
iv) Identify and discuss reasonable alternative treatments for each accounting issue and make a recommendation about how Graphite should account for each issue. Your discussion and recommendations should consider any relevant constraints, facts, and objectives.

Solutions to Study Problems

(Note that comments that appear in the solutions in *italics* are intended to provide explanations and clarifications to help you understand the material. These comments are not required as part of a complete solution)

Solution to Study Problem 1

a. The objectives of the retailer are likely tax minimization or to provide information to creditors, if any. However, the facts of the situation make consideration of the objectives unimportant. At the time the customer purchases the suit the four revenue recognition criteria are met. The revenue has been earned since the store has provided the customer with the suit and with the exchange the rights and risks of ownership have been transferred to the customer. (If the customer damages the suit or decides that he doesn't like it, it cannot be returned.) The amount of revenue is known since the suit has been paid for (and it can't be returned). Costs are known since the store would have purchased the suit from the manufacturer. The cost of any alterations to be provided in the future would have to be estimated if the owner wanted to accrue these costs, but the cost of alterations is likely small. Also, estimated future costs are not allowable for tax purposes so if the main objective were tax minimization and the main purpose of the statements was for tax purposes there would be no reason to accrue the cost. Collection is assured since payment has been made with a credit card.

b. The facts are quite ambiguous in this situation. Two possible points of revenue recognition are when production is complete and the goods are available for shipping to the customer and when the goods are actually shipped to the customer. The criterion that is mainly in question in this situation is when the revenue is earned. One could argue that once the goods have been made, are available for shipping, and have been safely stored in the warehouse, the manufacturer has fulfilled its responsibilities and revenue could be recognized. In this situation the manufacturer has met the obligations to the customer, all that is needed is the request for shipping by the customer. This revenue recognition point would be attractive in situations where higher revenue and/or income is desired. On the other hand, it could be argued that the rights and risks of ownership have not been transferred until the goods are delivered to the customer. A number of things could happen before delivery that would suggest that the rights and risks of ownership had not been transferred. For example, what would happen if the goods were damaged or destroyed while in the custody of the manufacturer? What if the customer decided that the goods were not required (i.e. the order was cancelled) or the customer would not accept the goods, perhaps because they did not meet specifications. From this perspective delaying revenue recognition until the goods were actually delivered makes sense. From an objectives standpoint this revenue recognition point would satisfy the tax minimization objective.

Solution to Study Problem 2

a. The owner-manager (sole shareholder) of a small incorporated business.

It is likely that an important objective of financial reporting would be tax minimization. As the sole owner and manager of the entity there is no need for communication with outside owners so paying as little tax as possible in any given year is attractive. It is also possible that the small incorporated business has creditors that receive the financial statements. The owner-manager would want to ensure that these creditors are prepared to maintain and provide the financing the business requires. If these creditors were the main focus of the owner-manager then the objective would be to provide liquidity and cash flow information so that the creditors could assess the business' ability to repay amounts owed.

b. Small shareholder of a large, publicly traded corporation.

Small shareholders rely on the annual reports of public companies (the general purpose financial statements) for information about the entity. Small shareholders have little influence on how management prepares those statements. Yet these small shareholders have important decision needs. Their objectives can include:

- management evaluation (is management doing a satisfactory job).
- performance evaluation (how is the company doing) and how will it be doing in the future (cash flow prediction, other predictions).
- stewardship.

Comment: A possible conflict can be seen here. While the small shareholders have information needs, management controls the information provided in the annual report. The managers may have objectives that are not consistent with the information needs of the small shareholders. For example, they may want to provide the minimum amount of information that is legally required (minimum compliance) or manage earnings for some reason.

c. A prospective lender considering whether to give a small business a large loan.

Lenders are concerned about whether the loans they make will be repaid, and in the event that the borrower cannot meet its payments that there is adequate security available. The lender will want to know whether the borrower will be able to generate adequate cash flows to make the required payments. Thus the objective is cash flow prediction.

Comment: Cash flow prediction is a future-oriented objective while financial statements tend to be historical (that is, they report what happened, not what will happen). Thus for cash flow prediction purposes there are limits to the usefulness of general purpose financial statements. In some cases the general purpose statements can provide a starting point for making predictions, but future-oriented information must be considered to forecast the future. A lender such as a bank might be able to request future-oriented information as part of the lending agreement. General purpose statements are also limited in usefulness for determining the availability of security for loans. The current value of assets that the lender might receive in the event a loan is not repaid is not provided (the general purpose financial statements provide valuations based on cost, not on current market values).

d. Managers of a privately owned business (the owners are not involved in day-to-day management) who are compensated in part on the basis of the business' net income.

Since part of the managers compensation is based on net income they would likely want to receive as much bonus as they reasonably could. This would mean that the accounting choices they would would tend to increase income.

Comment: Notice the conflict that can arise here. While the managers are interested in increasing income to obtain a larger bonus, the owners' interests are likely served by minimizing taxes. A tax minimization strategy means making income as low as possible while meeting the requirements of the Income Tax Act. This approach would not be satisfactory to the managers who would prefer net income being as high as it reasonably can be (to maximize the bonus), but at a minimum would want net income to be a reasonable reflection of their performance. As a result, the managers may be inclined to make accounting choices that increase income and their bonuses, rather than reduce taxes.

Solution to Study Problem 3

Part A

a.	Dr. Cash (asset +)	857,000	
	Cr. Gain on sale of land (income statement +)		307,000
	Cr. Land (asset -)		550,000
	To record the gain on the sale of land		

Comment: A gain is recorded in this case because the book value of the land ($550,000 is less than its selling price ($857,000). The amount of the gain equals the proceeds from the sale of the land less the land's net book value (NBV). In this case,

	Selling price	*$857,000*
-	*NBV*	*550,000*
=	*Gain*	*$307,000*

b.	Dr. Cash	925,000	
	Cr. Land		925,000
	To record the sale of land		

Comment: In this case there is neither a loss nor a gain because the land is being sold for its net book value. In this case,

	Selling price	*$925,000*
-	*NBV*	*925,000*
		$ 0

c.

		Dr.	Cr.
Dr.	Cash	1,100,000	
Dr.	Loss on sale of land (income statement)	650,000	
	Cr. Land		1,750,000

To record the loss on the sale of land

Comment: A loss is recorded in this case because the book value of the land ($1,750,000) is greater than its selling price ($1,100,000). The amount of the loss equals the proceeds from the sale of the land less the land's NBV. In this case,

	Selling price	*$ 1,100,000*
-	*NBV*	*1,750,000*
=	*Loss*	*($ 650,000)*

Part B

Comment: The purpose of this part of the problem is to ensure you understand how gains and losses are calculated. If you remember and understand the equation that is used to calculate gains and losses finding the missing information is straightforward. All you have to do is organize the information according to the equation. In the problem the data was not put in the order of the equation to make it a bit more challenging. The solution reorganizes the data so that it corresponds with the equation. Remember that when you use the equation if the Proceeds - NBV is negative there is a loss and if Proceeds - NBV is positive there is a gain.

	Selling price of land	-	NBV of land	=	Gain (loss) on sale of land
a.	142,000		115,000		27,000
b.	610,000		695,000		(85,000)
c.	250,000		250,000		0
d.	32,000		47,000		(15,000)
e.	380,000		258,000		122,000

Solution to Study Problem 4

a. and b.

Seabright Dry Dock Ltd.
Income Statements
(in thousands of dollars)

	Percentage of completion			Completed contract			Cash collection		
	2004	2005	2006	2004	2005	2006	2004	2005	2006
Revenue	$0	$12,925	$10,575	$0	$0	$23,500	$2,500	$8,000	$13,000
Cost of sales	0	9,075	7,425	0	0	16,500	0	9,075	7,425
Gross margin	0	3,850	3,150	0	0	7,000	2,500	(1,075)	5,575
Other expenses	0	1,200	1,200	0	1,200	1,200	0	1,200	1,200
Net income	$0	$2,650	$1,950	$0	($1,200)	$5,800	$2,500	($2,275)	$4,375
Gross margin percentage	-	29.8%	29.8%	-	-	29.8%	100%	-13.4%	42.9%
Profit margin percentage	-	20.5%	18.4%	-	-	24.7%	100%	-28.4%	33.7%

*Comment: The amount of revenue recognized under the percentage-of-completion method is based on costs incurred to date. In 2005 55% of the estimated costs were incurred ($9,075,000/$16,500,000) so 55% of the revenues ($23,500,000 * 55% = $12,925,000) are recognized. The remainder of the costs (45%) were incurred in 2006 so 45% of the revenue is recognized in 2006. The $1,200,000 of period expenses are expensed each year regardless of the percentage of revenues recognized. If the completed contract method is used no revenue is recognized until 2006 when the work has been completed. The period costs, costs that cannot be specifically matched to this project would be expensed as incurred. In the cash collection method expense are recorded as incurred. It would have also been possible to expense them based on the proportion of revenue recognized each year.*

c. The accounting method that Seabright uses has no effect on the underlying economic activity of the company. The costs and revenues associated with this contract, and the timing of the payments to Seabright will not be affected by the method. However, the method used does matter. The method used affects the timing of revenue and income. As can be seen in part a), revenue and net income varied significantly among the methods. These different measurements may have economic consequences for the entity and its stakeholders. The timing of tax payments, manager bonuses, compliance with contractual arrangements, among others could be affected.

d. There is not enough information to definitively decide which revenue recognition method Seabright should use. The facts would likely support the percentage-of-completion and completed contract methods, though the percentage of completion method would likely be preferred if reasonable estimates of costs and revenues could be made. The cash basis is probably not supportable unless there was a good case for collection problems. Especially difficult to justify would be the initial $2,500,000 payment, which would be recognized before any work was done.

   If Seabright's main objective was minimizing taxes the completed-contract method would be best. The method is allowed by CCRA (the contract is less than two years in length) and it would defer taxes until fiscal 2006. In addition, the costs that cannot be matched to the contract in 2005 could be used to reduce taxes further in 2005 (assuming Seabright has income from other sources). Minimizing taxes might be attractive to shareholders, but if managers received compensation on bonuses they would probably not like the choice. Presumably the managers would like to receive their bonuses as soon as possible. The completed contract method would delay any bonuses until 2006. Percentage of completion would be better since bonus payments would be received in 2005. If the cash collection method could be justified some bonus might be received in 2004. While attractive, it would likely be difficult to justify cash collection by the facts, as discussed earlier. The percentage-of-completion method would also be useful to evaluate Seabright's performance because it gives an indication of the ongoing economic activity. The cash collection method would probably be useful for stakeholders who were interest in seeing Seabright's cash flows. However, depending on the ongoing nature of the business the cash collection method might not be an indication of future cash flows, which lenders would be particularly interested in.

Comment: In this study problem not much information was given to allow an evaluation of the objectives of reporting. This was intentional. The idea here was to have you think about how the different methods could serve different legitimate uses without focussing on a single use. In reading the response notice how each alternative was tied to some use. Also notice that the facts and constraints were considered. Thus while some methods might be attractive for a particular objective, if the method is not allowable by the facts then the alternative would be rejected.

Solution to Study Problem 5

To the Members of the Board of Graphite Discount Building Supplies Limited:

This report provides accounting recommendations regarding the three outstanding issues that you brought to my attention. In my report I discuss the users of the financial statements and the uses they have, the financial reporting approach that I believe the Board should take, and discussion of the specific accounting issues.

Respectfully,

Accounting Advisor

Report to the Board of Directors of Graphite Discount Building Supplies Limited

i) Users and uses

I have identified the following users and uses of Graphite's financial statements. Identifying the users is necessary and important so that you can understand who will have access to the statements and what use they will put to them. This information is then useful in determining how to tailor the financial statements. While there are a number of different users and user groups relying on Graphite's general purpose financial statements, only a single set of general purpose statements can be prepared, even though these different users have different purposes for the statements.

User	Use
Previous owner	Determine the payment it will receive from the sale of Graphite, based on Graphite's income over the next three years
New owners	Evaluate performance of Graphite and its managers, minimize taxes, stewardship
CCRA	Calculation of taxes and ensure compliance with the Income Tax Act
New managers	Determine their bonuses, which are based on net income

Comment: Identification of users and the uses they have for information is an important step in analyzing accounting problems. This step identifies the stakeholders and defines their needs. In a preparer case (the board of directors in the question will determine Graphite's accounting policies) it is necessary to take stock of the users because the objectives emerge from the users and uses.

Comment: The previous owner will have access to the financial statements because the payments to the previous owner are based on accounting measures. Recognize that the interest of the previous owner in the financial statements will be limited to determining the payment it is to receive. The previous owner will not be interest in evaluating performance of Graphite since it no longer owns it.

ii) Objectives

The objectives of financial reporting represent the reporting focus that Graphite will take in its financial statements. Identifying the objectives is important because as was explained in the previous section of this report there are a number of users whose interests differ. Because only a single set of general purpose financial statements can be prepared, it will not be possible to satisfy all objectives. The possible objectives of financial reporting include:

Tax minimization (income minimization)—Under this objective accounting choices will be made with the purpose of lowering income and lowering taxes. This strategy will also have the effect of reducing payments to the previous owners because those payments are based on net income. The information I have been provided indicates that for purposes of determining the amount of the payment GAAP must be followed. No additional restrictions are stated. Therefore, any accounting choices that conform with GAAP are acceptable for purposes of determining the payment. This objective is attractive because in conserves cash by reducing tax payments and payments to the previous owner. However, a drawback to this objective is that it may have adverse effects on the managers because their bonuses will be lower than they might have been. The bonus plan was set up to provide incentives for managers and this objective may undermine the purpose of the plan.

Bonus determination—The new managers receive a bonus based in part on Graphite's net income. The managers themselves would prefer higher net income so that they could receive larger bonuses. From the board's perspective the bonus should represent compensation for the accomplishments of the managers. Thus for bonus purposes the objective would be for income and the other measures of performance used to determine the bonus to be linked to the accomplishments of management.

Management/Performance evaluation by absentee shareholders—Some of Graphite's new owners do not sit on the Board of Directors and will require information about Graphite for evaluation and stewardship purposes. Presumably, the Board of Directors will want the shareholders to have good information about the entity. This might require extensive disclosure of relevant information. The problem with extensive disclosure in the general purpose financial statements is that other stakeholders, in particular the previous owners, might receive more information than is desirable. However, it is possible to overcome this potential conflict by providing supplementary reports to the absentee shareholders, as required. As far as the reporting strategy goes, the same approach described for bonus determination would make sense because the measurements would be linked to the accomplishments of management as well as to the accomplishments of the company.

Comment: Note that the objective of management would be different from that of the board of directors for bonus determination. Managers want the largest bonus they can reasonably get whereas the board is more interested in reasonable compensation. The Board should not want to give away the keys to the vault. Some might argue that the Board would want to minimize the bonus. That objective seems unreasonable because the managers were recently hired and the bonuses were put in place as incentives. If the bonuses were intentionally reduced because of accounting choices the managers might be less motivated or might quit altogether.

Comment: Notice that the objectives are formulated from the perspective of the role. In this case the issues are being viewed from the perspective of the Board of Directors. If we were working for the previous owners and received financial statements that resulted in them receiving less than what they felt was appropriate, we would examine the choices made and challenge them.

Comment: The above discussion should make it clear that there are conflicts among the objectives. Income minimization will be useful for reducing taxes and minimizing the payments to the previous owners, but it may create motivational problems for managers, which could have negative implications for the performance of Graphite. In other words, it might be worthwhile to pay a little more in taxes and a little more to the previous owners in exchange for highly motivated managers. The Board must take this conflict into consideration.

Ranking: In my view the primary objective should be income minimization. Reducing payments to the previous owners over the three-year period would represent a real and permanent economic gain to the new owners. Delaying taxes also has economic benefits (conserves cash) which may be important given the small profits that Graphite has been generating (small profits may correspond with low cash flow). This recommendation results in the managers perhaps not receiving what they would see as a "fair" bonus. This may be a difficult problem to address. A contract exists between Graphite and the managers and changing the terms of the contract may not be easy. However, it might be possible to make a side deal with the managers. Otherwise it will be necessary to tradeoff the benefits and costs of this choice. I also suggest that disclosure be minimized in the general purpose statements to minimize information available to users such as the previous owner. The previous owner has no use for any information other than net income and there is no reason to provide unneeded details. Additional information can be provided to the new shareholders in special purpose reports. The managers will not require disclosure because as insiders they will be familiar with the activities of the company.

Comment: This ranking is only one of many possible ones. It would be reasonable to rank the manager bonus as most important. The actual ranking made is less important than the support provided for the ranking chosen. As has been mentioned, there can be many reasonable approaches to solving problems. A good analysis of objectives in this case should have the correct focus (view from the Board of Director's perspective), recognition and discussion of conflicts among objectives, and the ranking. This is not to say, however, that every ranking is acceptable. It is possible in cases to make rankings that do not make sense.

Comment: These cases tend to be more up front about the motivations of the preparers than one would expect to see in actual situations. While there is little doubt that the motivations of the preparers influence financial reporting decisions, one would not expect to see these motivations explicitly stated, and certainly not in documents that would have wide distribution. For example, a manager who makes accounting choices that will have a positive effect on the earnings of the entity (perhaps to increase a bonus or send a positive signal to the stock market) would couch the argument in terms of the accounting rationale. If the intent was explicitly stated the credibility of the information would be lost.

Comment: It is important to comment on ethical issues here. One could argue that the previous owner of Graphite is being cheated because of the income minimization objective. Clearly, the previous owner will not be receiving as much as it would have had another objective been chosen. However, the terms of the contract are being met—the payments are to be based on GAAP-based income. The choices recommended below are fully supportable by the facts. There is no fraud or misrepresentation. There is a lot of "gray", however, but this is the nature of accounting. In addition, we do not really know what the "right" amount of income is. The ultimate purpose of these cases is to make you aware of the impact of the accounting choices that managers can and do make so that you will understand the nature and limitations of accounting information.

iii) Constraints:
Clearly GAAP is a constraint because the financial statements are to be audited and have to be in accordance with GAAP. There is no indication that there are accounting restrictions written into the agreement with the previous owner for determining net income for purposes of the payment to the previous owner.

Issue 1—Membership fees
According to GAAP four criteria must be met if revenue can be recognized. These criteria are:

1. The revenue has been earned.
2. The amount of revenue can be reasonably measured.
3. The costs required to earn the revenue can be reasonably measured.
4. Collection of payment is reasonably assured.

The following analysis will be based on these criteria.

There are three possible revenue recognition points for the membership fees:

a) When a person joins
The key issues with recognizing revenue when a person joins are whether it is earned as of that time and the amount of revenue that is earned. First, what does the membership fee represent? If it represents the right to shop in the store then the revenue has been earned on joining. If, on the other hand, the membership fee represents the right to shop and to receive lower prices, this point is more debatable. A good case can be made that the membership fee simply represents the right to shop. If a customer never buys anything, he or she is not entitled to receive the membership fee back once the membership period is over. Once the year has expired Graphite can keep the money regardless of the amount of merchandise the member did (or didn't) buy. Also, the members still must pay for the merchandise they buy.

More problematic is the amount of revenue. While the amount that each customer pays is known, the amount of revenue that will be realized in total is not known because members can get their membership fees back at any time during the year. Management has estimated that 40% of members will ask for a refund of their membership fees. This estimate has to be considered very rough since this is the first year of doing business this way. There is little basis for supporting the 40% estimate. On the other hand, estimates are an inherent part of accounting so the 40% might be acceptable if at least some support can be given for it. The other revenue recognition criteria are met when a person joins. Cash has been collected so collectibility is assured. Costs related to promoting the store and processing memberships are measurable and should be treated as period costs.

This alternative will result in revenue being recognized at the earliest possible time, which will increase current income.

b) Gradually over the year
This alternative raises the same issues as the first alternative: when revenue is earned and the amount of revenue that will be realized. As was discussed in a), does a membership simply buy access to the store or is the membership fee part of the pricing strategy (i.e. the membership fee covers the lower prices). If the membership fee is tied to the pricing policy then recognition when a person joins is too early. If the membership fee is tied to the pricing policy then gradual recognition can be supported since a customer will benefit from the pricing policy over the life of the membership. As was the case in a), collectibility is not an issue here since cash has already been collected. The cost of the promoting membership are measurable and likely treated as period costs, and the cost savings given to customers as part of their membership are reflected when purchases are made. The problem with revenue remains with this alternative. Until the last day of a person's membership passes the amount of revenue that will be earned is not known because a member can ask for a full refund. The problem with estimating the proportion of members that will ask for refunds is the same as

was described in a). It is possible to make an estimate, as management has, but there is a great deal of uncertainty associated with it.

c) At the end of the year (when Graphite knows for sure that it will keep the fee)
Graphite can only reasonably measure the amount of revenue it is receiving from membership fees at the end of the year. The problem is that members have the right to obtain full refunds at any time. While management has attempted to estimate the percentage of members that will ask for a refund, the 40% is debatable since this is the first year that this business model has been used, so there is little basis for the amount. The 40% could be wildly inaccurate. Perhaps in the future, if a stable pattern emerges for the proportion of members asking for refunds it will be possible to accrue this cost. In the meantime, the uncertainty surrounding the amount would make the financial statements unreliable. Thus even though the other three revenue recognition criteria are met before the end of a member's year, the amount of revenue that will be realized is not known until that time and, therefore, revenue recognition should be delayed until the end of each member's year.

Analysis and Recommendations

The best alternative given the objective of minimizing income is to recognize revenue at the expiration of a member's year. This alternative eliminates the uncertainty about the amount of refunds and so the actual amount of revenue recognized is more reliable. This alternative delays revenue recognition to the latest possible point, but earlier recognition could make the financial statements misleading and result in too much money being paid in taxes and to the previous owner. If too much was paid to the previous owner the excess amount likely would not be recoverable.

Comment: The analysis of this issue should highlight an important point. Good cases can be made, based on the facts and constraints, for more than one alternative. One alternative is not always superior to the others. Yet one must be chosen if the financial statements are to be prepared. It is crucial to recognize that among the three alternatives for membership fees one is not definitively right and the others wrong. (In other words this isn't a trick...trying to see if you can get the "right" answer.) In this situation there is no right answer. Different managers, analysts, and stakeholders could argue passionately for different alternatives. From a user's perspective recognizing the existence of alternatives and their impact on financial statements is crucial for using the statements effectively.

Comment: Some readers may feel intimidated when reading this analysis. You may feel that the analysis is beyond your knowledge, skill, and ability at this stage. In some ways that's true, but analyzing accounting or any other type of problem requires more than just information from a book. What is needed is the ability to take knowledge and information and apply it to a situation. These types of exercises help develop the critical thinking and problem solving skills that are so important. The analysis above applies the four revenue recognition criteria to a set of realistic facts. It is very possible that in your attempt of this case that you didn't make all the same points that are discussed in this solution. That shouldn't be a source of discouragement. I tried to make this solution fairly complete so that you would see many of the issues. That said, some readers may have addressed issues or perspectives in their solutions that were valid but not addressed in this one. These cases are designed to get you thinking about accounting and to help you understand how it works. Don't be discourage if you don't know all there is to know yet, you have a long way to go! If you were able to analyze and interpret the information to craft a valid and useful recommendation, you are moving in the right direction.

Comment: Note that if a different objective was ranked as most important, a different alternative might have been preferred. If a different objective were selected the argument made in support would be different, but would still have to be valid.

Issue 2—Sales to customers
Sales to customers who pay cash or use major credit cards should be recognized on exchange—when a transaction takes place and the customer pays and takes his or her merchandise. The revenue has clearly been earned since the rights and risks of ownership have been transferred and Graphite has few obligations remaining. Revenue is known (the purchase has taken place) and cash collection is assured (cash has been collected or payment has been made with a major credit card, which is as good as cash). There will likely be some merchandise returned for refunds but the amount will likely be small and an allowance could be set up for estimated returns.

Comment: For this issue objectives do not play a role because the facts are clear. There is really no viable alternative to recognizing revenue in this situation, so the facts dictate the accounting treatment. However, observe that why the facts are clear was explained, not just asserted.

The credit arrangements with builders and contractors should also be recognized on exchange. These arrangements with the creditors appear quite typical and there would seem to be no undue risk associated with offering credit. There is uncertainty about the amount of cash that will be collected (because not all contractors will be willing or able to pay), but it should be possible to come up with a reasonable estimate. (Note that this argument is different from the one used for membership fees. Credit sales to customers are more typical and reasonable estimates more possible. However, if the uncertainty about the amount of bad debts were significant, delaying revenue recognition would be appropriate.) The revenue is earned at exchange. Graphite has done all it has to do to earn the revenue except collect the cash, and the rights and risks of ownership are transferred when the customer buys the merchandise and it is taken away or delivered. At the time of exchange the amount of revenue is known (the contractor agreed to a price) and most costs are known (cost of goods is known, most other costs are treated as period costs). The only uncertainty is cash collection and it is assumed that a reasonable estimate of bad debts can be made.

Comment: In most cases revenue would be recognized at exchange. However, note that there is some uncertainty about the facts. Specifically, the amount of cash that will be collected is uncertain.

There is more uncertainty with the sales to the struggling builders. These builders have a much higher likelihood of non-payment and payment is contingent on the sale of the houses being constructed. This means that it is not clear if or when cash will be received. If the houses aren't sold, Graphite will not receive its money. There are two possible points at which revenue could be recognized. First, revenue could be recognized on exchange, as was the case for the credit sales to less risky contractors and builders. Since collection from struggling builders is more uncertain a larger allowance for uncollectable amounts would be appropriate if revenue were recognized on exchange. The second alternative would be to recognize revenue when cash is collected. The rationale for this alternative is that collection is very unpredictable (since there is a small number of struggling builders the actual amount that is ultimately collected could be highly variable) and collection is contingent on the sale of houses. Without the sale of houses collection will not occur. (It could be argued that revenue could be recognized when the builder sells a house, but it would be difficult to verify when the sales occurred so this alternative is not practical.)

The second alternative is recommended given the significant amount of uncertainty of collection. This choice is superior for the objective of minimizing income because it delays revenue recognition until cash is collected. Recognizing revenue on exchange would increase income in more current periods, which would increase taxes and increase payments to the previous owner.

Comment: Even though the sales to the builders and contractors and to struggling builders are similar in nature, the facts for each are different. As a result, recognizing revenue at different points can be justifiable and appropriate.

Comment: Again notice that the discussion revolves around reasonable alternatives. Cases can be made for both.

Issue 3—Advertising costs
The issue here is whether the advertising costs should be capitalized or expensed. Normally under GAAP advertising costs are expensed as incurred because it is difficult to determine if a future benefit exists or the amount of the benefit. In other words, it is not possible to say that the advertising will result in additional sales and profits in the future. The other criteria for an asset are met by the expenditures made for advertising: There have been transactions with other entities and the amount spent for the advertising can be determined (see Chapter 2 for coverage of the definition of assets). Because Graphite is doing image building rather than short-term promotion of products, a case can be made for classifying the expenditures as assets because they are intended to have long-term benefits. In my view the argument for classifying these advertising expenditures as assets are weak since the existence of future benefits is questionable at best. Therefore, I recommend that the advertising costs be expensed as incurred. This treatment will satisfy the objective of minimizing income.

Comment: It is important in answering these cases to link the recommendation back to the main objective or objectives. The reason is that it makes sure that you are always aware of what you are trying to accomplish and why you are making the choices you are. In practice, the objectives or motivations for particular choices may be stated more subtly or even be unstated. The reason is that choices have to be supportable by the facts. The credibility of a choice hinges on the facts and the choice must be framed that way. It is actually not relevant to stakeholders what the objectives of the preparers are. Stakeholders are interested in information that is useful for their purposes. If the focus is on the objectives, a stakeholder who is opposed to the choice will argue that the choice is simply being made because of self-interests. For example, if the former owner of Graphite read this report and saw the explicit references to minimizing income to minimize payments to the previous owner, the credibility of the report would be impaired. That's not to say that the objectives are not relevant. They are very relevant. However, the arguments for achieving the objectives must be supported by the facts.

Chapter 5
Generally Accepted Accounting Principles

Chapter Overview

Chapter 4 emphasized two closely linked themes. First, the chapter explored some of the complexities surrounding income measurement and the recognition of revenues and expenses. The chapter demonstrated that an entity's economic activity can be reported in different ways (remember that an entity's underlying economic activity is not affected by alternative accounting approaches). However, the chapter explained that while the different reporting approaches do not change the entity's underlying economic activity, the different approaches can have economic consequences for the entity and its stakeholders.

The second theme addressed in Chapter 4 was the objectives of financial reporting and the different incentives that managers can have when approaching the preparation of the financial statements. This purpose of this part of the chapter was to provide a framework for understanding why and how managers of an entity would choose different ways of reporting the same underlying economic activity. Importantly, the discussions in Chapter 4 emphasized that different objectives and different reporting approaches could all take place within generally accepted accounting principles.

As Chapter 4 explains accounting choices are influenced by three broad factors: constraints, facts, and objectives. Chapter 5 focuses on one of the key constraints that many entities operate under in the accounting environment: generally accepted accounting principles. Chapter 5 introduces the underpinnings of GAAP. The emphasis of the chapter will be conceptual. Little attention will be paid here to the specific rules for treating particular transactions and economic events. Instead, the chapter will examine some of the key assumptions, characteristics, and conventions that constitute GAAP. The purpose is to introduce readers to the foundations of GAAP so they can understand the rationale for the specific rules of GAAP.

An important theme of Chapter 5 is that GAAP is not the one, the only, or the best way to account. Given different circumstances there could easily be different GAAPs. GAAP, including Canadian GAAP, are not without flaws. To be a sophisticated user of financial information it is necessary to know and understand what GAAP-based information tells you, how it can help you, and what its limitations are.

Study Points and Study Tips

What are Generally Accepted Accounting Principles (GAAP)

- Financial reporting in Canada and in most places around the world is played by a set of rules. These rules are known as generally accepted accounting principles (GAAP). GAAP are not universal. Different countries have different GAAP. International Accounting Standards (IAS) are a harmonized set of accounting standards that could be used around the world.

- GAAP are the characteristics, assumptions, principles, conventions, practices, procedures, and rules that define acceptable accounting practices and guide the preparation of financial statements in certain situations. If there were no rules it would be much more costly and difficult to make sense of the information contained in accounting reports because it would be necessary to learn and understand the rules that each entity was using. Canadian accounting standards are written in a way that requires the interpretation of the circumstances in applying a standard.

- GAAP are crucial to Canadian financial reporting. Having a common basis of communication that all stakeholders can know and understand makes it easier and more straightforward for an entity to communicate with its stakeholders. Stakeholders would have to invest heavily to learn and understand the accounting of each entity they are interested in.
- Despite the importance and value of a somewhat standardized set of rules, it is important to look at GAAP critically. This means recognizing that GAAP has significant limitations as well as benefits.
- All of GAAP is not documented in a single place. In fact, much of GAAP are not recorded at all. The most prominent source of GAAP is the *CICA Handbook*, but much of GAAP are simply what entities actually do in practice. There can be more than one way for accounting for a particular type of economic event or transaction, all of which can be considered GAAP. And because the world is always changing GAAP are always evolving and changing to meet the changing environment.
- Public corporations must follow GAAP. Corporations Acts also require that private corporations follow GAAP and have audited financial statements but the shareholders can waive this requirement if they agree unanimously to do so. As a result private corporations do not necessarily have to follow GAAP. Partnerships and proprietorships are not covered by any constraints that require them to follow GAAP. Following GAAP is voluntary by these types of entities.

The World According to GAAP

- The basic assumptions
  - Unit of Measure
    - The unit-of-measure assumption states that the economic activity of an entity can be effectively stated in terms of a single measurement basis. The unit-of-measure that is almost always used is money, and in Canada the monetary unit used is usually the Canadian dollar. The major benefit of using a single unit-of-measure is that it allows diverse information to be aggregated and summarized.
    - The drawbacks of using a single unit-of-measure include the loss of considerable information about the individual items being measured and characteristics of an entity that are not easily measured in terms of money are not accounted for. In addition, the unit-of-measure required under Canadian GAAP does not take into account the changing purchasing power of money over time.
  - Entity
    - Accounting systems are designed to provide information about some defined entity. When providing information about an entity, it is necessary to exclude transactions and economic events that do not pertain to the entity of interest from the accounting records and the financial statements. An accounting entity does not have to be a separate legal entity.
    - Partnerships and proprietorships are legitimate economic entities for accounting purposes, but they are not separate legal entities. In general, an entity is any economic unit that is of interest to a stakeholder.
  - Going Concern
    - GAAP accounting assumes that, absent information to the contrary, an entity operates as a going concern. This means that under GAAP an entity is expected to complete

its current plans, use its existing assets, and meet its obligations in the normal course of business.

- If the going concern assumption does not apply then it is not appropriate to use historical cost as the basis for valuing assets and liabilities. If an entity cannot be considered a going concern then assets and liabilities should be valued on a liquidation basis.
- Similarly, the classification of assets and liabilities as current and non-current is not meaningful if an entity is not a going concern because the entity will not be in existence beyond the short term. The going concern assumption is also the reason that capital assets are amortized over their useful lives.

➢ Periodic Reporting

- The periodic reporting assumption states that meaningful financial information about an entity can be provided for periods of time that are shorter than the life of an entity. To provide necessary information to stakeholders more frequently and regularly, financial statements are prepared more often than at the end of an entity's life. Accounting would be much easier if it was only necessary for an entity to prepare financial information once—at the end of its life.
- At the end of an entity's life everything about the entity's activities are known with certainty and there are no decisions or estimates to make about when to record and how much to record of assets, liabilities, revenues, and expenses. Once the life of an entity is broken down into small pieces, there can be difficulty determining in which periods revenues and expenses should be reported.
- The underlying economic activity is not affected by the different choices but the representation of that economic activity in financial statements can differ significantly. In addition, the shorter the time period that an entity reports on, the more difficult are the problems of allocating expenses and revenues among periods.

♦ The qualitative characteristics

➢ Understandability

- To be useful for decision making users must be able to understand the information presented to them in financial statements Understandability does not mean that information must be presented simply enough for the most unsophisticated user to understand.
- The *CICA Handbook* states that accounting information should be understandable to users who have a reasonable understanding of business and accounting, and a willingness to study the information provided, and if they do not, it is assumed that they will obtain advice. Targeting accounting information at moderately sophisticated users is a choice made by standard setters. What is important about the choice is that it has implications for the nature and sophistication of the information that is presented in accordance with GAAP.

➢ Comparability

- Accounting information is very difficult to evaluate in absolute terms. It usually must be evaluated relative to some benchmark. Broadly, there are two types of comparisons that users can make. First, an entity's accounting numbers can be compared with the accounting numbers of other similar entities, and second, the entity's numbers can be compared with its own accounting numbers from previous years.

- Comparability is a worthwhile goal in principle but there are many problems and concerns with achieving comparability in practice. GAAP frequently provides legitimate alternative accounting treatments for certain types of transactions. As a result, comparing the financial information of different entities must be done with a great deal of caution. If entities do not have the same set of constraints, facts, and objectives, then it is not reasonable to expect that the entities will use the same accounting methods. GAAP provide some protection for users by requiring entities to disclose the accounting policies they choose.

➢ Relevance

- Relevant information is defined as information that is useful for the decisions a stakeholder has to make—information that will influence the stakeholder's decisions. The objectives of financial statements that are stated in the *CICA Handbook* narrows the focus of the financial reporting for for-profit organizations to primarily present and potential debt and equity investors.
- The *Handbook* goes on to state that debt and equity investors are interested in predicting an entity's ability to earn income and generate cash flows. The *Handbook* is explicit that it is not practical for financial statements to satisfy all the information needs of all users.
- The *Handbook* adds three characteristics that contribute to the relevance of information:
  - Predictive value: Predictive value is the ability to predict future earnings and future cash flows. Despite the stated importance of prediction GAAP financial statements focus on reporting transactions and economic events that have happened, not on what will happen. GAAP financial statements are useful for prediction because they can be used as a benchmark for predicting the future. Users are expected to begin with previous periods' financial statement information and by incorporating future-oriented information from other sources and by making assumptions, make the predictions they require.
  - Feedback value: When users make predictions, they require information that allows them to evaluate their predictions and to revise, update, correct, and adjust them. GAAP-based accounting is reasonably well suited for providing feedback because it presents the results of what happened.
  - Timeliness: For information to be useful for decision making, it must be available to stakeholders in time to influence their decisions. Information that does not arrive on a timely basis will have little impact on decision making.

➢ Reliability

- For information to be useful to users, it must provide a reasonable representation of what it is intended to measure. The *CICA Handbook* describes the following components of reliability.
  - Verifiability: Information is verifiable if independent and knowledgeable observers can come up with the same results for the measurement of an attribute. In an accounting context, historical cost, transaction-based information is quite

verifiability. Because financial statement amounts can be traced back to documents that underlie a transaction, the amounts are relatively easy to verify.

- Representational faithfulness: Representational faithfulness refers to the association between underlying activity being measured and the representation of that information in the financial statements. Financial statements are a representation of the underlying economic activity of an entity. If the statements are to be representationally faithful, then they must capture the economic activity of an entity. This means that all the assets, liabilities, revenues, and expenses must be reflected in the statements.
- Neutrality or freedom from bias: Information is neutral or free from bias if it is not presented in a way that is designed to influence or manipulate users' decisions. This characteristic seems to be inconsistent with the objectives of financial reporting. While neutrality is a worthwhile characteristic to have, evidence from research and casual observation of events reported in the popular press strongly suggests that preparers do use the accounting choices available to them to pursue their objectives and can thus not really be thought of as being free of bias.

- The measurement conventions
  - Valuation
    - There are many different ways that assets and liabilities can be valued. The replacement cost of an asset is the current price that would have to be paid to purchase an identical or equivalent asset.
    - Replacement cost is a market-value measure, not a historical measure. However, replacement cost is sometimes used under GAAP for reporting inventory on the balance sheet if the market value of the inventory is lower than its cost.
    - Net realizable value is the amount of cash that is expected to be received from the sale or realization of an asset, after taking into consideration any additional costs. Accounts receivable are normally valued at their net realizable value on an entity's balance sheet. The present value of future cash flows represents the amount of cash that would be paid today for cash flows that will be received in the future.
    - Historical cost or the transaction cost is the primary method used to measure financial statement elements under GAAP. Historical cost requires that transactions and economic events be valued in the financial statements at the actual dollar amounts involved when the transaction or economic event took place. The dominance of historical cost emerges from the assumptions and qualitative characteristics.
    - Historical cost is consistent with reliability. In almost all situations, the historical cost of an asset, liability, revenue, or expense is at least as reliable as any of the other possible alternatives. The terms of most transactions and economic events are usually easily determined at the time they occur and these terms can usually be readily verified. The use of historical cost in GAAP accounting indicates the tradeoff that often exists between reliability and relevance is often resolved in favour of reliability. Historical cost is also consistent with the going concern assumption.
  - Full disclosure
    - For financial statements to fulfill their objective of providing relevant information to users, the statements must include all relevant information about the economic

activities of the entity. The principle that financial statements should provide this information is known as full disclosure.

- In reality, financial statements do not provide all the information users require. However, the information in the financial statements should be adequate so as not to mislead users. Under GAAP, certain disclosures are explicitly required while in other cases the preparers must use their judgment when deciding if there should be disclosure of certain information and how that information should be disclosed.
- Whether information is disclosed only in the notes to the financial statements or reflected in the statements themselves can matter if financial statement numbers are used to determine an outcome such as managers bonuses, the selling price of a business, whether a borrower has met the terms of a loan agreement, or the amount of tax that should be paid, measurement is important.
- For the capital markets and highly sophisticated users of accounting information, how the information is incorporated into the financial statement package is less important than whether it is incorporated. Sophisticated users can readily take information from various sources, including the financial statements and the notes, and organize it in ways that is appropriate for their decisions.

➢ Recognition

- Recognition refers to when any financial statement element—asset, liability, equity, expense or revenue—is entered into the accounting system and reported in the financial statements. For example, revenue recognition represents the point when a sale transaction is recorded.

➢ Matching

- Under GAAP, matching is the process of associating costs with the revenue the costs help generate so that income can be determined. Matching makes sense, at least for some objectives of accounting, and it is consistent with the objectives of GAAP accounting as stated in the *CICA Handbook*. As long as there is a clear link between the revenue and the costs, there is no problem with matching. However, matching the cost some assets, for example capital assets, to revenues can be problematic.
- Clearly, capital assets can contribute to the generation of revenue over a number of periods but what the relationship is between revenue and a particular capital in a particular period can be thought of as being somewhat arbitrary.
- Accountants find some costs so difficult to associate with particular revenues that no attempt is made to match them with revenues. For example, research and advertising costs. These costs are treated as period costs and are matched to a period of time—usually the period that the costs are incurred.

➢ Conservatism

- Conservatism requires that measurements in financial statements should be made to ensure that assets, revenues, and net income are not overstated and that liabilities and expenses are not understated.
- Conservatism does not mean that there should be a deliberate understatement of assets, revenues, and net income or the deliberate overstatement of liabilities and expenses. Conservatism requires that losses be recognized when they are identified. In contrast gains are only recognized when they are realized—that is when the gain is

supported by a transaction. One of the problems with conservatism is that today's conservative choices can lead to the opposite effects in later periods

- Conservatism tends to be one of the dominant accounting conventions. Conservatism can be used to justify deviating from the historical cost convention and reliability. One of the problems with conservatism is that it requires judgment by the preparers and these types of judgements can be highly subjective. As a result, managers can abuse conservatism by using it to manage the earnings of their companies.

➢ Non-arm's length transactions

- Financial reporting under GAAP assumes that the transactions that give rise to assets, liabilities, revenues, and expenses occur at arm's length. An arm's length transaction is a transaction that takes place between unrelated parties, each of whom is acting in his or her own self interests and, therefore, trying to get the best deal for him or herself.
- When a transaction takes place at arm's length, the exchange amount is considered to be the fair market value. The exchange or transaction amount is the basis of most valuation issues in GAAP accounting.
- A non-arm's length transaction occurs between related parties. Related parties exist when one entity has the ability to influence the decision making of another. Non-arm's length transactions can cause serious problems for interpreting financial statements.
- The *CICA Handbook* requires that information about non-arm's length or related party transactions be disclosed in the financial statements. Non arm's length transactions are not illegal or unethical. However, their existence can have significant implications for the financial statements and users should be very aware of that fact.

➢ Materiality

- Materiality describes the significance of financial information to users. Information is material if its omission or misstatement would affect the judgement of a user of the information.
- All material information should be disclosed in financial statements because its absence may affect the decisions made by users. Matters that are not material do not have to be treated in accordance with GAAP.
- Materiality is a matter of judgment and it is difficult to establish firm rules. Materiality will depend on the size of the entity, the risks it faces, and the identity and needs of the users of the financial statements. In addition, as is typically the case with general purpose financial statements, it is not really possible to define a level of materiality that is appropriate for all decisions and users.

The Auditors' Report

♦ The auditors' report gives the external auditors' opinion on the entity's financial statements. Auditors examine an entity's financial statements and the accounting records that were used to prepare the financial statements to evaluate whether the financial statements are properly prepared in accordance with the relevant accounting rules.

♦ There are four opinions that auditors can give on financial statements: an unqualified opinion, which says the financial statements satisfy the standards the auditor is using, and three opinions that indicate problems with the financial statements or the audit—a qualified opinion, an adverse opinion, and a denial of opinion.

- An unqualified auditors' report always has three paragraphs in it. The first paragraph is called the introductory paragraph. The introductory paragraph tells the reader what the auditor did. The introductory paragraph also tells readers that preparation of the financial statements is the responsibility of the management of the entity. The second paragraph of an unqualified auditors' report is called the scope paragraph. The scope paragraph describes how the auditor conducted the audit. In the third paragraph of an unqualified auditors' report, the auditor provides his or her opinion on the financial statements. The opinion paragraph states that the financial statements present fairly, in all material respects, the financial situation of the entity, in accordance with GAAP. To be fair, financial statements must comply with GAAP.
- Other forms of assurance accountants can provide:
  - Audits are only one of the forms of assurance that accountants can provide. A review engagement provides less assurance to users about whether an entity's financial statements are in accordance with GAAP than audit does.
  - Accountants can also provide reports on financial information other than financial statements or on compliance with an agreement or regulations.

Study Problems

Study Problem 1 (Examining relevance and reliability) You and your housemates are trying to decide on an all-inclusive holiday destination during the upcoming reading week. You receive a package of information from a resort in Mexico that contains the following:

a. A letter endorsing the country from the Mexican Tourism Board.
b. A brochure from a major Canadian travel agency with a ranking of all resorts in Mexico.
c. Testimonials from other students from your school who have stayed at this resort in the past three years.
d. Some currency exchange rate tables with conversion rates from U.S. dollars and Euros to Mexican pesos.
e. A letter from management of the resort stating that their resort is the best in Mexico.
f. An annual report for both the resort and charter airline that provides transportation.
g. A brief history of the region.
h. An article from the local newspaper (in Mexico) that claims the town nearest the resort has the "best shopping in all of Mexico."

Required:

Evaluate the relevance (including predictive value, feedback value, and timeliness) and reliability (including representational faithfulness, verifiability, and neutrality/freedom from bias) of each piece of information for purposes of choosing a holiday destination.

Study Problem 2 (Identifying accounting assumptions, qualitative characteristics, and measurement conventions) For each of the following situations, identify the accounting assumptions, qualitative characteristics, and/or measurement conventions that Green Turtle Corp. (Turtle) would be violating by the accounting choices that it made. Explain your answer. Turtle is a semiconductor manufacturing company with fabrication facilities across Canada.

a. The Chief Financial Officer (CFO) of Turtle decided to increase the value of a building the company was holding for resale because the amount originally recorded significantly understated the value.

b. Turtle's sole shareholder used Turtle employees, raw materials, and machinery to build her cottage in Muskoka . All costs incurred were reported on Turtle's income statement as other expenses.
c. A raging forest fire potentially threatens one of Turtle's manufacturing facilities in British Columbia (Okanagan region). This region has a history of hazardous fires and researchers are predicting another dangerous summer in the province. Turtle has not provided any information about the possibility of this fire in its financial statements because the company is still having discussions with local firefighters and is hopeful that "things will work out".
d. Turtle recently signed a contract to produce and sell "state-of-the-art" high performance microprocessors to a high-tech firm. Turtle's engineering staff just began working on production and it is hoped that these microprocessors will be delivered in two and a half years. Turtle recognized the revenue when the contract was signed with the high-tech firm.
e. Turtle expenses the cost of raw materials inventory when the inventory is received from the supplier.
f. Turtle decided to change the method of recognizing revenue on some of its long-term contracts from the completed-contract method to the percentage-of-completion method to be consistent with competitors. Due to certain complexities, Turtle is not changing the revenue reported in previous years.
g. Turtle purchased new machinery for its production lines. The machinery itself cost $500,000. Delivery, installation and employee training costs (to allow the machinery to be installed and operated) cost an additional $50,000, which were expensed when incurred.
h. Some of Turtle's inventory was seriously damaged in a flood after some pipes burst in one of their fabrication facilities. The company is currently looking for a buyer and is hoping to receive about 15% of the original cost of the inventory. Turtle's controller is not writing down the inventory because "it has not been sold yet."

Study Problem 3 (Examining materiality) For each of the following situations, explain whether you think the amount involved is material.

a. A life insurance professional achieves the qualifying level of 'Management Club' if their personal income exceeds $350,000. In 2004 Brian Harrington (Brian), a life insurance professional received a T4 slip for $345,454, but his company payroll department made a bookkeeping error and his actual income was $354,545. Is the error material?
b. A life insurance professional achieves the qualifying level of 'Management Club' if their personal income exceeds $350,000 or 'Leaders Club' if their personal income falls between $300,000 and $349,999. In 2004 Brian received a T4 slip for $329,000 but his company payroll department made a bookkeeping error and his actual income was $330,000. Is the error material?
c. Gator Inc. (Gator) with annual sales of $15,000,000, net income of $2,250,000, and total assets of $7,500,000 accidentally did not include a $1,500,000 sale made near the end of the year in its current year's income statement. All costs associated with this sale were expensed in the current year's income statement. Is the $1,500,000 omission material?
d. Gator did not include a $5,000 sale made near the end of the year in its current year's income statement. All costs associated with the sale were expensed in the current year's income statement. Is the $5,000 omission material?
e. An agreement to sell a subsidiary is set at a selling price 10 times the average net income. A $10,000 disbursement that is normally expensed when incurred was capitalized. Net income, without considering the capitalized $10,000 item, was $500,000.

f. In 2005, Sovereign PLC (Sovereign), a British pharmaceuticals company spent $7,000,000 on research and development. In 2006 because the company was short of cash, it spent only $1,050,000 on research and development. Since the amount spent in 2006 was relatively small, management decided to include research and development in the general and administrative account on the income statement instead of reporting it separately as it did in its 2005 financial statements. In the 2006 financial statements, the 2005 amount was restated for consistency purposes so that it was also included in general and administrative expenses.
g. Loon Lake Imaging Inc. (an operating company) leases office space for $7,000 per month in a building owned by Looney Louis Ltd. (a holding company). The shares of both corporations are owned 100% by the same shareholder.

Study Problem 4 (Examining non-arm's length transactions) For each of the following transactions entered in by Gertrude's Mussels Ltd. (Mussels), a banquet and catering business in the maritime provinces, indicate whether it should be considered a non-arm's length transaction (related party transaction). In each case indicate whether information about the transaction should be disclosed separately according to GAAP. Explain your thinking. Assume you are a small shareholder in Mussels.

a. The Chief Executive Officer (CEO) of Mussels purchases a company vehicle owned by Mussels so that her husband can utilize the vehicle in the general contracting business he owns and controls.
b. Forty percent of Mussels' sales are to a single company that employs several thousand people and holds weekly functions throughout their fiscal year.
c. Mussels' obtains its fresh seafood from a fishery operated by the majority shareholder's sister. All transactions occur at standard terms for the industry.
d. A number of Mussels' employees are close relatives of the majority shareholder. These people receive compensation that is the same as the other employees carrying out similar duties.
e. The ex-husband of Mussels' CEO is the "special consultant to the CEO." The special consultant has special training or experience in the field but is rarely seen in Mussels' offices.
f. A friend of the CEO is Mussels' main supplier of kitchen equipment.
g. Mussels' provides banquets and retirement parties for provincial and federal government ministries.
h. The CEO is compensated with a bonus based on Mussels' monthly reported net income. One month, the majority shareholder directed the payroll department to move back employee payroll expenses from the 1st of the next month to the 31st of the current month.

Study Problem 5 (Examining conservatism) Electric Lemonade Ltd. (Electric) is a fast growing chain of juice bars and also a producer of 'smart drinks' with a customer base in southwestern Ontario. Electric purchases equipment and hires entrepreneurs to manage their store locations. Electric has a policy of capitalizing the costs of delivery and installing the equipment and amortizing the cost over 10 years. In the last year and a half Electric has not been performing well and in late 2005 the shareholders of the company, none of whom are involved in the management, decided to replace the existing management with a new team of managers. Electric is in the process of preparing its December 31, 2005 financial statements. In light of the company's recent poor performance, the new management has decided to write off the entire $40,000 of store opening costs that were recorded as an asset on the balance sheet.

a. If a new store incurred $2,500 in delivery and installation costs, what journal entry would Electric make to capitalize the delivery and installation cost as an asset? Assume that $1,000 of these costs was in cash and the remainder is a liability.

b. What journal entry would Electric record when it writes off the $40,000 in delivery and installation costs? What is the effect on income in 2005 of writing off the delivery and installation costs?
c. What accounting concepts justify the write-off of the delivery and installation costs?
d. What possible motivations could Electric's new management have for writing off the delivery and installation costs in 2005?
e. If Electric had not written off the delivery and installation costs, it would have incurred about $4,000 in amortization expense for the delivery and installation costs in each of fiscal 2005, 2006, and 2007. Assuming that the income included all revenues and expenses except for the delivery and installation costs in 2005 was $35,000, and was estimated to be the same for 2006 and 2007, calculate net income in 2005, 2006, and 2007:
   i. Assuming that Electric wrote off delivery and installation costs in 2005.
   ii. Assuming that Electric did not write off delivery and installation costs in 2005 and amortized $4,000 in each year.
f. Using your results in (e), explain the effect of the write off in 2005 on future years' earnings and the problems users might have interpreting financial statements as a result of the write-off.

Solutions to Study Problems

Solution to Study Problem 1

	Relevance	Reliability
a.	Knowing pertinent facts about the country of destination would be important information. The information could give an indication about weather trends, crime rates and local culture and customs. However, if information is outdated or about traditional resort areas, the information may not be relevant to you. For example, if the information highlighted Acapulco, Puerto Vallarta and Cancun but your intention was to visit the Mayan Riviera or Los Cabos the information may have no significance. Also, information concerning traditional resort areas is backward-looking and by not incorporating future oriented information, it may not be predictive.	The reliability is somewhat dubious since the Mexican Tourism Board may portray a misleading impression. The fact that only traditional resort areas may have been highlighted raises doubt regarding their representation of the sample. In other words, the information would not be neutral. It would be possible to verify the factual information through independent news services such as Reuters. Thus the information about Mexico would be verifiable but it might not be neutral or represent good faith. The information may not be representative of the new wave of tourism to areas in Mexico that are growing rapidly and still under development.
b.	The article may provide relevant information if the ranking is based on criteria that are important to you. For example, the ranking may be based on stunning beaches and beautiful natural surroundings when you are looking for quality dining and first class accommodations. Also, several key chefs may have left the resort, so the ranking	The reliability could be high, if the criteria are objective. If the criteria are subjective, they may reflect personal opinions of biased individuals.

	lacks predictive value. The article may not be published until after the deadline for booking the holiday, so again, it would lack predictive value.	
c.	The testimonials may be relevant if they include positive comments on criteria that are of interest to you. The information might help you predict whether the resort is suitable for you.	The testimonials are unlikely to be reliable, since they may have been solicited by the resort and selected from among a group that probably included less positive letters. Also tourists that have chosen a specific resort may have personal bias about their holiday having been to the same resort more than once or been given some incentive (room upgrade to an ocean view, etc.) to give positive feedback.
d.	The currency exchange rate tables would not be relevant since you would need to convert Canadian dollars into Mexican pesos.	The currency exchange rate tables are likely fairly reliable, although exchange rates change frequently. By investigating exchange rates at different financial institutions you may also find that rates vary significantly (at different financial institutions).
e.	The letter is probably designed to be as relevant as possible to the criteria that the management expects you to apply when choosing your holiday destination.	The letter is undoubtedly biased, perhaps to the extent that it is of limited usefulness.
f.	The annual reports could be very useful as it may help assess the financial health of the resort and charter airline. The annual report itself would not be enough and it would be necessary to obtain additional information from business newspapers and magazine articles.	The information that is included, such as profitability and cash flow is likely objective and verifiable. In 2002, many Canadian tourists lost their money when Canada 3000 bankrupt rendering their airline tickets worthless. However, several negative articles had been published leading up to the bankruptcy and tourists should not have been surprised by the announcement.
g.	The history may have some limited relevance.	The history is likely reliable since it is mostly factual. Negative information such as crime rates would not be included if negative.
h.	The relevance will depend on your criteria. The predictive value will depend on the incoming consumers.	It is not likely that the claim reflects any objective assessment of all towns in the region since the article appeared in the local newspaper nearest the resort.

Solution to Study Problem 2

a. The historical cost principle is violated. Recognition is also violated because a gain is being recognized before it is realized. An increase in the market value of the building that is not supported by a transaction with an outside party is called an unrealized gain. This treatment is also not conservative. Under GAAP, gains are recognized only when they are realized.

b. The entity principle is violated since personal expenses are presented as expenses of the company. Transactions that do not pertain to Turtle should be excluded from Turtle's financial statements. In this case it was clear that for tax purposes it is desirable to expense as much as possible to minimize the amount of tax that must be paid by Turtle (although not legitimate).

c. The full disclosure principle is violated because information that would affect a decision to invest in the firm is not being disclosed. If a fire ravaged the manufacturing facility, production would be dramatically affected. Relevance is also violated since this information could be very important to stakeholders.

d. The revenue recognition principle is violated since the revenue has not been earned. The treatment used by Turtle is not conservative. Also, consideration of the nature of the industry needs to be given. The technology sector has been uncertain in recent years and many companies that purchased goods and services on credit no longer exist to make payments to the suppliers (who have already recognized the revenue).

e. The matching principle is violated since the costs are not expensed in the same period as the revenue is recognized. Expenses should be recorded and reported in the same period as when the revenue those expenses help earn is recorded and reported.

f. The qualitative characteristic of comparability is violated because the company is not accounting for similar transactions in the same manner. A change in revenue recognition method is a change in accounting policy that needs to be applied retroactively and must be disclosed in the financial statements.

g. The historical cost principle is violated, since the purchase is recorded at an amount that does not fully reflect cost. However, in some cases a user might not object to the choice due to conservatism. The cost of an asset that is reported on an entity's balance sheet should include all of the costs associated with purchasing the asset and getting it ready for use. Turtle's delivery, installation and employee training costs should all be capitalized.

h. Turtle's treatment is not conservative since the asset, which is clearly overvalued, has not been written down. The inventory must be reported on the balance sheet at the lower of cost and market value (in this case market value). The amount of the write-down is the difference between the inventory's cost and market value and is reported as a loss on the income statement in the period that the market value of the inventory falls, not when it is sold.

Solution to Study Problem 3

a. The difference is material since attaining the level of 'Management Club' qualifies Brian for a sales convention in Las Vegas. The difference also has an affect on his recognition and credibility within the organization from his peers, and possibly a promotion within the company.

b. Whether the error is material depends on how the information is reported. If only the qualifying level is reported, it is not material. If the income level is also conveyed to a decision-maker, it may be material, as the employer may use their own decision rule that, for example, distributes bonuses based on increments of $10,000.

c. The amount is certainly material, since the income would be $1,500,000 (67%) higher if it was corrected. Total assets would also increase by 20% and presumably equity by a larger percentage. There is no doubt that most users of the financial statements would view the company differently.

d. No, the difference with or without the error is not large enough to affect the views of any users of the financial statements. An exception might be if the absence of the $5,000 in revenue put the entity in violation of a covenant. Information is material if its omission or misstatement would affect the judgement of a user of the information. If materiality was not considered the cost of having 100% perfect information may significantly outweigh the benefits to the user.

e. The amount is small, only 2% of net income, but in this instance it does have a $100,000 impact on the price at which the subsidiary would change hands and cannot be considered immaterial.

f. The $1,050,000 amount may be small for a large pharmaceuticals company, but the fact that the Sovereign decreased spending on research and development has significance for anyone predicting the future profitability of the firm. The real information here is the $5,950,000 difference. Full disclosure would require that readers of the financial statements be informed. The change in reporting is material.

g. This is a related party transaction, which is important not just in terms of the amount but the fact that such transactions exist. The *CICA Handbook* requires that information about related party transactions be disclosed in the financial statements. If this is the only transaction, that fact would be of interest to the users of the financial statements.

Solution to Study Problem 4

a. This is clearly a non-arm's length transaction since it is between the CEO and the entity. There is reason to doubt whether the purchase of the vehicle took place at market value or special arrangements were made between Mussels and the CEO. Disclosure of the transaction in the notes would be appropriate.

b. While the relationship between the holding company and Mussels may be at arm's length the extent of the business relationship suggests a power imbalance between the entities. Mussels' survival may depend on the continued commitment of this customer. As a result one could argue that Mussels is dependent on the business and therefore this relationship and dependence should be disclosed.

c. GAAP does not consider transactions with a sibling to be non-arm's length and therefore no disclosure is required. However in reality it is reasonable to expect that transactions between an entity and the CEO's sibling could have terms that are not typical of arm's length transactions. It would likely be useful if this relationship were disclosed along with the terms of the transactions but GAAP does not require it.

d. How close are the close relatives? The *CICA Handbook* limits the definition of close relatives to spouses and dependent children. This provides a large loophole of people with influence to use. People can have close relationships with brothers, non-dependent children, cousins, etc., that could lead to transactions having terms and conditions that are not available to actual arm's length parties. If the definition of close relatives meets the requirement of the *Handbook,* the transactions should be disclosed in the notes. This information would be of interest to shareholders since they may have concerns that the employees may be more willing to cooperate in carrying out actions that benefited the majority shareholder at the expense of the minority shareholders. The fact that the transactions occur at market value does not preclude disclosure of the transactions.

e. The ex-spouse of a senior manager would not be considered a related party and the transaction would be considered arm's length because transactions between ex-spouses could reasonably be expected to be driven exclusively by market forces (for example, the consulting contract would not be considered a way for the CEO to obtain additional compensation without approval by the board of directors). Information about the existence of the consulting arrangement does not need to be disclosed. Stakeholders would like to assess the propriety of the arrangement and whether value-for-money is being obtained by the consultancy relationship, but Mussels' need not disclose such information in this case.

f. According to GAAP this would be considered an arm's length transactions. It is difficult to evaluate the existence and implications of friendships. However, it is possible that the friend may have received terms that were not available to other suppliers. Nevertheless, no recognition of the relationship or the transactions is required according to GAAP.

g. This transaction appears to be at arms-length although scrutiny may be necessary since the revenue from these events comes from the public sector.

h. According to the matching concept expenses are reported on the income statement in the same period as the revenue that those expenses help earn. In this case it appears as though the majority shareholder does not want the CEO to receive a monthly bonus. The majority shareholder may hold voting control at the board meetings but this does not mean that controlling shareholders have the power to contravene GAAP.

Solution to Study Problem 5

a.	Dr.	Delivery and installation costs (asset +)	2,500	
		Cr. Cash (asset -)		1,000
		Cr. Accounts payable (liability +)		1,500
b.	Dr.	Write-off delivery and installation costs (income statement -)	40,000	
		Cr. Delivery and installation costs (asset -)		40,000

The write-off would decrease income by $40,000 (less the amount of delivery and installation costs that would have been amortized in the absence of the write-down) in fiscal 2005.

c. If it is clear that the asset no longer has value, representational faithfulness would require that no amount be presented as an asset on the balance sheet. Conservatism requires that the loss be recognized as soon as it becomes known.

d. As the new managers of Electric, your performance evaluations will be based on the performance of the company after you take over and will likely be compared to the profitability under the previous managers. Therefore you have an incentive to understate the profitability of the past, and one way to do that is to write off assets of uncertain value. The second result is to increase future profitability since the delivery and installation costs will not be an expense in the future.

   This is often termed a "big bath." There is empirical evidence that supports new managements taking a big bath soon after they have been installed. The big bath gives the new managers a leg up on satisfying the demands of stakeholders to improve performance from the previous managers.

e.

i)	**2005**	**2006**	**2007**
Income before delivery and installation costs	$35,000	$35,000	$35,000
Delivery and installation costs	40,000	0	0
Net income (loss)	$(5,000)	$35,000	$35,000

ii)	**2005**	**2006**	**2007**
Income before delivery and installation costs	$35,000	$35,000	$35,000
Delivery and installation costs	4,000	4,000	4,000
Net income (loss)	$31,000	$31,000	$31,000

f. The write off increases the earnings in future years because the delivery and installation costs do not have to be amortized. This could affect the perceptions that users of the financial statements have of the company's profitability. If the user is fully aware of the accounting choices made, an adjustment is easy to make. An investor who obtained the 2006 or 2007 financial statements without referring to the 2005 financial statements would not know the exact amount of delivery and installation costs involved, although the accounting policy would likely be disclosed in the notes to the financial statements. Further complicating the task of interpreting trends in year-to-year comparisons is the fact that the number of deliveries and installations, and their costs, might be fairly constant or fairly uneven. The distortion in net income resulting from the write-off would be much less if expenditures on deliveries and installation were constant. Financial ratios will be affected by the write off. For example, in 2006, Electric's profit margin would be higher if the write off occurred in 2005 than if it continued to amortize the delivery and installation costs over the three year period.

Chapter 6
Cash Flow, Profitability, and the Cash Flow Statement

Chapter Overview

Accrual accounting is the basis of GAAP and general purpose reporting in Canada. Chapters 3, 4, and 5 placed a heavy emphasis on accrual accounting. It is easy to forget that accrual accounting is not the only way to account. Accrual accounting can mask an entity's cash flow—the amounts reported on an accrual income statement (for sales, expenses, net income) may be very different from the actual cash inflows and outflows (cash collected from customers, cash paid to various suppliers, net cash flows). It's important to remember that cash pays the bills. An entity without adequate cash, cash flow, or access to cash cannot survive. Even if an entity has a large net income, if cash is not available it will soon grind to a halt when suppliers stop delivering supplies and employees stop working. Therefore it is important for most of an entity's stakeholders to be aware of its cash flow situation.

In Chapter 6 we take a step back from accrual accounting and focus on cash flow. The chapter examines differences between cash and accrual accounting and looks at how cash cycles through an entity. Most of the coverage in Chapter 6 is devoted to understanding and preparing the cash flow statement.

Study Points and Study Tips

Cash versus Accrual Accounting and the Cash Cycle

- Accrual accounting is the predominate method of accounting in Canada and in most other places in the world.
  - While accrual accounting is almost a necessity once economic activity becomes the least bit complex, accrual accounting measures can often obscure an entity's cash flows. However, adequate cash and cash flow is essential for an entity's survival since cash pays the bills.
  - Cash flow differs from accrual measures because accrual accounting attempts to reflect economic impact of transactions and economic events. Cash flow reflects the movement of cash in and out of the entity.
  - Cash accounting requires much less judgement than accrual accounting because it is the inflow and outflow of cash that trigger the recording process. This is in contrast with accrual accounting where judgement must be used to determine when to recognize revenue and expenses.
  - Earnings is not a substitute for cash flow. Earnings can be very different from cash flow and it cannot be assumed that they are the same.
  - It is very dangerous to ignore cash flow. Entities need cash to operate and survive.
- The cash cycle is the process whereby an entity begins with cash, invests in resources, uses those resources to provide goods or services to customers, and then collects cash from customers.
  - Usually there is lag between the time cash is invested in resources and cash is collected from customers. An entity must have cash to finance this lag.

- An entity that requires capital assets (such as equipment, buildings, licenses, patents, rights, etc.) must obtain those assets before they can be used to help generate revenue. To purchase these assets cash must be raised (debt or equity) to pay for them. The assets will help generate cash over their useful lives; however the assets (and the cash to acquire them) must be obtained first.
- Similarly, inventory is bought and usually paid for before it is sold. Suppliers often help finance inventory by providing credit for a period of time. However, if the inventory is not sold before the supplier is paid then the entity must finance the inventory from the time the supplier is paid until cash is collected from customers.
- Often revenue is recognized before cash is received. The entity incurs the costs of the sale but does not receive the cash until later.
- If cash flows were perfectly predictable (sales were known in advance, customers paid exactly what they owed when they were supposed to) there would be no cash flow problems. Entities would be able to obtain the cash they need to finance the cash lag knowing the cash was forthcoming—it would simply be a matter of arranging financing to manage the cash lag. There would be no risk that lenders wouldn't be repaid.
    - In reality cash flows and other future events are not perfectly predictable and as a result anticipated cash flows may not arrive. For example,
        - If sales are lower than expected cash flows will be lower than planned. As a result there may not be enough cash available to repay loans and other obligations as they come due.
        - Market conditions might change which affect the selling prices of goods and services.
        - Customers may experience financial difficulties and may not pay amounts owed or may not pay when expected to.
        - Costs of operating the business may be different than expected. Labour costs may increase or the cost of inputs may be higher than expected.

Understanding the Cash Flow Statement

- The cash flow statement explains how cash was obtained and used by an entity. The definition of cash used in a cash flow statement is not always the physical cash an entity has. Cash in a cash flow statement can include, in addition to cash on hand and in bank accounts, cash equivalents (a security that can be converted to a known amount of cash quickly). In addition cash can be netted against short-term borrowing.
- The cash flow statement divides cash flows into three categories:
    - Cash from operations (CFO) is the cash an entity generates from or uses in its regular business activities. Cash inflows from operations include cash collected from customers along with other receipts of cash that are related to operations. Cash outflows from operations include cash payments made to generate operating cash inflows, for example, payments to suppliers and employees.
    - Cash flows from investing activities is the cash an entity spends on buying capital and other long-term assets and the cash it receives from selling those assets.

- Cash from financing activities is the cash an entity raises and pays to equity investors and lenders.
- See Figure 6-3 in the text (page 324) for examples of each category of cash flow.

♦ There are two ways that CFO can be calculated and reported in a cash flow statement:

- The direct method reports CFO by showing cash collections and cash disbursements related to operations during the period.
    - The direct method is a much more intuitive approach to disclosing cash from operations but it is very rarely seen in practice. The direct approach also provides clearer information about operating cash flows by explicitly showing cash collected from customers and cash paid to employees, suppliers of goods and services, and so on.
- The indirect method reconciles from net income to CFO by adjusting net income for non-cash amounts that are included in the calculation of net income and for operating cash flows that are not included in the calculation of net income.
    - The indirect approach is not very intuitive but is the method is used almost exclusively in practice (even though the *CICA Handbook* encourages the use of the direct method). As a result it is important to understand the adjustments that are made when reconciling from net income to cash from operations.
    - There are two types of adjustments that are made when reconciling from net income to cash from operations.
        - Adjustments to remove the effect of transactions and economic events that are included in the calculation of net income but have no effect on cash flow (for example, amortization, write-downs and write-offs of assets, gains and losses, future taxes).
            - ♦ These types of transactions and economic events have no effect on cash flow. They are part of the calculation of net income so they must be removed when reconciling from net income to cash from operations so that the non-cash components of net income are eliminated.
        - Changes in non-cash working capital accounts. The non-cash working capital accounts reflect cash flows that are not captured by the income statement.
            - ♦ For example, sales on the income statements does not reflect cash collected from customers (some credit sales recognized during a period have not been collected as of the end of the period, some credit sales recognized in a previous period are collected in the current period, some sales recognized in the current period may have been collected in a previous period). These differences between cash inflow and sales are reflected in accounts receivable and unearned revenue.
            - ♦ Similarly, cost of sales and other expenses may not correspond with the actual amount of cash expended during the period (cash associated with expenses may occur before, after, or at the Allisone time the expense is recognized).
            - ♦ The intuition for these relationships is that the income statement reflects accrual amounts, not cash flows. The differences between the accrual amount on the income statement and the related cash flow amount has to be captured

on the balance sheet. For example, if revenue is recognized at a time other than when cash is received a balance sheet account is affected (accounts receivable or unearned revenue). This intuition can be seen in the textbook in the Kamloops Inc. example on page 332 and the Rollingdam Ltd. example on page 333. Review these two examples carefully to understand the connection between income statement and balance sheet amounts and cash flows.

Preparing a Cash Flow Statement

- The six steps for preparing a cash flow statement are:

  Step 1: Obtain balance sheets as of the beginning and end of the period and the income statement for the period, along with any other information that is available about the cash flows of the entity.

  Step 2: Prepare a spreadsheet with a column for each balance sheet and income statement account, plus columns to number and classify entries. Enter the amounts from the beginning and ending balance sheet amounts and from the income statement amounts on the spreadsheet.

  Step 3: Make entries to the spreadsheet that explain the changes in each account.

  Step 4: For each entry that affects the cash account, classify it as an operating, financing, or investing cash flow.

  Step 5: Prepare the cash flow statement by organizing the amounts in entries that affected the cash account into CFO, investing activities, and financing activities.

  Step 6: Calculate totals for each of operating, financing, and investing cash flows and calculate total cash flow for the period.

- Some points to remember with this approach
  - Entries to the cash column of the spreadsheet provide the information need to prepare the cash flow statement. All that is required is to classify each entry to the cash column (operating, financing, or investing) and organize the amounts into a form suitable for a cash statement.
  - This approach is appropriate for preparing a cash flow statement that shows cash from operations using the direct approach.
  - When trying to make entries to the spreadsheet that explain the changes in each account (step 3) keep things as simple as possible. Make your assumptions as simple as possible while remaining consistent with the information provided. For example, assume all sales and purchases are on credit unless you told otherwise.
  - Step 3 involves figuring out missing information. This can be done using the following equation:

Ending balance in the account	=	Beginning balance in the account	+	Transactions and economic events that increase the balance in the account	-	Transactions and economic events that decrease the balance in the account

- You have to know three of the four elements of the equation and then solve for the fourth. The beginning and ending balance sheets provide you with the beginning and ending balances in an account. Information about increases and decreases to the account will come from the income statement or from other information.
    - For example, the income statement gives the increase to accounts receivable (sales, or more correctly credit sales). With sales plus the beginning and ending balance in the accounts receivable account from the balance sheet the amount of cash received from customers during the period can be calculated.
    - Similarly, with the wage expense from the income statement and the beginning and ending balances in the wages payable account on the balance sheet the amount of cash paid to employees can be calculated.

Interpreting the Cash Flow Statement

- The cash flow statement provides important information about an entity's liquidity. The ability of an entity to generate cash flow from its operations determines its ability to meet its obligations as well as pay dividends and make required acquisitions of capital assets.
- The cash flow statement is an historical statement. Users can use the cash flow statement as a basis for predictor of future cash flows but it cannot be assumed that future cash flows will be the Allisone as the historical ones.
- Negative cash from operations means that by operating an entity consumes cash. This situation can be reasonable in some situations, for example an entity that is expanding, but it is not sustainable. If operations are consuming cash the entity will have to obtain cash to finance its operations either by borrowing or issuing equity, or by selling assets.
- New companies must have adequate cash reserves or access to cash to operate during the start-up phase of the business. When the cash lag was discussed I pointed out usually cash outflows must occur before cash inflows are realized.
- An important piece of information about an entity's future cash flows is not reported on the cash flow statement. If a bank has provided the entity with a line of credit then there is liquidity available even if the current liquidity position of the entity and its projected cash flows are not strong.

Manipulating Cash Flow and the Effect of Accrual Accounting Choices on the Cash Flow Statement

- One of the advantages attributed to cash flow information is that it is not affected by the judgement of the managers. In fact, this is only partially true.
    - Accounting choices made by managers do not affect an entity's cash flow. However, managers can make decisions that affect the timing of cash flows.
        - Managers can advance or delay expenditures on repairs and maintenance on equipment, advertising, research, and so on.
        - They can take more time to pay the entity's accounts payable.
        - These types of choices have real economic implications for an entity. That is, delaying spending on maintenance can have real implications. Compare that with the decision to expense or capitalize the money spent on maintenance

- Accounting choices may affect the classification of a cash flow in the statement of cash flow. An amount that is expensed is classified as cash from operations whereas if the expenditure is capitalized as an asset it is classified as an investing activity.
- Accrual accounting choices do not have a direct effect on an entity's cash flows. In some circumstances there may be a secondary effect if the accrual accounting choice affects the amount of tax the entity must pay or the bonus paid to managers.

Study Problems

Study Problem 1 (Classifying transactions) Chiswick Inc. is a manufacturer of fine wood furniture. For each of the following, specify whether the item should be classified as an operating, financing, or investing cash flow, (or whether it would not be reported on the cash flow statement) whether the item represents a cash inflow or outflow, and the amount of the transaction. Explain your reasoning.

a. Chiswick paid $250,000 to repurchase some of its own shares back from shareholders.
b. Chiswick paid suppliers $2,450,000 during the year for raw materials that it uses to make furniture.
c. Chiswick reported an amortization expense of $150,000.
d. Chiswick paid $51,000 for electricity during the year.
e. Chiswick paid consultants $75,000 for a report on how to improve the efficiency of its operations.
f. Chiswick paid dividends to shareholders totaling $200,000.
g. Cheswick purchased new manufacturing facility for $1,000,000. The seller of the facility took back a mortgage on a property.
h. Chiswick's employees were used to get the new manufacturing facility ready for use. $100,000 in employee wages were capitalized as part of the cost of the new facility.
i. Chiswick paid $11,000 in interest on its bank loan.

Study Problem 2 (Calculating cash flows from accrual information) Use the information shown below to calculate the following cash flows for the year ended December 31, 2005.

a. Cash collected from customers
b. Cash paid inventory
c. Cash paid to employees

Accounts receivable on December 31, 2004	$27,000
Accounts receivable on December 31, 2005	31,000
Inventory on December 31, 2004[1]	53,000
Inventory on December 31, 2005	50,000
Accounts payable on December 31, 2004	41,000
Accounts payable on December 31, 2005	46,000
Wages payable on December 31, 2004	17,000
Wages payable on December 31, 2005	9,000
Sales during 2005 (all sales were credit sales)	325,000
Cost of goods sold for 2005	103,000
Wage expense for 2005	78,000
[1] Assume all inventory purchases are on credit	

Study Problem 3 (Calculating cash from operations using the indirect method) You are provided the following information about Pageant Inc. (Pageant) for 2005:

Net loss	=	$(275,000)
Accounts receivable on January 1, 2005	=	245,000
Accounts receivable on December 31, 2005	=	201,000
Inventory on January 1, 2005	=	307,000
Inventory on December 31, 2005	=	355,000
Prepaid expenses on January 1, 2005	=	33,000
Prepaid expenses on December 31, 2005	=	21,000
Accounts payable on January 1, 2005	=	215,000
Accounts payable on December 31, 2005	=	249,000
Amortization expense	=	188,000
Gain on the sale of capital assets	=	57,000
Write-down of development costs	=	90,000

Required

Calculate CFO for Pageant for 2005. Use the indirect method. Explain why net income differs from cash from operations.

Study Problem 4 (Preparing a cash flow statement from balance sheet and income statement information) Wynard Inc. (Wynard) is a high-technology company. In 2004 Wynard raised $5,000,000 in cash by selling equity in the company to a group of private investors. Management had determined that Wynard would require a dramatic change in direction if it was going to survive and the additional cash was required to implement the dramatic new business model. The company's plan was to find new markets for its existing products and to invest heavily in modifying existing products and developing ones so that its line would be at the leading edge of the market. The new business model was implemented in late 2004 and management was satisfied with the progress in 2005. During 2005 Wynard lost significant sales in its previous markets but made good progress in developing new markets. In addition, Wyndard's research and development program was, in the eyes of the managers, proving to be productive and successful. Examine Wynyard Inc.'s (Wynyard) balance sheets and income statement below:

Wynyard Inc.
Balance Sheets
As of December 31,
(in thousands of dollars)

	2005	2004		2005	2004
Assets			**Liabilities and Shareholders' Equity**		
Current assets			*Current liabilities*		
Cash	$401	$4,432	Accounts payable	$450	$540
Accounts receivable	800	952	Wages and salaries payable	120	175
Inventory	1,480	1,202	Promotion, marketing, and selling costs payable	55	70
Prepaids	41	53	Unearned revenue	32	92
Total current assets	2,722	6,639	Total current liabilities	657	877
			Long-term debt	700	210
Capital assets	3,820	3,050			

Accumulated amortization	(1,012)	(692)	Capital stock	8,000	7,400
	2,808	2,358	Retained earnings	(3,827)	510
				4,173	7,910
Total assets	$5,530	$8,997	Total liabilities and shareholders' equity	$5,530	$8,997

Wynyard Inc.
Income Statement
For the years ended December 31,
(in thousands of dollars)

	2005	2004
Sales	$4,771	$6,350
Cost of sales	1,450	1,600
Gross margin	3,321	4,750
Expenses:		
Salaries and wages	1,050	1,300
Research and development	2,050	450
Amortization	450	410
Promotion, marketing and selling	2,325	1,950
Interest	47	37
General and administrative	1,855	1,420
Other	543	490
Loss on sale of capital assets	138	0
Income before income taxes	(5,137)	(1,307)
Income taxes	(800)	(250)
Net Income	($4,337)	($1,057)

Additional information:

a. During 2005 Wynyard wrote off $240,000 of inventory. The amount is included in cost of sales
b. $400,000 of Wynyard's sales were for cash. The remainder of the sales were made on credit.
c. All of Wynyard's purchases of inventory were made on credit. Purchases of inventory on credit are reflected in the accounts payable account.
d. During 2005 Wynyard sold capital assets that cost $310,000 and had a net book value of $180,000 for $42,000. (Remember that when amortizable capital assets are sold the cost of the asset and the accumulated amortization associated with the asset must be removed from the books. In this situation, the capital asset account would be reduced by $310,000 and the accumulated amortization account would be reduced by $130,000.)
e. Costs associated with research and development and general and administrative expenses were fully paid in cash during 2005. Other expenses are paid in cash when incurred, except for prepaid expenses. During 2005, Wynyard expensed $75,000 of prepaid items.
f. The long-term debt is held by the founders of the company. Interest in paid annually on December 31.
g. Wynyard's founders purchased $600,000 in commons shares from the company during fiscal 2005.

h. The unearned revenue on the December 31, 2004 balance sheet was recognized as revenue during 2005.
i. Because of its losses Wynyard refilled its previous years' tax returns and received a refund of previous amounts paid of $800,000.

Required:
i) Use the information provided to prepare a cash flow statement for Wynyard for the year ended December 31, 2005. Use the direct method for calculating cash from operations.
ii) Assume the roll of a lender who is evaluating Wynyard's situation. Analyze and interpret the cash flow statement you prepared and prepare a report to your manager about what you learned about Wynyard from the statement.

Study Problem 5 (Calculating cash from operations using both the direct and indirect methods) You are provided the following balance information and summarized income statement for Zadow Ltd.:

Zadow Ltd.
Current operating assets and liabilities as of December 31,

	2006	2005		2006	2005
Accounts receivable	1,406,100	1,223,200	Accounts payable	1,731,840	1,844,325
Inventory	3,195,100	3,679,000	Accrued liabilities	189,600	167,500
Prepaid insurance	36,000	22,000	Wages payable	69,627	64,057

Zadow Ltd.
Income Statement
For the year ended December 31, 2006

Revenue	$11,876,600
Cost of goods sold	6,545,950
Gross margin	5,330,650
Wage expense	1,531,800
Selling, general, and administrative	2,310,000
Amortization expense	790,500
Insurance expense	150,000
Other expenses	412,500
Gain on sale of capital assets	(181,500)
Write-down of assets	1,180,600
Net loss	($863,250)

Accounts payable pertains exclusively to the purchase of inventory. Accrued liabilities pertains exclusively to Selling, general, and administrative expenses. Other expenses were fully paid in cash during the year.

Required:

a. Prepare Zadow's cash from operations section of the cash flow statement for the year ended December 31, 2006 using the direct method.
b. Prepare Zadow's cash from operations section of the cash flow statement for the year ended December 31, 2006 using the indirect method.
c. Explain the difference between net income and cash from operations. Why did Zadow have a profit on its income statement but had negative cash from operations?

Study Problem 6 (Application problem) In spring 2002 Allison Flatt decided that instead of finding a summer job working for someone else that she would start a business of her own to make money to finance her education. She decided that she would design and sell tee shirts to the residents and many vacationers visited the area near where Allison lived.

Allison incorporated a company called Trendy Tee-Shirts Inc. (Trendy). She decided that she would operate the business out of a modified van that Trendy purchased. The van would allow her to move around from location to location so that she could be where the customers were. Allison used her own computer to design the tee shirts and purchased equipment to print the designs on the shirts. To start up the business Allison invested $6,000 of her own money and borrowed $10,000 from her parents. Her parents told her that they wanted to have the money repaid in the next two to three years.

Trendy's first year in business was successful. She earned enough money to pay for her schooling and to take a nice vacation during the winter. In fact, Allison thought Trendy was so successful that she expanded the business in 2003. For 2003 Allison bought a second van that was operated by an employee and some additional equipment. She also increased the number of designs and the quantity of tee shirts she produced because in the summer of 2002 she found himself running short of shirts. (Note that Trendy did not have the cash to pay for the second van at the beginning of the summer but was able to arrange financing until operations generated enough cash to pay for it. This financing is not reflected in the cash flow statement.)

It is now October 2003 and Trendy has ceased operations for the year. Allison feels very satisfied with the performance of her business for the year. Trendy had net income of $14,250 for the year ended September 30, 2003. (Allison's father is an accountant and he prepared an income statement for him.) However, Allison was shocked to find that when she finally got around to looking at Trendy's bank statements for the last few months (she didn't bother to look at them over the summer because she was so busy) that there was only $2,820 in the bank. There was not enough money to pay for school, to take another vacation, or repay the bank. Trendy's cash flow statements for the last two years (shown on the next page) confirmed her fears—there isn't enough cash to meet her needs—and Allison can't figure out why.

Required:

a. Use the cash flow statement to explain to Allison how her business can be successful yet she doesn't have enough cash to meet her needs.
b. Allison is thinking about going to the bank to borrow additional money. If you were the banker would you lend money to Trendy? Explain.

Trendy Tee-Shirts Inc.
Cash Flow Statement for the years ended October 31,

	2003	2002
Operations		
Net income	$14,250	$9,430
Add: amortization expense	8,100	3,250
Less: increase in inventory	3,510	1,250
Cash from operations	18,840	11,430
Financing		
Loan from parents	(6,000)	10,000
Bank loan	7,500	
Common stock issued		6,000
Dividends paid		(12,500)
Investing		
Purchase of van	17,000	11,000
Purchase of equipment	2,200	2,250
Increase in cash	1,140	1,680
Cash balance at the beginning of the year	1,680	0
Cash balance at the end of the year	$2,820	$1,680

Solutions to Study Problems

(Note that comments that appear in the solutions in *italics* are intended to provide explanations and clarifications to help you understand the material. These comments are not required as part of a complete solution)

Solution to Study Problem 1

a) The repurchase by an entity of its own common stock is a financing activity because it is a transaction involving Cheswick's equity investors.

Comment: Whether a cash flow is an inflow or an outflow does not affect the classification. Since the repurchase of the shares involves Cheswick's own equity the cash flow is classified as a financing activity. Note that if Cheswick had paid cash to purchase the shares of some other company the cash flow would be classified as an investing activity because the purchase of another company's shares is an investment.

b) The purchase of raw materials (inventory) is an operating cash flow.

c) Amortization expense does not affect cash flow and would therefore have no impact on the cash flow statement

Comment: Remember that amortization appears in the calculation of cash from operations using the indirect method because net income is being adjusted for non-cash events. Amortization is a non-cash event.

d) The amount paid to the consultants is an operating cash flow. The fact that consulting fees may not be paid regularly does not change the fact that this outlay pertains to operations. The payment is related to Cheswick's regular business activities and so is included in cash from operations.

e) Electricity is required to operate the business so cash paid for electricity is an operating cash flow.

f) Dividends are a financing activity. Dividends represent a distribution to shareholders.

g) The purchase of the manufacturing facility did not involve cash. The vendor of the facility financed the purchase by taking back a mortgage from Cheswick. Because no cash changed hands this transaction is not shown in the cash flow statement.

Comment: According to the CICA Handbook financing and investing transactions that do not involve the exchange of cash should not be reported in the cash flow statement. The Handbook section does require that these types of transactions be disclosed elsewhere in the financial statements. Interestingly, if Cheswick had arranged the mortgage through another party, such as a bank, the mortgage and the purchase of the property would have appeared in the cash flow statement because there would have been cash exchanges. One cash exchange would have been the cash obtained from the mortgage and the second would have been the cash paid to the seller of the manufacturing facility.

h) The amount paid to the employees for work done getting the manufacturing facility ready is an investing activity. Because the work is capitalized as part of the cost of capital asset (an investing activity), the cost of the work is classified as an investing cash flow.

Comment: The key here is that the wages were capitalized as part of the cost of a capital asset. Had the wages been expensed they would have been included in cash from operations.

i) Interest is classified as an operating cash flow (even though it is a payment made in respect of a financing activity).

Solution to Study Problem 2

Comment: This question is designed to help you understand the relationship between cash flows and the accrual amounts that are reported in the balance sheet and income statement. The numbers at the top of each column in the solutions below correspond with the general equation shown on page 338 of the textbook. In each of the situations notice that the manipulation of that general equation can differ, depending on the information that is missing. When working through these solutions do not simply focus on the reorganization of the equation. It is essential to understand the intuition in the relationship between the accrual information and the cash flow amount. The intuition is explained some below. Another way to gain some insight into the relationship between the flow of cash and accrual information is to construct a spreadsheet.

a) Cash collected from customers

4		3		2		1
Cash collected from customers	=	Sales	+	Beginning accounts receivable	-	Ending accounts receivable
	=	$325,000	+	$27,000	-	$31,000
	=	$321,000				

Comment: Sales is an accrual concept. The difference between accrual sales and cash flow is reflected in accounts receivable. During 2005 cash would have been collected from customers who owed money at the end of 2004. The amount owing at the end of 2004 would not be included in 2005's sales (it would have been recorded in 2004) but is a cash inflow in 2005. As a result beginning accounts receivable balance is added to sales. Ending accounts receivable represents sales recorded in 2005 but not collected in cash during 2005. This amount is deducted so that the amount of sales recorded that did not correspond with a cash inflow is removed.

b) Cash spent on inventory

3		**4**		**1**		**2**
Inventory purchased during 2005	=	COGS	+	Ending inventory	-	Beginning inventory
	=	$103,000	+	$50,000	-	$53,000
	=	$100,000				

4		**3**		**1**		**2**
Cash paid for inventory	=	Inventory purchased during 2005	+	Beginning accounts payable	-	Ending accounts payable
	=	$100,000	+	$41,000	-	$46,000
	=	$95,000				

Comment: This situation is the Allisone as the one shown in the textbook on pages 339-340. There are two steps that must be taken—first to determine the amount of inventory purchased and the second to determine the amount of inventory paid for. The first step is needed to find out how much inventory is purchased on credit. The second step determines the cash flow.

Comment: In parts a) and b) it is assumed that all purchases and sales of inventory are on credit. This assumption simplifies the calculation but is not essential. Information could be given that broke sales into credit and cash components (also for purchases) and the calculation of cash flows could be done. The amount of cash flow would be the Allisone.

c) Cash paid to employees

3		**4**		**2**		**1**
Cash paid to employees	=	Wage expense	+	Beginning wages payable	-	Ending wages payable
	=	$78,000	+	$17,000	-	$9,000
	=	$86,000				

Comment: Here the wage expense represents wages earned by employees in 2005. Wage expense does not necessarily correspond with the amount of cash paid to employees during 2005. The amount in beginning wages payable represents wages expensed in 2004 but not paid until 2005 represents an additional cash outflow not reflected in the wage expense. As a result the amount in beginning wages payable is added to the wage expense. The ending wages payable balance represents amounts earned by employees during 2005 but not paid during 2005. This amount does not reflect a cash outflow during 2005 and so the amount is subtracted from wage expense in the calculation of the actual amount of cash paid to employees.

Solution to Study Problem 3

Pageant Inc.
Cash from operations for the year ended January 31, 2005

Net loss	$(175,000)	
Add: Amortization expense	188,000	
Add: Write-down of development costs	90,000	
Less: Gain on sale of capital assets	(57,000)	
		$46,000
Changes in current operating accounts		
Accounts receivable	44,000	
Inventory	(48,000)	
Prepaid expenses	12,000	
Accounts payable	34,000	42,000
Cash from operations		$88,000

For 2005 Pageant Inc. reported a loss of $175,000 but has positive cash from operations of $88,000. The main reason for the difference between the two amounts is the $188,000 amortization expense and $90,000 write-down of capital assets. These amounts are deducted in the calculation of net income but do not have any effect on cash flows. The effect of these two items is offset by the $57,000 gain on the sale of capital assets. The gain increases net income but the cash associated with the sale of capital assets is treated as an investing activity. The gain itself is just the difference between the net book value of the capital assets and the amount received from their sale—the amount is not a cash flow.

Changes in the current operating accounts also contribute to the difference between the net loss and cash from operations. Pageant's cash from operations was also higher than its net loss because (a) it collected more receivables that were incurred in 2004 than it had outstanding at the end of 2005, which means sales on the income statement were less than the actual amount of cash collected from customers; and (b) it used up more prepaids that were paid for before 2005 than it paid for in 2005, which means that the amount of prepaids expensed during 2005 is more than the actual amount of cash expended on prepaid expenses. Inventory and payables taken together show that Pageant spent $4,000 more on inventory and other items than was expensed during 2005. (The previous sentence refers to inventory and other items because accounts payable likely includes amounts owing to suppliers other than suppliers of inventory.)

Solution to Study Problem 4

Comment: This is a comprehensive problem to give you practice preparing a cash flow statement from balance sheet and income statement information and allow you to interpret the statement you prepare. The solutions follows the steps described in the text and explanations are provided for each of the entries in the spreadsheet.

Step 1: Obtain balance sheets as of the beginning and end of the period and the income statement for the period, along with any other information that is available about the cash flows of the entity.

Wynyard's balance sheets, income statements, and other information are provided in the question. Note that the income statement for 2004 is not needed to prepare the cash flow statement but may provide some insights when analyzing Wynyard's it.

Step 2: Prepare a spreadsheet with a column for each balance sheet and income statement account, plus columns to number and classify entries. Enter the amounts from the beginning and ending balance sheet amounts and from the income statement amounts on the spreadsheet.

The spreadsheet is shown in Exhibit A. Row 1 of the spreadsheet shows the beginning balances as found in Wynyard's December 31, 2004 balance sheet. Row 28 of the spreadsheet shows the amounts in each balance sheet account as found in Wynyard's December 31, 2005 balance sheet.

Step 3: Make entries to the spreadsheet that explain the changes in each account.

Rows 2—6: Recognition of revenue and collection of accounts receivable

Row 2 recognizes the $400,000 of revenue from cash sales. This information was provided in item (b) of the additional information. Because specific information was provided about cash sales that information must be followed exactly. Row 3 is a bit of a trick. Wynyard had $92,000 of unearned revenue on its December 31, 2004 balance sheet and item (h) tells us that that amount was recognize in 2005. This means that the unearned revenue account has to be decreased by $92,000 and the revenue account increased by that amount. If this event was not properly accounted for the calculation of the amount of cash collected from customers would have been in error. Row 3 does not have any effect on cash flow but it is relevant for the calculation of the amount of cash that was collected from customers. Row 4 records the credit sales during 2005. This entry has no effect on cash flow but is necessary to calculate the amount of cash that was collected from customers. Row 5 records the amount of receivables that were collected from customers during 2005. Using the spreadsheet is another way of applying the equation on page

Comment: The information in item (h) was placed towards the end for a reason. Information is not usually provided in the most useful order to a person. It is important to assess all the information available before beginning an analysis so that one can know what is available.

Step 4: For each entry that affects the cash account, classify it as an operating, financing, or investing cash flow.

The second column of the spreadsheet shows the classification of each cash flow. Only the rows that have an entry in the cash column are classified because all we are interested in a cash flow statement is cash. If there is no effect on the cash column there is no cash flow to be considered. The reason for the classification was included in the discussion of each entry in step 3.

Step 5: Prepare the cash flow statement by organizing the amounts in entries that affected the cash account into CFO, investing activities, and financing activities.

Step 6: Calculate totals for each of operating, financing, and investing cash flows and calculate total cash flow for the period.

The completed cash flow statement is shown in Exhibit B. The information in the cash column of the spreadsheet was organized by type of cash flow (operating, investing, or financing) and totals calculated for each type. At the bottom of the statement the ending balance in the cash account is calculated by adding the decrease in cash during 2005 to the opening cash balance that was reported on the December 31, 2004 balance sheet.

Exhibit A

	Type of cash flow	Cash	Accounts receivable	Inventory	Prepaids	Capital assets	Accumulated amortization	Accounts payable	Wages and salaries payable	Promotion, marketing, and selling costs payable	Unearned revenue	Long-term debt	Capital stock	Retained earnings	Sales	Cost of sales	Salaries and wages	Research and development	Amortization	Promotion, marketing and selling	Interest	General and administrative	Other	Loss on sale of capital assets	Income taxes
1.		4,432	952	1,202	53	3,050	(692)	540	175	70	92	210	7,400	510											
2.	O	400													400										
3.											(92)				92										
4.			4,279												4,279										
5.	O	4,431	(4,431)																						
6.	O	32									32														
7.				(240)												(240)									
8.				(1,210)												(1,210)									
9.				1,728				1,728																	
10.	O	(1,818)						(1,818)																	
11.	I	42				(310)	130																	(138)	
12.							(450)												(450)						
13.	I	(1,080)				1,080																			
14.	F	490										490													
15.	F	600											600												
16.	O	(2,050)																(2,050)							
17.	O	(175)							(175)																
18.	O	(930)							120								(1,050)								
19.	O	(70)								(70)															
20.	O	(2,270)								55										(2,325)					
21.	O	(47)																			(47)				
22.	O	(1,855)																				(1,855)			
23.					(53)																		(53)		
24.					(22)																		(22)		
25.	O	(63)			63																				
26.	O	(468)																					(468)		
27.	O	800																							800
28.		401	800	1,480	41	3,820	(1,012)	450	120	55	32	700	8,000	510	4,771	(1,450)	(1,050)	(2,050)	(450)	(2,325)	(47)	(1,855)	(543)	(138)	800
29.														(4,337)	(4,771)	1,450	1,050	2,050	450	2325	47	1,855	543	138	(800)
30.		401	800	1,480	41	3,820	(1,012)	450	120	55	32	700	8,000	(3,827)	0	0	0	0	0	0	0	0	0	0	0

Exhibit B—Cash Flow Statement for Wynyard Inc.

Wynyard Inc.
Cash Flow Statement
For the years ended December 31, 2005
(in thousands of dollars)

Cash from operations		
Cash collected from customers (rows 2 + 5 + 6)	$4,863	
Cash paid to employees (rows 17 + 18)	(1,105)	
Cash paid for inventory (row 10)	(1,818)	
Cash paid for research and development (row 16)	(2,050)	
Cash paid for promotion marketing and selling (rows 19 +20)	(2,340)	
Cash paid for interest (row 21)	(47)	
Cash paid for general and administrative expenses (rows 22)	(1,855)	
Cash paid for other expenses (rows 25 + 26)	(531)	
Cash received as a refund of income taxes (row 27)	800	
Cash from operations		($4,083)
Investing activities		
Proceeds from sale of capital assets	42	
Purchase of capital assets	(1,080)	
		(1,038)
Financing activities		
Proceeds from the issue of long-term debt	490	
Proceeds from the issue of capital stock	600	
		1,090
Decrease in cash during 2005		(4,031)
Cash balance on December 31, 2004		4,432
Cash balance on December 31, 2005		$401

Exhibit C—Cash Flow Statement for Wynyard Inc. (CFO calculated using the indirect method)

Wynyard Inc.
Cash Flow Statement
For the years ended December 31, 2005
(in thousands of dollars)

Cash from operations		
Net income	($4,337)	
Add:		
Amortization expense	450	
Loss on the sale of capital assets	138	
Changes in current working capital accounts		
Decrease in accounts receivable	152	
Increase in inventory	(278)	
Decrease in prepaids	12	
Decrease in accounts payable	(90)	
Decrease in wages and salaries payable	(55)	
Decrease in promotion, marketing, and selling costs payable	(15)	
Decrease in unearned revenue	(60)	
Cash from operations		($4,083)
Investing activities		
Proceeds from sale of capital assets	42	
Purchase of capital assets	(1,080)	
		(1,038)
Financing activities		
Proceeds from the issue of long-term debt	490	
Proceeds from the issue of capital stock	600	
		1,090
Decrease in cash during 2005		(4,031)
Cash balance on December 31, 2004		4,432
Cash balance on December 31, 2005		$401

Solution to Study Problem 5

a.

Zadow Inc.
Cash Flow Statement
For the year ended July 31, 2005

	Notes		
Cash from operating activities:			
Cash inflows:	(1)		$11,693,700
Cash outflows			
Cash payments to suppliers	(2)	(6,174,535)	
Cash payments to employees	(3)	(1,526,230)	
Cash payments for selling, general, and administrative	(4)	(2,287,900)	
Cash payments for insurance	(5)	(164,000)	
Other cash expenses		(412,500)	(10,565,165)
Cash from operations			$1,128,535

Notes:

(1)

Cash collections from customers	=	Sales	+	Beginning AR	-	Ending AR
	=	$11,876,600	+	$1,223,200	-	$1,406,100
	=	$11,693,700				

(2)

Inventory purchased	=	Cost of goods sold	+	Ending inventory	-	Beginning inventory
	=	$6,545,950	+	$3,195,100	-	$3,679,000
	=	$6,062,050				

Cash paid to suppliers	=	Purchases	+	Beginning AP	-	Ending AP
		$6,062,050	+	$1,844,325	-	$1,731,840
		$6,174,535				

(3)

Cash payments to employees	=	Wage expense	+	Beginning wages payable	-	Ending wages payable
	=	$1,531,800	+	$64,057	-	$69,627
	=	$1,526,230				

(4)

Cash payments for insurance	=	Insurance expense	+	Ending prepaid insurance	-	Beginning prepaid insurance
		$150,000	+	$36,000	-	$22,000
		$164,000				

(5)

Cash payments for selling, general, and administration	=	Selling, general, and administrative expenses	+	Beginning accrued liabilities	-	Ending accrued liabilities
		$2,310,000	+	$167,500	-	$189,600
		$2,287,900				

b.

Zadow Ltd.
Cash Flow Statement
For the year ended May, 2005

	Notes		
Cash from operating activities:			
Net Income		($863,250)	
Add:			
Amortization expense		$790,500	
Write down of assets		1,180,600	
Decrease in inventory	(1)	483,900	
Increase in wages payable	(2)	5,570	
Increase in accrued liabilities	(3)	22,100	2,482,670
Deduct:			
Gain on sale of capital assets		(181,500)	
Increase in accounts receivable	(4)	(182,900)	
Increase in prepaid insurance	(5)	(14,000)	
Decrease in accounts payable	(6)	(112,485)	(490,885)
Cash from operations			$1,128,535

Notes:

Item	2005	2004	Change	Category	Note
Inventory	3,195,100	3,679,000	(483,900)	O	(1)
Wages payable	69,627	64,057	5,570	O	(2)
Accrued liabilities	189,600	167,500	22,100	O	(3)
Accounts receivable	1,406,100	1,223,200	182,900	O	(4)
Prepaid insurance	36,000	22,000	14,000	O	(5)
Accounts payable	1,731,840	1,844,325	(112,485)	O	(6)

d. Net income is an abstract economic concept used to measure performance under accrual accounting. It is intended to measure the change in wealth of the owners of a profit-oriented entity by recognizing revenue when it is earned and matching expenses to the revenue. Cash flows can occur before, after, or at the same time that revenues and expenses are recognized. Cash receipts are recorded when they are received and disbursements when cash is paid. Rather than measure flows of wealth, cash flow is intended to capture cash receipts and disbursements. Inevitably differences arise between the net income and cash flows

The main reason that Zadow Ltd. reported a loss on its income statement but has positive cash flow from operations is the write down of assets. A write down causes a reduction in net income because it represents an economic cost or loss to the entity—the entity's shareholders' wealth has decreased because of the decline in value of the assets. However, the write down does not have a cash cost associated with it—no cash leaves the entity to "pay" for the write down. A write down is simply an internal adjustment. The increase in current assets must be financed and are therefore a use of cash. This pattern suggests a growing company but more information is needed to confirm this. The situation could also be indicative of a struggling company that bought too much inventory and relaxed it credit terms.

Solution to Study Problem 6

a) Report to Allison Flatt regarding the performance of Trendy Tee Shirts Inc.

Dear Allison:

I am writing to try to clarify your confusion regarding the cash position of Trendy Tee Shirts Inc. compared with its accrual accounting performance. Your business performed well—earning an income of $14,250—but your cash position is poor—only $2,820 on hand at the end of the year before paying yourself a dividend. To begin the explanation it is first important to understand the difference between accrual accounting and cash flow. Accrual accounting reflects economic flows, not just cash flows. The idea is to measure the wealth and change in wealth of an entity, not to measure cash and change in cash. As a result the amount of income you report does not necessarily correspond with your business' cash flow.

During 2002 Trendy generated cash from operations—the cash an entity generates from its ordinary business activities—of $11,430. This means that Trendy generated $11,340 from operations, cash that can be used for purposes such as paying off debts, paying dividends, expanding operations, making investments in capital assets, and so on. This amount was different from your net income of $9,430 for two reasons. First, in the calculation of net income an amortization expense of $3,320 was deducted. This amount does not involve the outlay of cash; it is simply part of the cost of the van and equipment that is deducted in the calculation of net income. The idea is that part of the cost of assets that help earn revenue over more than one year is expensed each year. (It is important to note that Trendy did spend $13,200 in cash on the van and equipment in 2002. I will have more to say about this shortly.) The second difference between cash from operations and net income was the investment in inventory you had at the end of the year. This inventory had been paid for by the end of 2002 but it had not been expensed in 2002 because it had not been sold.

A similar analysis can be provided for 2003. Your cash from operations in 2003 was $18,840, a fair bit higher than in 2002. The Allisone adjustments that I described above were needed to explain the difference between cash from operations and net income. Trendy's income statement reported $8,100 in non-cash amortization expense and an additional $3,510 was invested in inventory that was unsold as of the end of the year. The bottom line is that your business is generating decent cash flow. So why don't you have enough cash on hand to meet your needs?

There are several reasons. First, you have spent a significant amount of money purchasing assets that will help you make money over an extended period of time—the vans and the equipment. So while your business is generating cash, you have had to invest a significant amount of money to get your business going. If you do not expand in future years these assets will contribute to sales without costing you any cash. However, when a business first starts up or expands, cash outlays are required. In your first two years in business Trendy spent $32,450 on these assets.

Second, Trendy has invested $4,760 in inventory. This amount is reflected in cash from operations, as discussed above. However, it represents consumption of cash. As an aside, $4,760 seems like a lot of money to be tied up in inventory. Does this amount represent tee shirts that have not yet been printed on or are they tee shirts that have designs on them? If it is the latter will these shirts be saleable? Don't designs go out of style? If this is the case and the inventory cannot be sold the income of your business may, in fact, be overstated because the cost of unsaleable inventory should be expensed. If the inventory is shirts without designs then it can be used in future, but it seems like a lot of money to be tied up for materials that can be easily purchased at any time. You might consider returning some of these goods if you can to free up some cash. Third, in 2002 Trendy spent $12,500 paying a dividend.

In 2002 Trendy generated the cash to pay the $13,250 required for the van and equipment and the $12,500 from operations ($11,430), borrowing ($10,000), and your own investment ($6,000). In 2003 you generated the cash to pay $19,200 for the second van and some additional equipment and $6,000 to repay the loan from your parents from operations ($18,840) and from bank borrowing ($7,500). The problem in 2003 was that there was much less cash generated from financing activities—borrowing and equity investment—than in 2002. In essence, your dividend in 2002 was paid for by borrowing and a return of the money you invested in Trendy to start with. In 2003 you did not have much additional investment. The $7,500 bank loan was mainly to replace the loan from your parents. As a result the investments in the second van and the additional equipment were paid from operations and the opening cash balance of $1,680. By using all the cash generated by operations to purchase the van and equipment there was no cash available for your personal needs.

This should be a short-term problem for you. Assuming that your business continues to be as successful as it has been and if you control your inventory Trendy should be generating about $20,000 a year in cash from operations. That amount will allow you to pay off your $7,500 bank loan in 2004 and have plenty of cash available for your own needs. This also assumes that you will not spending significant amounts of cash on additional assets such as vans and equipment. In the meantime, you will have to find an alternative source of cash to meet your personal needs this year. Perhaps you can borrow from your parents or obtain a bank loan.

b) As a banker I would give serious consideration to providing a loan to Trendy on the basis of its operations. Trendy generates a lot of cash and it would be able to support a loan—both the interest and principal—assuming that it continues to perform as it did in 2003. That said, tee shirts can be a risky business. What is popular one year might not be popular in another, so there are some risks should the business become less successful. On the other hand, tee shirts have had over the years sustained popularity so this mitigates some of the risk. Even if business were to contract by 25% there would still be significant cash flow to support the loan. Trendy has its two vans and the equipment along with the inventory to use as collateral for a loan. It is not clear, however, what how much cash those items would raise if they had to be sold. An estimate would have to be made to determine the amount. Of significant concern is that Trendy does not really need cash for the business. Assuming that no additional purchases of capital assets are required (no additional expansion is planned) and that little cash is need for working capital (for example to purchase inventory and supplies) the main purpose of the loan would be to allow Trendy to pay a dividend. If that is the case the amount of equity that Allison would have in the business would be $7,180 (initial equity investment + net incomes - dividends = $6,000 + $9,430 + $14,250 - $12,500 - $10,000 (assuming an additional bank loan of $10,000)). This would be in comparison with liabilities of $21,500 ($4,000 + $7,500 + $10,000 (assuming an additional bank loan of $10,000)). This represents a relatively small amount of equity relative to debt (debt-to-equity ratio = $21,500/$7,180 = 2.99). If Allison neglects his business for some reason in the future or chooses not to continue in business our bank and the other lenders stand to lose much more than Allison does (although Allison's parents will lose $4,000 of their money). All told, I would be inclined to recommend a loan to Trendy. I think that the business has shown an ability to generate cash in the past and stands to do so in the future. I recommend that if any assets have not been secured against the other bank loan that we should take those assets as security against our loan. In addition, we should obtain personal guarantees from Allison and from his parents if possible. This will provide the bank with additional protection. Finally, the terms of the loan should prevent Trendy from purchasing additional capital assets until the bank loans have been reduced or paid off. This is appropriate because additional purchases will use up cash from operations and reduce or eliminate cash needed to pay off the bank loan. Additional purchases will also result in a repetition of the current situation where Allison is not able to draw enough cash from Trendy to meet his personal needs. In addition, further expansion may add to the bank's risk since it is not known whether there is enough demand for more of Trendy's products and it is not clear whether Allison will be able to effectively manage an expanded business.

Comment: Notice the focus of the discussion in part b). The banker is interested in what will happen, not what has happened. This is very important to keep in mind. Historical information can sometimes be a useful basis for predicting future cash flows (and earnings) but the future will usually not be the Allisone as the past. As a result the bank must consider "what if" scenarios. What if sales decrease? What if profit margins decrease? Without this type of assessment it is difficult for the bank to evaluate the risks that it is facing.

Chapter 7

Cash, Receivables, and the Time Value of Money

Chapter Overview

Cash and receivables is a more straightforward topic than the liabilities chapter (Chapter 10). By placing the coverage of the time value of money in this chapter you have the opportunity concentrate on the time value of money concepts. By the time you get to Chapter 10 you will be prepared to tackle the topics where the time value of money is significant. In addition, the introduction of the time value of money supports the discussion of long-term receivables.

Time value of money is a crucial topic for business students and a powerful tool for you to know since in most business schools it is addressed in other courses such as corporate finance. If you do not understand the time value of money concept early on, topics in Chapter 10 such as bonds and leases will seem more complicated.

The purpose of covering hidden reserves in this book is to demonstrate how managers can influence the numbers in financial statements in a way that is very difficult for users to detect. The discussion of hidden reserves establishes an important link between the textbook and the real world. Hidden reserves are at the heart of some accounting controversies and introducing the topic at this time will help you understand how these controversies occur. The coverage also shows how the estimates required under accrual accounting provide opportunities for managers to achieve their reporting objectives.
Discuss accounting for cash including cash management and controls over cash, bank reconciliations, and the changing purchasing power of money. Introduce time value of money concepts. Explain accounting for receivables, including accounting for uncollectible amounts and long-term receivables. Explain how managers can use hidden reserves to massage accounting information while providing little disclosure to users of the financial statements. Further explore liquidity by examining the current and quick ratios and introduce the accounts receivable turnover ratio

The introduction points out that the focus of the book changes in Chapters 7. Chapters 7 through 11 address accounting topics by balance sheet classification. While the chapter titles suggest that attention is paid only to the balance sheet, the related income statement implications of these balance sheet topics are fully discussed. Chapter 7 covers accounting for cash and receivables, and introduces the basic tools for time value of money analysis.

Summary of Key Points

- Cash on the balance sheet usually includes cash equivalents, which are short-term investments that can be converted into a known amount of cash easily and quickly (e.g. GICs, treasury bills, and money market funds).

  - Internal controls are the policies and procedures that management implements to protect the entity's assets and ensure the integrity of the accounting information system.
  - Bank reconciliations are internal control procedures used to explain differences between the accounting records and the bank records. The chapter identifies three purposes for a bank reconciliation:

1) Helps determine the cash balance that should be reported on the balance sheet at the end of a period;
2) Serves to identify accounting and bank errors;
3) May help detect theft of cash by employees.

➢ Canadian GAAP uses the nominal dollar as the unit of measure; that means changes in the purchasing power of money are not captured by financial statements in Canada.

♦ The chapter covers:

- Future value
- Present value
- Present value of an annuity

➢ Present value and future value techniques make it possible to compare different streams of cash flows on a common basis.
➢ The approach in the book relies on traditional present value and future value tables to demonstrate time value of money concepts. The formulas for future and present values are provided in the book and these can be programmed into spreadsheets or calculators.

♦ The main focus of the discussion of receivables is on amounts owed by customers, but amounts can also be owed by shareholders, employees, and CCRA and provincial tax authorities.

➢ Accounting for uncollectible receivables - Selling on credit introduces the possibility that amounts customers promise to pay may not be fulfilled. It is therefore necessary to account for amounts that are estimated to not be collected.
➢ There are three methods described for accounting for uncollectible amounts:
    1) Direct write-off method
    2) Percentage-of-receivables method
    3) Percentage-of-credit sales method

➢ If a receivable is due in more than a year or an operating cycle, it is classified as a long-term asset. If a long-term receivable does not require the payment of interest or if the interest rate is less than the market rate, the amount of revenue that is recognized and the receivable are too high if the time value of money is ignored.

♦ Chapter 13 of the book pulls together the financial statement analysis tools from all the chapters in the book into a more comprehensive discussion.

➢ Hidden reserves are excess accruals made in good times for use in bad times to boost financial statement numbers. Hidden reserves are included because they help make the study of accounting real. There are several examples of problems in the contemporary accounting environment as many of the accounting scandals of recent times relate to hidden reserves.
➢ The discussion of the current and quick ratios builds on the material on liquidity from Chapter 2. The current ratio was introduced in Chapter 2 and the quick ratio is added to the mix here.
➢ The current and quick ratios are static measures of liquidity because they are balance sheet measures that do not take into consideration an entity's cash flow. An entity

that has a reliable cash flow can tolerate much lower current and quick ratios than an entity that has erratic cash flows.

- Accounts receivable turnover ratio and the average collection period of accounts receivable indicate how quickly receivables are incurred and replaced.

Study Points and Study Tips

Cash

- It is important to note that cash is not always liquid. Sometimes the use of cash is restricted to specific purposes. Restricted cash (not available for day-to-day operations) must be disclosed in the financial statements.

  - For example, colleges and universities set aside cash for specific purposes such as research activities that are not utilized in day-to-day operations.
  - There is an opportunity cost to retaining cash because it is not a productive asset. Cash is a crucial asset, but an entity does not earn significant returns by holding cash in a bank account. By holding cash an entity can earn a risk-free rate of return such as the yield on Government of Canada Treasury Bills (T-Bills). This return compensates the entity for the loss of purchasing power due to inflation, but not for taking risks. Of course entities need some money in cash reserves. In 2004, Government of Canada T-Bills paid less than 2% interest.
  - Some companies like Apple Computer Inc. (Apple) hold billions of dollars in cash and short-term investments (in 2003 cash and short-term investments accounted for over 2/3 of Apple's total assets). In years when sales are weak Apple's high interest revenue presents a misleading operating income to users.
  - Management must balance the need to ensure that the liquidity requirements of the entity are met without holding excess cash. Although in some industries, such as the securities industry, firms are required by regulatory bodies to hold excess cash to uphold investor confidence.

- Protecting assets is part of the internal controls that an entity maintains. Establishing effective internal controls is a multi-step process that includes the input from the board of directors, auditors, management and employees.

  - Strong internal controls provide assurance to stakeholders that the entity's assets cannot be stolen, used inappropriately, used without proper authorization, and that the information produced by the accounting system can be relied on.
  - Transactions and other economic activities reported by Canadian entities often take place in currencies other than Canadian dollars. For the financial statements to have all amounts stated in Canadian dollars, it is necessary to convert these transactions and economic activities into Canadian dollars. Foreign cash amounts are converted into Canadian dollars using the exchange rate in effect on the financial statement date.
  - Imagine the complexity of preparing the consolidated financial statements for Magna International Inc. Magna has core operating groups in Canada, the U.S., Mexico, South America, Europe and Asia and are required to consolidate all of this information into Canadian financial reports.

The Time Value of Money

- Entities prefer payment today rather than in the future because of the interest available to be earned. If an amount is received today rather than in the future it can be invested, and the resulting amount will be larger than if the same amount was received in the future (due to interest earned).

- If you have a student loan, you must determine the amount of payments on the loan. You may not realize it but the amount of the loan payment is based on the present value of the loan, a time value of money concept. In fact, the longer that you can defer payments on the loan, the more powerful the time value of money benefit becomes.

Receivables

- Most companies offer credit to remain competitive which allows customers more flexibility. The majority of receivables result from selling goods and services to customers on credit. Stakeholders need to beware when companies record a substantial amount of credit sales to risky customers.

  - In the last five years offering credit has backfired dreadfully on telecommunications equipment suppliers such as Nortel, Cisco and Motorola. Users beware of this type of 'catch 22': 1) the economy begins to go in the tank 2) companies like Nortel need to remain competitive so they increase receivables (or lengthen the collection period) to ensure current sales growth 3) banks tighten their lending policies 4) Nortel's customers are faced with a shortage of funding which puts even more pressure on Nortel to extend receivables 5) "dot-com" sector implodes and Nortel is faced with writing-off billions of dollars in receivables.
  - If receivables are managed properly companies financing customer accounts can use credit as a strategy to increase total revenue. Canadian Tire Bank now offers credit card services and a close look at Canadian Tire's consolidated statements shows that credit charge receivables are greater than accounts receivable on their balance sheet.

- Accounting for receivables ties into the coverage of revenue recognition from Chapter 4. When revenue is recognized determines when an account receivable appears on the books. The main focus of this section is accounting for uncollectible amounts. Long-term receivables are introduced where the time value of money is linked to the accounting for receivables.

  - <u>Direct write-off method</u>—expense is recognized when management determines that an amount owing will not be collected.
  - <u>Percentage-of-receivables method</u>—expense is determined by estimating the amount of the outstanding receivables at year end that will not be collected. An aging schedule can be used to assist in this process. This method focuses on the balance sheet so the net amount of receivables reflects the net realizable value of the receivables. In this method the bad debt expense is a "plug" because it is equal to the amount that must be credited to the allowance account to come up with the desired balance in the allowance account.
  - <u>Percentage-of-credit sales method</u>—expense is determined by estimating the portion of credit sales that will not be collected. This approach focuses on the income statement because the expense represents an estimate of the amount of credit sales that will not be collected. In this method the credit to the allowance account is a "plug" because it is equal to the amount that must be expensed in the period.

    - If there is a persistent bias in the bad debt expense (the expense is over- or understated year after year) the valuation of receivables becomes badly distorted (the allowance account balance will be too high or too low) and so net accounts receivable will not be a good estimate of their net realizable value.

- The percentage-of-credit sales and percentage-of-receivables methods are accrual methods that match the cost of uncollectible amounts to the revenue to which they relate. The direct write-off method is not an accrual method because a receivable is written off only when management decides that it is uncollectible. The expense is not necessarily recognized in the same period as the revenue is recognized.

  - All three methods require that management exercise judgement. With the direct write-off method management must decide when an amount is not going to be collected. With the two accrual methods management must decide how much to expense each period.
  - In principle the two accrual methods should yield the same result—same bad debt expense, same balance in the allowance account each period. In practice they will not, unless the estimated amount of bad debts proves to be accurate every year. Research In Motion Limited (RIM) makes their estimate based on specifically identified accounts, historical experience, and other current information such as economic conditions.
  - With the two accrual methods write-offs of accounts receivable do not affect the net amount of accounts receivable.

- Errors in estimating bad debts do not necessarily imply management of accounting information. It is reasonable to expect that the estimate will rarely match the actual. Even understated or overstated estimates for a few years may not imply a bias. This is why entities do not change the basis of their estimates after one or two years of "bad" estimates.

  - Absent other information, management may feel the amounts estimated will average out over time.

- The discussion of long-term receivables integrates accounting for receivables with time value of money concepts.

  - The amount of revenue that should be recognized should be the present value of the cash flows to be received from the customer. (If the customer is required to pay interest at the appropriate market rate, the present value of the cash that will be received (including interest) will equal the selling price of the goods or services at the date of the transaction.)
  - By discounting the cash payments the amount of revenue recognized and the receivable recorded when revenue is recognized will be less than the amount of cash received. The difference between the amount of revenue recognized and the amount of cash ultimately received is recognized as interest revenue over the period the receivable is outstanding.
  - An example is provided (beginning on page 402) to show the process of recording a long-term receivable at its discounted value and how interest revenue is recognized over the period the receivable is outstanding. The example shows how the receivable builds up to the actual number of dollars that will be received from the customer.

Financial Statement Analysis Issues

- With hidden reserves the important point to understand is that over time income is the same. All that the managers' choices are doing is changing the periods in which the earnings appear. This is the same theme that was discussed in Chapter 4 in the coverage of revenue recognition.

  - In 1998 Arthur Levitt, Chairman of the SEC in the US, addressed in the strongest terms the use by companies of what he called "cookie jar" reserves. What makes hidden reserves especially problematic is that they are very difficult for users to detect. As a result it is not possible for users to fully understand the earnings and other financial statement numbers that are reported because it is not clear if or the extent to which they reflect the economic activity of the entity.

- While using hidden reserves for earnings management purposes is undesirable, users face the challenge of understanding the motivation of the managers (which is not observable). Changes in estimates are not necessarily made to manage earnings. Some reflect legitimate changes in an entity's accounting environment and are important for conveying managers' private information to stakeholders.
- The example uses the allowance for doubtful accounts as the basis for how management could hide profits in the "cookie jar." There are many other places where earnings can be stashed. Certainly any type of accrual can serve the purpose: warranty provisions, environmental accruals, returns allowances, accrued liabilities, and coupon provisions.
- You may also be confused by how it is that these accounting treatments can be hidden. It is important to realize that the aggregation of information in the financial statements and the absence of comprehensive disclosure make it possible to hide things in the financial statements. The material in textbooks tends to make the accounting process transparent, which contributes to the confusion.
- Recently Adidas-Salomon reported extraordinary profits which originated through the use of hidden reserves. With increased earnings, the management of Adidas-Salomon had to expect shareholders would request an increase in the dividend payout ratio. Once shareholders realized that the increased profit was due to prior hidden reserves, a compromise was achieved.

- Figure 7-2 (page 408) provides seven-year averages for the current ratios and quick ratios for 11 different industries. This figure demonstrates that norms are not uniform across different industries. Also, smaller companies should have higher current ratios to meet unexpected cash requirements.

  - There are a number of problems with calculating and interpreting the accounts receivable turnover ratio and average collection period of accounts receivable.
  - Correct application of the ratio requires credit sales. However, the financial statements of most companies do not provide separate credit and cash sales numbers. For businesses in industries such as retail where there is a significant amount of cash sales, interpreting the accounts receivable turnover ratio can be challenging. For industries where cash sales are a relatively minor part of total sales, using total sales instead of just credit sales is not a big problem.
  - The accounts receivable turnover ratio can be affected by how the average accounts receivable is calculated. For seasonal businesses, using the year end amounts will yield different ratios than if quarterly or monthly receivables are employed.
  - The credit terms an entity offers its customers and franchisees are not found in the annual report. The credit terms are a benchmark for evaluating the effectiveness of the entity's collections. Compounding the problem is the fact that an entity may not offer all customers the same credit terms. It is possible to find out credit terms from other sources.

Study Problems

Study Problem 1 (Calculating present values) Answer the following questions:

a. Andrew McCulloch purchases $15,000 worth of computers. The goods will be paid for in cash in three years. How much revenue should be recorded on the date the goods are delivered, assuming a discount rate of 7%?

b. Slick Willy is presented with an investment opportunity that will pay you $0 in the first year, $1,000 in two years, and $5,000 in three years. At a discount rate of 5%, would you pay $5,000 for this investment?
c. A "zero coupon bond" also known as a "strip bond" is a type of long-term debt that pays no interest, but simply pays a single amount on the date the bond matures. The province of Saskatchewan is offering zero coupon bonds that will pay $50,000 in 30 years. How much would you pay for the bond today, if your discount rate were 8%?
d. You have just signed a contract with a publishing company that specializes in educational products for university students. The company has offered you $10,000 in one year, $5,000 in two years, and $2,500 in three years. At a discount rate of 4%, what would you require today to make the deal worthwhile for your efforts?

Study Problem 2 (Preparing a bank reconciliation) On April 30, 2005 the accounting records of Lobster Ltd. (Lobster) showed a cash balance of $14,330.29. The balance reported in Lobster's April 30, 2005 bank statement was $9,346.01. Examination of the bank statement and the accounting records showed the following:

a. Two cheques had been written and mailed by Lobster, and recorded in Lobster's accounting records, had not been cashed by the entities to which the cheques had been written. The outstanding cheques were numbers #129 for $2,354.99 and #130 for 140.91.
b. Lobster deposited $7,900.71 in cash and cheques to its bank account through a bank machine late April 30, 2005. The deposits were not recorded by the bank until May 1, 2005 and as a result did not appear in the April 30, 2005 bank statement.
c. The bank collected $1407.41 on behalf of Lobster from one of Lobster's customers. Lobster did not record this collection in its accounting records.
d. Bank service charges for April 2005 were $73. The amount was deducted from Lobster's bank account but not recorded in the accounting records.
e. A cheque received from one of Lobster's customers was insufficient funds (NSF) by the bank because the customer did not have enough money in its bank account to cover the cheque. The amount of the cheque was $749.02. Lobster had recorded the cheque as a debit to cash when it was deposited.
f. Lobster was paid $14.23 in interest during April. The amount was deposited in Lobster's bank account but not recorded in the accounting records.
g. The bank made an error by removing $179.09 from Lobster's bank account that should have been taken from another entity's bank account.

Required:

1) Prepare a bank reconciliation April 30, 2005.
2) What amount should Lobster report for cash on its April 30, 2005 balance sheet?
3) Prepare any journal entries required as a result of the bank reconciliation and review of the bank statement.

Study Problem 3 (Calculating accounts receivable) Use an accounting equation spreadsheet and the following information to calculate accounts receivable for Chucky's Chicken Schwarma Ltd. (Chucky) on June 30, 2005. Chucky's fiscal year runs from July 1st to June 30th :

	June 30, 2005	June 30, 2004
Accounts receivable	A	$ 75,000
Allowance for uncollectible accounts	$ (5,000)	(3,750)
Unearned revenue	22,000	15,000
Revenue recognized during fiscal 2005*	340,000	B
Payments of accounts receivable during fiscal 2005	370,000	C
Bad debt expense for 2005	3,500	D
Cash received from customers for services to be provided in the future during 2005	12,000	E
Amounts of accounts receivable written off during 2005	4,600	F

* Includes recognition of revenue classified as unearned in previous periods. All other revenue is on credit.

Study Problem 4 (Comparing the percentage-of-receivables and percentage-of-credit sales methods) The following information has been obtained about Fashion Fad Inc. (Fashion) for 2005. The information was obtained before any year-end adjusting entries were made. Fashion's fiscal year end is September 30:

Accounts receivable on September 30, 2005	$ 700,000
Credit sales for the year ended September 30, 2005	2,500,000
Allowance for uncollectible accounts on September 30, 2005 (credit balance)	5,000

Required:

a. Calculate the bad debt expense that Fashion would record for the 2005 fiscal year, assuming that management expects that 4% of year-end accounts receivable will not be collected. What would the balance in Allowance for uncollectible accounts on September 30, 2005? Prepare the journal entry to record bad debt expense.
b. Calculate the bad debt expense that Fashion would record for the 2005 fiscal year, assuming that management expects that 1.0% of credit sales during fiscal 2005 will not be collected. What would be the balance in Allowance for uncollectible accounts on September 30, 2005? Prepare the journal entry to record the bad debt expense.
c. What would your answers in (a) and (b) be if the balance in Allowance for uncollectible accounts on September 30, 2005 (before any year-end adjusting entries) was a debit of $5,000? Explain any differences you find.

Study Problem 5 (Comparing the effects of different methods of accounting for bad debts) You have obtained the following information about Harte Ltd. (Harte) from the company's 2006 annual report:

a. Harte's year end is August 31st.
b. Sales for the year ended August 31st, 2006 were $17,750,000; 75% of sales were credit sales.
c. The balance in Accounts Receivable on August 31, 2006 was $6,450,000.
d. The balance in Allowance for Uncollectible Accounts on August 31, 2005 was $590,000.
e. During fiscal 2006, Harte wrote off $575,000 of accounts receivable.
f. The bad debt expense can be estimated as 2.5% of credit sales or 7.0% of year-end accounts receivable.

g. Net income for the year ended August 31, 2006, including all revenues and expenses except for the bad debt expense, was $2,250,000.

Required:

1) Determine the bad debt expense for the year ended 2006, assuming that Harte used:
   I. The direct write-off-method for accounting for uncollectible accounts.
   II. The percentage-of-credit sales method for accounting for uncollectible accounts.
   III. The percentage of receivables method for accounting for uncollectible accounts.
2) What would be the balance in Allowance for Uncollectible Accounts on August 31, 2006 using the 3 methods identified in part (1)?
3) Prepare the journal entry required to record the bad debt expense under each of the 3 methods identified in part (1).
4) What would net income be for 2006 using the 3 methods identified in part (1)?
5) Explain why the three methods identified in part (1) provide different bad debt expenses.
6) Which method of determining the bad debt expense and the allowance for uncollectible accounts is best? Explain.

Solutions to Study Problems

Solution to Study Problem 1

a. $15,000 $(1.07)^{-3}$ = $12,244.47 or using the tables $15,000 * 0.8163 = $12,244.50

b. $0 + $1,000 $(1.05)^{-2}$ + $5,000 $(1.05)^{-3}$
= $5,226.22

or using the tables ($0 * 0.95238) + ($1,000 * 0.90703) + ($5,000 * 0.86384)
= $5,226.23

Yes you would pay $5,000 for the investment. The present value of the cash flow indicates that you will have more purchasing power three years from now than your $5,000 currently has. $5,226.22 is the amount that would make you indifferent between having $5,000 now and the series of cash flows stated in the question.

c. $50,000 $(1.08)^{-30}$ = $4968.87 or using the tables $50,000 * 0.09938 = $4,969.00. This figure represents the amount that you would give to the province of Saskatchewan today, in return for $50,000 in 30 years (at 8%).
Zero coupon bonds have cash flow advantages for the issuer since they are not required to pay semi-annual interest throughout the life of the bond.

d. $10,000 $(1.04)^{-1}$ + $5,000 $(1.04)^{-2}$ + $2,500 $(1.04)^{-3}$
= $16,460.66

or using the tables ($10,000 * 0.96154) + ($5,000 * 0.92456) + ($2,500 * 0.8890)
= $16,460.70

You would be indifferent in choosing to receive either $16,460.66 today or the stream of payments offered by the publishing company (at an assumed discount rate of 4%).

Note that differences between the two calculation approaches shown are due to rounding errors in the table.

Solution to Study Problem 2

a.

Lobster Ltd.

Bank Reconciliation for April 30, 2005

Balance per accounting records		**Balance per bank statement**		
on April 30, 2005	$14,330.29	on April 30, 2005		$9,346.01
Add: Interest earned	14.23	Add: Outstanding deposits		7,900.71
Add: Collections by bank	1,407.41	Add: Bank errors		179.09
Subtract: Bank service charges	(73.00)	Subtract: Outstanding cheques		
Subtract: Returned cheque	(749.02)		#129	(2,354.99)
			#130	(140.91)
Adjusted cash balance	$14,929.91	Adjusted cash balance		$14,929.91

b. The amount of cash Lobster should report on its April 30, 2005 balance sheet is $14,929.91.

c.

	Dr.	Cr.
Cash	14.23	
Interest earned		14.23
To record interest earned on bank account.		
Cash	1,407.41	
Accounts receivable		1,407.41
To record amounts collected by the bank on Lobster's behalf.		
Bank service charges	73.00	
Cash		73.00
To record bank service charges on bank account.		
Accounts receivable	749.02	
Cash		749.02
To record returned cheque (NSF).		

Solution to Study Problem 3

	Cash	**Accounts receivable**	**Allowance for uncollectible accounts**	**Unearned revenue**	**Revenue**	**Bad debt expense**
Beginning balances 06/30/04		75,000	(3,750)	15,000		
		B 335,000		**A (5,000)**	340,000	
	12,000			12,000		
	370,000	(370,000)				
			(3,500)			(3,500)
		(4,600)	4,600			
Ending balances 06/30/05	**D 382,000**	**C 35,400**	(2,650)	22,000	340,000	(3,500)

A = -15,000 – 12,000 + 22,000 = **(5,000)**
B = 340,000 – 5,000 = **335,000**
C = 75,000 + 335,000 – 370,000 – 4,600 = **35,400**
D = 12,000 + 370,000 = **382,000**

Solution to Study Problem 4

a. Bad debt expense = $700,000 (4%) - $5,000 = $23,000
Allowance for doubtful accounts = $700,000 (4%) = $28,000

	Dr	Cr
Bad debt expense	23,000.00	
Allowance for doubtful accounts		23,000.00

b. Bad debt expense = $2,500,000 (1.0%) = $25,000.00
Allowance for doubtful accounts = $25,000.00 + $5,000 = $30,000.00

	Dr	Cr
Bad debt expense	25,000.00	
Allowance for doubtful accounts		25,000.00

c. Bad debt expense = $700,000 (4%) + $5,000 = $33,000
Allowance for doubtful accounts = $700,000 (4%) = $28,000

	Dr	Cr
Bad debt expense	33,000.00	
Allowance for doubtful accounts		33,000.00

Bad debt expense = $2,500,000 (1.0%) = $25,000.00
Allowance for doubtful accounts = $25,000.00 - $5,000 = $20,000.00

	Dr	Cr
Bad debt expense	25,000.00	
Allowance for doubtful accounts		25,000.00

A debit balance in the allowance for doubtful accounts indicates that the estimate of bad debts was too low. Under the percentage of receivables method, the focus is on reporting receivables at their net realizable value. This means that the allowance must reflect the amount of receivables estimated to be uncollectible. It follows that the allowance must be credited an additional $5,000, resulting in a higher bad debts expense.

Under the percentage of credit sales method, the focus is to report an accurate bad debt expense. It follows that the bad debt expense for the period will not be changed. However, the allowance for doubtful accounts will be $5,000 lower, and accounts receivable will not be stated at their estimated net realizable value on the balance sheet. With the percentage credit sales method it is possible for the allowance balance to become unrepresentative of the amount of receivables that will not be collected if there is an error that persists in one direction (i.e. the bad debt expense is continually overstated or understated).

Solution to Study Problem 5

1)

i. $575,000
ii. 2.5% (17,750,000 x 75%) = $332,812.50
iii. 7.0% (6,450,000) = $451,500
451,500 – (590,000 - 575,000) = $436,500

2)

i. $0 (There is no allowance for doubtful accounts under the direct method)
ii. 590,000 – 575,000 + 332,812.50 = $347,812.50
iii. $451,500

3)

i.	Bad debt expense	575,000	
	Accounts receivable		575,000

To record the bad debt expense under the direct-write-off method.

ii.	Bad debt expense	332,812.50	
	Allowance for doubtful accounts		332,812.50

To record the bad debt expense under the percentage-of-credit-sales method.

iii.	Bad debt expense	436,000	
	Allowance for doubtful accounts		436,000

To record the bad debt expense under the percentage-of-receivables method.

4)

i. $2,250,000 – 575,000 = $1,675,000
ii. $2,250,000 – 332,812.50 = $1,917,187.50
iii. $2,250,000 – 436,000 = $1,814,000

5) The differences arise because each method of determining bad debts has a different focus. Under the direct method, bad debts are charged to income as they occur, which means matching does not occur. Under the percentage-of-credit-sales method, the focus is to report a reasonably accurate bad debt expense. Under the percentage-of-receivables method, the focus is to report accounts receivable reasonably close to their net realizable value. If the estimates using the latter two methods are not correct year after year

differences in the methods will occur because the percentage-of-receivables method adjusts the balance in the allowance account to ensure that the net accounts receivable approximates its NRV. The percentage-of-credit-sales method does not consider the NRV of accounts receivable, only the expense for the period.

6) No method is inherently better or worse, each one involves a trade-off. The direct method provides accurate information about the amount of bad debts, but does not match the expense to the revenue it helped generate. The percentage-of-credit-sales method does match the expense to the revenue it helped generate, but it is not necessarily accurate. The percentage-of-receivables method also matches the expense to the revenue it helped generate and provides an approximation of the receivables net realizable value, but the amount of bad debts may be even less accurate than the percentage-of-credit-sales method. It must be stressed that if the estimates are unbiased (over time estimation errors average to zero) the methods should yield similar results. Differences between the methods are caused by errors in estimating bad debts.

Chapter 8
Inventory

Chapter Overview

Chapter 8 provides an in-depth coverage of accounting for inventory. Coverage is provided from conceptual and procedural vantage points and considers the perspective of users and preparers. Concepts include perpetual and periodic inventory control systems, inventory valuation methods, the lower of cost and market rule, consignment inventory, and direct and absorption costing. Probably the most unusual part of the chapter is the section on valuing inventory using non-cost methods. The purpose of that section is to get you thinking about accounting outside the traditional model. It is easy to stick to standard GAAP approaches to accounting to the exclusion of everything else, but that approach can be narrow minded. It is important to know and understand GAAP but also important to recognize that GAAP approaches do not represent all possibilities. The section on non-cost valuation methods can help you realize some limitations and strengths of GAAP approaches, and also learn that non-GAAP information can provide useful information to users.

Other than describing the coverage of the chapter, the introduction makes two points. First is the centrality of inventory to most businesses, including service businesses. Second, the introduction explains that accounting for inventory is not nearly as straightforward as one would think or been led to believe so far in the book. This point lays the groundwork for the discussion of the cost flow assumptions and well as other inventory accounting choices that impact cost of sales and inventory valuation.

Crucial concepts in Chapter 8 include: how inventory costs move through an entity; how different methods of accounting for inventory affect balance sheet and income statement valuations (including cost flow assumptions, the lower of cost and market rule, and direct and absorption costs; introduction of a non-GAAP approach to accounting for inventory; the important relationship between different cost flow assumptions and how they affect financial reporting for tax purposes; tools for interpreting and analyzing inventory information in the financial statements

Summary of Key Points

- Different types of businesses including retailers, manufacturers, and service providers have different types of inventory.

- GAAP does not provide a lot of guidance about how to account for inventory. As a result, there are many acceptable ways of accounting for inventory, which allows for many different measurements of the same underlying economic resource.

  - The *Handbook* requires that inventory be accounted for at cost. However it is not specific about which costs should be included in inventory

- The entry to cost of sales is an adjusting entry in a periodic system and a transactional entry in a perpetual system.

  - The main advantage of a perpetual inventory control system is the improved internal controls that it provides.
  - Physical counts of inventory are required under both systems. In a periodic system the count is needed to determine the cost of goods sold. In a perpetual system the count is needed because the accounting records may not agree with the count (because of recording errors, theft, loss, etc.).

- Cost flow assumptions are necessary because it is too costly or difficult to track the costs associated with actual physical units of inventory.

  - The four best-known cost assumptions are:
    - Specific identification
    - Average Cost
    - First in, First out (FIFO)
    - Last in, First out (LIFO

    - The movement of costs through inventory to cost of sales does not necessarily reflect the actual physical movement of the inventory. Once a cost enters the accounting system the flow of the costs is separated from the physical flow of the inventory (unless the specific identification method is used).

- The lower of cost and market rule requires that inventory be reported on the balance sheet at market value when the market value at the end of a reporting period is lower than cost. The LCM rule violates the historical cost measurement convention to satisfy conservatism. The loss is recognized before it is realized.

- There are two broad categories of costs:
  - Prime costs
  - Overhead

- There are three methods of costing inventory:
  - Prime costing – only prime costs are included.
  - Direct costing – prime costs plus variable overhead.
  - Absorption costing – all costs are included (prime and overhead).

- It is important for accountants and users of accounting information to think beyond the traditional model so that they understand the alternatives. Without this broader horizon you may think that Canadian GAAP accounting is the only basis for reporting.

- There are alternatives to historical cost for valuing inventory on the balance sheet, primarily replacement cost and net realizable value.

  - These non-cost methods often sacrifice reliability for relevance.
  - The use of a market value method for valuing inventory eliminates the need for cost flow assumptions because the inventory is valued at the same amount, the market value.

- Accounting and income taxes are very closely linked. While the Income Tax Act is specific with respect to some requirements for tax reporting purposes (for example, determination of CCA), in many situations the same accounting is used for tax and financial reporting purposes.

- Managing inventory is an important responsibility for an entity's management. Too much or too little inventory can be costly for an entity.

  - The inventory turnover ratio and the average number of days that inventory is on hand provides information about how efficiently inventory is being managed by measuring how quickly the entity is able to sell its inventory.

- In a seasonal business these measures can be misstated if the years beginning and ending inventory are the only amounts used to calculate average inventory because this average may not represent the average over the entire year (because of seasonal variations). However, consistent application will allow assessment of trends.
- Different accounting treatments (cost flow assumptions, inventory costing methods) will provide different measures of the inventory turnover ratio and the average number of days inventory on hand, even though the underlying economic activity of the entity is not affected by these accounting choices. Differences in accounting among entities can affect comparability. Comparisons over time for a particular entity are possible if accounting choices are applied consistently.

Study Points and Study Tips

What Is Inventory?

- Different cost flow assumptions are acceptable under GAAP (FIFO, LIFO, average cost). Different cost flow assumptions result in different measurements for cost of goods sold and inventory.

What GAAP Say

- There is flexibility about which costs should be included in inventory for manufacturers and processors. The *Handbook* requires that direct materials and labour be included in inventory plus an applicable share of overhead. The interpretation of "applicable" is flexible and different entities could treat similar costs differently. As a result, costing methods ranging from direct costing to full absorption costing can be used.

Perpetual and Periodic Inventory Systems

- While perpetual and periodic inventory systems usually yield different cost of sales and inventory amounts, the choice will likely not be used by managers to achieve their financial reporting objectives.

  - While the specific identification method eliminates the need for assumptions about the flow of costs, it does not necessarily result in better measurement or financial reporting. If management can choose which unit of inventory it is selling it can manage its earnings and balance sheet valuation of inventory by selecting the "appropriate" unit to sell.
  - The *CICA Handbook* and GAAP do not express a preference for one cost flow assumption over the others. The *Handbook* requires that inventory be valued at cost and that the method an entity uses to value its inventory results in the "fairest" matching of costs to revenues. In most cases, it is difficult to argue conclusively that one cost flow assumption results in a fairer matching than the others, so the choice is up to the preparer of the financial statements.

Inventory Valuation Methods

- Cost is not the only basis by which inventory can be valued but it is the only one GAAP allows. There are methods that use measures of current market value to value inventory, such as replacement cost and net realizable value.

  - The choice of a cost flow assumption does not have any effect on the underlying economic activity of the entity (though it may have tax implications, as discussed later), but the reporting on the balance sheet and the income statement can be significantly different depending on the cost flow assumption used. The cash flows of the entity (again ignoring income taxes and other cash flows affected by financial statement numbers) are not affected by the cost flow assumption. The payments made to suppliers are the same regardless of how inventory is accounted for.

- Tables 8-1 through 8-7 and associated text demonstrate the mechanics of the four cost flow assumptions. Figure 8-5 summarizes the different methods. This figure is very useful for showing how the numbers on the income statement and balance sheet are affected by the cost flow assumption. The results in this table apply to situations when prices are rising.
- The *CICA Handbook* and GAAP do not express a preference for any cost-based cost flow assumptions. The *CICA Handbook* merely requires that the method an entity chooses for determining inventory costs should be "one which results in the fairest matching of costs against revenues." The problem with this matching argument is that it is not clear what we are trying to match. All of the cost flow assumptions match a cost to the revenue, although what is being matched depends on the method.
- One method is not better than the others. The different methods provide different measurements of the same underlying economic activity. Ultimately the best choice comes down to the users' needs of the information and the objectives of financial reporting.
- The retail method is widely used in retail businesses because inventory in stores is indicated on the merchandise, so it is easier to start with the retail price and back out the cost of the inventory. The retail method can get quite complex. When Canadian Tire acquired Mark's Work Warehouse, inventory was accounted for using the retail method.

The Lower of Cost and Market rule

- Once inventory has been written down to its market value it cannot be written back up if the market value subsequently increases.

  - Entities can use different cost flow assumptions and different definitions of market for different categories of inventory. Leon's Furniture Limited (a retail company) values inventory at the lower of cost, determined on a first-in, first-out basis and net realizable value. However, Research In Motion (RIM) (a manufacturing company) records raw materials inventory at the lower of cost and replacement cost and work in process and finished goods inventory at the lower of cost and net realizable value. Canadian Tire uses the average cost method for valuing its merchandise inventory.
  - For tax purposes entities are allowed to deduct write-downs of inventory to its market value. You may interpret the LCM rule to mean that the lowest possible inventory valuation is to be used from all possible alternatives. However, the LCM rule simply means that the lowest valuation using the cost flow assumption and definition of market selected by the entity is selected. You should recognize that it is possible that a lower inventory valuation is possible if a different cost flow assumption or market definition is used.

Direct and Absorption Costing

- The costing method used by an entity can affect the amount of expenses and the net income that are reported in a period. In addition, the costing method also has an affect on the balance sheet since the inventory account is also affected. Keep in mind that the costing method used affects both financial reporting and taxation.

  - Inventory on the balance sheet will always be higher with absorption costing because more costs are included in inventory. Net income will be different under the 3 costing methods because of the timing of the overhead expenses. Over the life of the entity cost of sales and net income will be the same. In any given period net income will not necessarily be higher or lower under one costing method or another. The effect on net income depends on changes in the amount of inventory.

- GAAP only provide vague guidance about the costs that should be included in inventory. As previously mentioned, the *CICA Handbook* requires that the cost of materials and direct labour be included in inventory, along with "an applicable share of overhead." The *CICA Handbook* clearly requires the inclusion of direct materials and labour, along with some overhead. This means that prime costing will not be seen when an entity is constrained by GAAP.
- Prime costing will not be seen when an entity is constrained by GAAP since the *CICA Handbook* requires the inclusion of direct materials and direct labour, along with some overhead.

Valuing Inventory at Other than Cost

- Using these (replacement cost and net realizable value) methods, when inventory costs are rising means that economic gains are recognized before they are realized (the revenue recognition criteria are violated). Recording inventory at market value gives rise to holding gains and losses, changes in the market value of the inventory from the time it was acquired until the time sold or the end of the period.

  - If a holding gain or loss occurs on inventory that has not been sold by the end of the period, it is an unrealized holding gain or loss.
  - If the value of inventory changes from the date it is purchased (or from the beginning of the period) to the date it sold, there is a realized holding gain or loss because the inventory has been sold.

Examples of Inventory Disclosures in Financial Statements

- This section provides two examples of inventory disclosures that are provided in financial statements. You will see that all the information you require is not necessarily in one place. Instead, the information might be in several places. The second example is a commercial real estate company whose inventory is "Properties under development, construction, and held for sale."

Consignment Inventory

- The textbook description of consignment arrangements is straightforward. However, the economics of the transactions can sometimes be murky.

  - A recent case involving channel stuffing by Bristol-Myers Squibb is an example. Bristol-Myers Squibb, in an attempt to increase revenues and earnings to meet market expectations, offered inducements to wholesale customers to overbuy the company's product. The SEC in the US has established requirements for when such overselling occurs. In these cases the seller is required to account for the excess inventory as consignment inventory and not recognize the transfer of the goods to the buyer as a sale until the goods are actually sold to the final consumer.
  - eBay is beginning to set up hundreds of consignment businesses. For example Circuit City, an electronics retailer based in the United States is the first large retailer to help consumers sell their products on eBay. When thousands of internet businesses went bankrupt, eBay was able to survive since it did not have to invest in inventory and was able to keep its costs down.

Inventory Accounting and Income Taxes

- LIFO cannot be used for tax purposes in Canada, which explains why so few companies in Canada use LIFO when compared with the US. US firms face a trade-off because if inventory prices rise they get tax benefits from using LIFO but they have lower income for financial reporting purposes. In the US the IRS requires firms to use the same cost flow assumption for tax they use for financial reporting. The differential use of LIFO between Canada and the US gives some insight into how economic consequences affect the accounting choices of managers.

  - You may come to the conclusion that LIFO is not allowed in Canada because it is not permitted for tax purposes. You should understand the Canadian GAAP allows the use of LIFO. The limitations on its use are only for tax purposes.
  - For tax purposes both absorption and direct costing are allowable. Deferring taxes is better achieved using direct costing.
  - Tax rules allow the use of the lower of cost and market rule for inventory. Write- downs are not allowed for tax purposes for most other assets (i.e. capital assets).
  - Tax minimization probably provides the most effective and clear way to explain how objectives of financial reporting affect accounting choices. Students have little difficulty understanding that taxes are related to income measurement and that accounting choices will affect the amount of tax paid. Tax minimization can be effectively contrasted against other objectives (such as bonus maximization) to highlight the economic consequences of accounting choices and the decisions that managers have to make.

Interpreting and Analyzing Inventory Information on the Financial Statements

- While bankers sometimes accept inventory as collateral for a loan, it is usually not very desirable collateral. If an entity has trouble selling its own inventory, how well can a bank be expected to do? Usually when inventory is used as collateral the bank will not lend the full balance sheet amount—only a percentage of the amount is loaned.

  - The inventory turnover ratio and the average number of days inventory on hand can be difficult to interpret if an entity has different types of inventory (as in an entity with more than one line of business).

Study Problems

Study Problem 1 (Using the retail method) Grafton Street Inc. (Grafton) sells hand crafted Mennonite furniture in Nova Scotia. Grafton uses the retail method for determining its ending inventory. The store has a September 30 year end. On October 1, 2005 Grafton had opening inventory with a cost of $750,000 and retail value of $900,000. During the year Grafton purchased inventory for $1,075,000. The inventory purchased during the year had a retail value of $1,890,000. When the inventory was counted on September 30, 2006, there was $640,000 of inventory on hand valued at its retail price. Sales during the year ended September 30, 2006 were $2,150,000.

Required:
Estimate the cost of inventory on September 30, 2006 using the retail method.

Study Problem 2 (Calculating the inventory turnover ratio and the average number of days inventory on hand) You are provided with the following information about the bookstore at Mount St. Bernard University (Mount):

Cost of sales for the year ended June 30, 2006	$ 510,000
Inventory balance on June 30, 2005	125,000
Inventory balance on June 30, 2006	165,000

Required:

a. Calculate Mount's inventory turnover ratio for the year ended June 30, 2006.
b. What is the average length of time that it took to sell its inventory in 2006?
c. Is Mount's inventory turnover ratio satisfactory? What would you need to know to fully answer this question?

Study Problem 3 (Lower of cost and market) Clemson Ltd. (Clemson) uses the lower of cost and market rule to value its football equipment inventory. Clemson defines market as net realizable value. Clemson's inventory on January 31, 2005 had a cost of $1,200,000 and an NRV of $1,125,000.

Required:

a. By how much should Clemson's inventory be written down?
b. Prepare the journal entry that Clemson should prepare to record the write-down.
c. What amount should be reported for inventory on Clemson's January 31, 2005 balance sheet?

Study Problem 4 (Inventory cost flow assumptions when prices are falling) Parkwood Holdings Inc. (Parkwood) operates a Gift shop, Tea Room and summer Tea House where the cost of inventory (souvenirs) has been falling recently. The cost of inventory purchased by Parkwood over the last year is summarized below. Parkwood values its inventory at the lower of cost or market and defines market as net realizable value. Assume that purchases are made at the start of a month before any sales occur during that month.

Date	**Quantity**	**Cost per unit**	**Selling price per unit.**
Purchases			
Opening Inventory	1750	$4.75	
October 1, 2005	3600	4.50	
January 2, 2006	2700	4.30	
April 1, 2006	2100	4.05	
July 2, 2006	4250	3.85	
Sales			
October-December, 2005	4050		$8.55
January-March, 2006	2900		8.10
April-June, 2006	2150		7.75
July-September, 2006	3950		6.95

Required:

a. Calculate cost of sales for the year ended September 30, 2006 and ending inventory on September 30, 2006 for Parkwood using the FIFO, average cost, and LIFO cost flow assumptions.
b. Which cost flow assumption is most attractive for an accounting objective of income maximization.
c. Which cost flow assumption is most attractive for an accounting objective of tax minimization.

d. Compare the relative values under the three cost flow assumptions of ending inventory and cost of sales in this situation versus a situation where prices are rising. What is different between the two situations?

e. Apply the lower of cost and market rule to year-end inventory. Assume that Parkwood's selling costs for inventory are $1.50 per unit.

Study Problem 5 (The impact of cost flow assumptions on ratios) Macewan Corp. (Macewan) Weldon Ltd. (Weldon), and Bloomfield Inc. (Bloomfield) are small butcher shops specializing in catering. They are identical in every respect-same amount of sales, same quantity of inventory sold, and same number of employees. Everything is the same except that Macewan uses FIFO as its cost flow assumption, Weldon uses average cost and Bloomfield uses LIFO.

Income Statements
For the Year Ended June 30, 2006

	Macewan	**Weldon**	**Bloomfield**
	(FIFO)	**(Average Cost)**	**(LIFO)**
Revenue	$774,375.00	$774,375.00	$774,375.00
Cost of sales	483,210.00	543,611.25	583,878.75
Gross margin	291,165.00	230,763.75	190,496.25
Other expenses	211,750.00	211,750.00	211,750.00
Net income (loss)	**79,415.00**	**19,013.75**	**(21,253.75)**

Balance Sheets
For the Year Ended June 30, 2006

	Macewan	**Weldon**	**Bloomfield**
	(FIFO)	**(Average Cost)**	**(LIFO)**
Assets			
Cash	$15,405.00	$15,405.00	$15,405.00
Accounts Receivable	72,450.00	72,450.00	72,450.00
Inventory	303,312.50	225,544.90	157,982.40
Other Current Assets	12,075.00	12,075.00	12,075.00
Total Current Assets	403,242.50	325,474.90	257,912.40
Capital Assets (net)	433,262.50	433,262.50	433,262.50
Total Assets	**$ 836,505.00**	**$ 758,737.40**	**$ 691,174.90**
Liabilities & Owner's Equity			
Bank Loan	$24,375.00	$24,375.00	$24,375.00
Accounts Payable	217,062.50	217,062.50	217,062.50
Other Current Liabilities	18,687.50	18,687.50	18,687.50
Total Current Liabilities	260,125.00	260,125.00	260,125.00
Long-term debt	75,325.00	75,325.00	75,325.00
Other non-current liabilities	14,375.00	14,375.00	14,375.00
Total liabilities	349,825.00	349,825.00	349,825.00
Capital Stock	57,500.00	57,500.00	57,500.00
Retained Earnings	429,180.00	351,412.40	283,849.90
Total Liabilities & Owner's Equity	**$ 836,505.00**	**$ 758,737.40**	**$ 691,174.90**

You also learn that on June 30, 2005 the balances in Inventory for the three butcher shops were:

Ending Inventory balances on June 30, 2005

	Macewan	Weldon	Bloomfield
	(FIFO)	(Average Cost)	(LIFO)
Inventory	$108,000.00	$90,000.00	$65,000.00

Required:

a. calculate the following ratios:
   i. current ratio
   ii. quick ratio
   iii. inventory turnover ratio
   iv. average number of days inventory on hand
   v. gross margin percentage
   vi. profit margin percentage

b. Which of the three butcher shops has the strongest liquidity position?

c. Which of the three butcher shops is most profitable?

d. Which of the three butcher shops manages its inventory most effectively?

e. The three butcher shops' bankers lend money based on the amount of accounts receivable and inventory on hand. Which butcher shop will be able to obtain the largest loan? From the banks' point of view, is the butcher shop that receives the largest loan the best credit risk? Explain.

Case Study

Zohar's Zinc Alloys Inc. (Zohar) manufactures small, high-precision die cast components and small component assemblies. Its components are manufactured in Oshawa, Ontario (North American operations) and Swansea, Wales (European operations). The company is wholly owned and managed by Dr. Safa Zohar. Recently, Dr. Zohar has been considering a career change and has applied for a position in the Department of Business Administration at a Canadian university. Dr. Zohar has been approached by a prospective buyer who has requested a set of financial statements so that he can analyze the company. The buyer is an experienced entrepreneur. Since the business was formed, the financial statements have been prepared for calculation of income taxes and Zohar's prospective lenders.

In your conversation with Dr. Zohar, you learn the following:

1) Zohar manufactures three different types of die cast components. The company carries enough inventory to be able to respond to most orders quickly. When a customer places an order with Zohar for these components, the components are shipped within days.
2) Zohar also carries a sizeable inventory of zinc alloys used in the production of the components. On a recent examination of the inventory, Dr. Zohar noticed that there were some raw materials that had been on hand for some time, including materials relating to components that are no longer manufactured.

Required:

Dr. Zohar has come to you requesting advice on the selection of appropriate accounting policies (accounting for inventory) for the financial statements that will be prepared for the prospective buyer. In case the buyer questions the choice, they would like full explanations for the recommendations you make.

Solutions to Study Problems

Solution to Study Problem 1

	Cost	Retail	Cost/Retail
Beginning inventory	$ 750,000	$ 900,000	
Purchases	1,075,000	1,890,000	
Goods available for sale	1,825,000	2,790,000	0.654
Less sales		2,150,000	
Ending inventory at retail		640,000	

Ending inventory at cost = .654 x 640,000 = $418,560.

Solution to Study Problem 2

a. Average inventory = ($125,000 + 165,000)/2 = $145,000.

   Inventory turnover = cost of sales / average inventory =

   $510,000 / $145,000 = 3.52

b. The average length of time to sell inventory = 365 /3.52 = 103.7 days.

c. You cannot assess whether the turnover is satisfactory without having benchmarks. Information that could be helpful includes the typical turnover for other university bookstores and the turnover for the Mount in recent years, to identify trends. Also, any changes in the accounting environment that might explain or affect the turnover period would be useful.

Solution to Study Problem 3

a. The inventory should be written down by $1,200,000 - $1,125,000 = $75,000.

b.

		Debit	Credit
Dr.	Cost of sales	75,000	
	Cr. Inventory		75,000

c. The inventory should be presented on the balance sheet at $1,125,000.

Solution to Study Problem 4

a. **Cost of goods available for sale:**

1750 units at $4.75	$ 8,312.50
3600 units at $4.50	16,200.00
2700 units at $4.30	11,610.00
2100 units at $4.05	8,505.00
4250 units at $3.85	16,362.50
Total COGAS	$60,990.00

14,400 units available for sale
13,050 units sold
1,350 units in ending inventory

Perpetual system (assumed):

FIFO

Sale #1

Cost of goods available for sale	1750 units at $4.75 and 3600 at $4.50
Cost of goods sold	1750 units at $4.75 and 2300 at $4.50
Remaining inventory	1300 units at $4.50

Sale #2

Cost of goods available for sale	1300 units at $4.50 and 2700 at $4.30
Cost of goods sold	1300 units at $4.50 and 1600 at $4.30
Remaining inventory	1100 units at $4.30

Sale #3

Cost of goods available for sale	1100 units at $4.30 and 2100 at $4.05
Cost of goods sold	1100 units at $4.30 and 1050 at $4.05
Remaining inventory	1050 units at $4.05

Sale #4

Cost of goods available for sale	1050 units at $4.05 and 4250 at $3.85
Cost of goods sold	1050 units at $4.05 and 2900 at $3.85
Remaining inventory	1350 units at $3.85

Total ending inventory = 1350 units at $3.85 = $5,197.50
Total cost of goods sold = $60,990 – $5,197.50 = $55,792.50

Average Cost

Sale #1

Cost of goods available for sale	1750 units at $4.75 and 3600 at $4.50
Average cost	(8,312.50 + 16,200)/5,350 = $4.58
Cost of goods sold	4050 units at $4.58 = $18,549
Remaining inventory	1300 units at $4.58 = $5,954

Sale #2

Cost of goods available for sale	1300 units at $4.58 and 2700 at $4.30
Average cost	($5,954 + 11,610)/4,000 = $4.39
Cost of goods sold	2900 units at $4.39 = $12,731
Remaining inventory	1100 units at $4.39 = $4,829

Sale #3

Cost of goods available for sale	1100 units at $4.39 and 2100 at $4.05
Average cost	($4,829 + 8,505)/3200 = $4.17
Cost of goods sold	2150 units at $4.17 = $8,965.50
Remaining inventory	1050 units at $4.17 = $4,378.50

Sale #4

Cost of goods available for sale	1050 units at $4.17 and 4250 at $3.85
Average cost	($4,378.50 + 16,362.50)/5300 = $3.91
Cost of goods sold	3950 units at $3.91 = $15,444.50
Remaining inventory	1350 units at $3.91 = $5,278.50

Total ending inventory = 1350 units at $3.91 = $5,278.50
Total cost of goods sold = $60,990 - $5,278.50 = $55,711.50*

*Note: Adding the cost of goods sold for the four sales results in $55,690. The difference is due to rounding. Ending inventory in this case is $60,990 - $55,690 = $5,300.

LIFO

Sale #1

Cost of goods available for sale	1750 units at $4.75 and 3600 at $4.50
Cost of goods sold	450 units at $4.75 and 3600 at $4.50
Remaining inventory	1300 units at $4.75

Sale #2

Cost of goods available for sale	1300 units at $4.75 and 2700 at $4.30
Cost of goods sold	200 units at $4.75 and 2700 at $4.30
Remaining inventory	1100 units at $4.75

Sale #3

Cost of goods available for sale	1100 units at $4.75 and 2100 at $4.05
Cost of goods sold	50 units at $4.75 and 2100 at $4.05
Remaining inventory	1050 units at $4.75

Sale #4

Cost of goods available for sale	1050 units at $4.75 and 4250 at $3.85
Cost of goods sold	3950 units at $3.85
Remaining inventory	1050 units at $4.75 and 300 at $3.85

Total ending inventory = 1050 units at $4.75 and 300 at $3.85 = $6,142.50
Total cost of goods sold = $60,990 – 6,142.50 = $54,847.50

	FIFO	**Average**	**LIFO**
Revenue	$102,232.50	$102,232.50	$102,232.50
Cost of sales	55,792.50	55,711.50*	$54,847.50
Gross margin	$46,440.00	$46,521.00	$47,385.00
Ending inventory	$5,197.50	$5,278.50	$6,142.50

* See the note under Average Cost on the previous page.

b. To maximize income, you would choose LIFO.
c. To minimize taxes, you would choose FIFO because under FIFO cost of sales is largest.
d. When prices are falling, the relative effects of the three methods are reversed from what is seen when prices are rising because lower costs are in ending inventory and higher costs are expensed under FIFO; when prices are rising, higher costs are in ending inventory and lower costs are expensed under FIFO.
e. Market value for inventory is 1350 units x (6.95 – 1.50) = $7,357.50

Ending inventory	FIFO	Average	LIFO
Cost	$5,197.50	$5,278.50	$6,142.50
Market	7,357.50	7,357.50	7,357.50
Lower of cost and market	$5,197.50	$5,278.50	$6,142.50

In all three cases cost is lower than market so cost is used to value ending inventory.

Solution to Study Problem 5

	Macewan (FIFO)	Weldon (average)	Bloomfield (LIFO)
Current ratio	403,242.50/260,125 = 1.55	325,474.90/260,125 = 1.25	257,912.40/260,125 = 0.99
Quick ratio	87,855/260,125 = 0.34	87,855/260,125 = 0.34	87,855/260,125 = 0.34
Inventory turnover ratio	483,210/((108,000 + 303,312.50)/2) = 2.35	543,611.25/((90,000 + 225,544.90)/2) = 3.45	583,878.75/((65,000 + 157,982.40)/2) = 5.24
Average days inventory on hand	155	106	70
Gross margin %	38%	30%	25%
Profit margin %	10.3%	2.5%	(2.7%)

b. The current ratio indicates that Macewan is the most liquid but in fact they are all equally liquid. Bloomfield seems to have stronger liquidity as a result of its better inventory management (inventory turns over faster). The quick ratio is the same for all three firms. However, in reality the liquidity of the three firms is the same despite the differences in the measurements in the table. The apparent differences are purely a result of the different ways that inventory is accounted for and do not reflect any real economic differences among the firms.

c. Macewan appears to be the most profitable because it has a higher profit margin percentage. However, in reality the profitability of the three firms is the same despite the differences in the measurements in the table. The apparent differences are purely a result of the different ways that inventory is accounted for and do not reflect any real economic differences among the firms.

d. Bloomfield appears to manage its inventory better than the other firms because it has a higher inventory turnover ratio, but they all manage inventory equally well. The apparent differences are purely a result of the different ways that inventory is accounted for and do not reflect any real economic differences among the firms.

e. Whether the three firms have a different likelihood of obtaining a loan from their banks depends on whether the lending officers are able to fully unravel the impact of accounting choices. Since the terms described in the question indicate that the loans are based on accounts receivable and inventory Macewan will obtain the largest loan because it reports the most inventory (accounts receivable is the same for all three). The three firms are equally risky despite what the numbers show. Since the firms are described to be "identical in every respect" they must be equally risky (this assumes the three have similar customers, operate in similar markets, etc.). So while Macewan will receive the largest loan all three firms are equally risky and it could be justified that the same loans should be given to each.

Solutions to Case Study

In this case the owner of Zohar has sought advice as to how to prepare the financial statements for use by a prospective buyer. To date the financial statements have been prepared for tax purposes and it can be assumed that the intent has been to lower income for tax purposes. These statements would clearly not be appropriate for a prospective buyer because they would understate the performance of the company. The prospective buyer would want the financial statements to give a realistic impression of the entity so that he could evaluate how much he is prepared to pay. The vendors might want to be optimistic to aggressive so as to get more out of the business. It is important to remember that valuations are subjective.

In approaching the financial statements, choices can be made conservatively, where the bias is to report lower rather than higher income and assets, or optimistically, where the bias would be in the other direction. Clearly an unbiased approach is preferred for all users, but this is not really very realistic to expect. It is important that any choices made be supported, and reasonable in the circumstances.

Role:
- Consultant to Dr. Zohar - planning on selling his business.
- Report should be written in a way that is suitable for readers who are not financial experts.

Key users:
- The only relevant user in this question is the prospective buyer. This is a special purpose report prepared for the prospective buyer.

Key facts:
- Previous financial statements were prepared mainly for tax purposes. These statements would not be appropriate for evaluating the performance of Zohar because they will tend to understate the performance of the company.
- Prospective buyer is sophisticated - not likely to be fooled by tricky accounting techniques. Prospective buyer will likely be able to identify sensitive areas on the financial statements for follow-up questioning.
- Financial statements will be part of a special purpose report designed for specific use by the prospective buyer. Objective of tax minimization can still prevail in the general purpose financial statements.

Constraints:
- None, because Zohar is a private company. GAAP might be preferred by the prospective buyer.

Objectives:
- Main objective will be to show Zohar is a profitable (successful) while staying within the bounds of reasonable and supportable accounting choices. Preference will be to report higher rather than lower net income and revenue and lower expenses since this may provide the prospective buyer with a more favourable perception of Zohar.

Issues:

Inventory costing issues

- Different inventory costing methods result in different cost of goods sold, inventory, and net income amounts.
- Might be desirable to switch to a method that improves income but such a switch might be too costly to make.
- Inventory costing likely expenses as many costs as possible to minimize tax. While desirable for tax this may result in poor matching and misstate the performance of Zohar.
- Should attach as many costs as possible to inventory to increase inventory value and increase income. This includes attempting to attach

fixed costs to inventory in some rational way (full costing).

- Actual impact on income not certain—depends on whether inventory is increasing or decreasing. However, over a number of periods the effect of this change on net income will be positive.
- Full costing approach is more desirable for assessing performance in this case because it results in better matching of expenses and revenue.
- Variable costing while more attractive for tax purposes may not serve the interests of the Zohar if it reduces income and measures related to income.

Obsolete inventory

- Implication is that inventory is overstated and income is (or has been in the past) overstated.
- If impairment in value occurred in previous periods Zohar paid too much tax because inventory can be written down for tax purposes.
- There are a number of approaches for accounting for the obsolete inventory. The most appropriate will depend (in part at least) on the circumstances surrounding the obsolete inventory
- Must ascertain if the discovery of obsolete inventory is common or unusual. If common, then writing off the amount as on ordinary operating expense makes sense.
- If the discovery of obsolete inventory is unusual or if the amount discovered is unusually high then alternative treatments might be appropriate.
- One approach would be to disclose the full amount of impaired inventory in the current period as an unusual item. That means the amount of the write-down will not be included as a part of ordinary operations and so your prospective buyer will not view the write-down as an ordinary cost of business. This presumably will result in a higher value being assigned to the company.
- Another approach would be to allocate the amount of obsolete inventory to the current and prior periods. This is not done normally under GAAP but would be appropriate for this special purpose report because each year's income would represent the economic costs of the obsolete inventory.
- Another alternative would be to do nothing—do not account for the obsolete inventory. This would not be appropriate under GAAP since conservatism requires that inventory be valued at the lower of cost and market. However, I would advise caution in identifying obsolete inventory. It would be appropriate to establish a definition for obsolete inventory so that criteria can be applied. Clearly any inventory that is not saleable should be expensed. But simply because inventory is slow moving does not make it obsolete.

Chapter 9
Capital Assets

Chapter Overview

In Chapter 2, assets were introduced as the economic resources controlled by a company. In Chapter 7 and 8 you were introduced to cash / receivables and inventory. Those two chapters focused on current assets. The reason entities acquire capital assets, the focus of Chapter 9, is to derive a benefit for their use in the long-term. Entities that operate in capital intensive industries such as manufacturing, shipping and transportation, exhibit a large proportion of capital assets to total assets on their balance sheets. Capital assets comprise roughly 50% of the total assets of Dofasco Inc., an industrial products and steel manufacturer headquartered in Hamilton, Ontario. Capital intensive industries are often cyclical in nature. Since capital assets represent a significant long-term investment for entities, how capital assets are accounted for can have a dramatic effect on the quality of information available for users to make informed decisions.

Most accounting students do not have difficulty understanding tangible assets since they have a physical existence. However, intangible or knowledge assets often represent a substantial part of the total assets of Canadian and global entities, and traditional accounting has not been very effective in dealing with knowledge assets, such as patents, copyrights and goodwill. In addition, human capital is not accounted for on an entity's balance sheet. Most intangible assets, such as goodwill, appear on financial statements only if purchased. For many companies in sectors such as pharmaceuticals and biotechnology, intangible assets may be the primary source of revenue, but acknowledgment of these assets in financial statements is often excluded. For example, prior to 2001 Eli Lilly was deriving more than 25% of its revenue from Prozac which was protected by a patent. Leading up to the patent expiration in 2001 Eli Lilly stock dropped 30% since competitors were then able to produce similar drugs stealing market share.

In the early going, the limitations to historical cost accounting are presented and alternative valuation approaches described. Although capital assets are recorded on the balance sheet, they also affect the income statement because their costs are charged to amortization expense. For some organizations this expense may be one of the largest expenses on the income statement. Given that capital assets benefit multiple accounting periods, the costs of long-term assets must be systematically allocated to those accounting periods. The discussion of amortization describes the arbitrary nature of amortization and the implications on measurements such as income, assets, gains, losses, and write-downs. Amortization is a non-cash item and therefore has no effect on cash flow. However, the impact of amortization on the income statement can be very significant.

Summary of Key Points

- Capital assets have a useful life greater than one year. These assets are purchased for use in the business operation and are not intended for resale to customers. Since capital assets are not intended for resale and do not directly generate revenue for an entity, they are considered to make an indirect contribution to the entity.

- The use of historical cost accounting for measuring capital assets reveals many limitations. One such limitation involves Trent University in Peterborough, Ontario. In 1962, Canadian General Electric donated the core 100 acres to Trent University and that amount is still recorded at a historical cost of $0 on the financial statements, even though the property would be worth several million dollars in market value. In most cases, at the date of acquisition, historical cost equals market value.

- Alternatives to historical cost are:
  - Net realizable value
  - Replacement cost
  - Value-in-use

- The cost of an asset that is reported on an entity's balance sheet should include all necessary and reasonable expenditures with acquiring the asset and getting it ready for use. Only necessary costs should be capitalized such as shipping and installation costs. Costs that are not related to the acquisition—such as repairs or unnecessary work caused by poor planning, etc.—should not be capitalized.

- Amortization is the general term used to describe the allocation of the cost of a capital asset to expense over time. The purpose of amortization is to match the cost of capital assets to revenues over the life of the assets. Amortization is a non-cash expense that reduces net income. Four different amortization methods are considered:
  - Straight-line (most common)
  - Accelerated
  - Usage-based
  - Decelerated

- The Income Tax Act uses the term Capital Cost Allowance (CCA) to describe amortization for tax purposes. Amortization and (CCA) are separate and distinct. The two systems serve different purposes resulting in different expense and deduction calculations.

- An intangible asset is long-term but has no physical existence. The value of the intangible asset comes from the legal rights that it gives to its owner. Currently, internally generated intangible assets are not reported as assets because of measurement problems and conservatism.

- Capital assets are written down when their net book value is greater than their net recoverable amount. The asset's net recoverable amount is the undiscounted net cash flow the asset is expected to generate over its remaining life, plus its residual value. Do not confuse the write-down concept for capital assets with the lower of cost and market rule applied to inventory and other current assets.

- Management has considerable discretion in deciding the timing and amount of a write-down because determining the impairment of a capital asset is very subjective. Frequent news reports prove that managers time write-downs of capital assets to accomplish their reporting objectives. To satisfy reporting objectives, in recent years, management of telecommunication companies have written down significant capital assets as part of a wave of big bath transactions.

- Changes in accounting policies, such as the amortization method used for capital assets, are accounted for retroactively and are required to be disclosed in the financial statements. Users need to monitor whether these changes were voluntary or mandated. Accounting changes can occur from changes in the objectives of the preparers or changes in the economic circumstances surrounding a transaction or economic event. Accounting policy changes initiated by preparers need to be scrutinized to ensure justification.

- Changes in accounting estimates, such as the residual value and useful life used for capital assets, are revisions of judgements made by managers about uncertain future events. Accounting estimates may change as better information comes available, however, estimates may also change due to self interests of the preparers. Changes in accounting estimates are accounted for prospectively and are often not disclosed in financial statements, making it difficult for users to fully understand changes in the statements.

- Choice provides preparers the opportunity to present information in ways that are useful to several different stakeholder groups, all with varying objectives. Choice also provides an effective means for preparers to achieve their own reporting objectives. A system that allows choice opens itself up for abuse by preparers. A system with no choice reduces the likelihood for abuse but may render financial statements useless. This does not necessarily mean that preparers always intend to mislead and manipulate financial accounting information however, an informed user should be aware that the potential for deception is inherent in the reporting process.

- The proceeds from the sale of a capital asset are classified as investing activities on the cash flow statement. Gains and losses from the sale of capital assets do not represent cash flows. As a result, gains must be subtracted from the net income calculated from the income statement and losses must be added back to net income. This is done to reconcile from net income to cash from operations on the cash flow statement.

- Write-downs of capital assets also have no effect on cash flow. They must be added back to net income when reconciling from net income to cash from operations.

Study Points and Study Tips

Measuring Capital Assets and Limitations to Historical Cost Accounting

- There are a few alternative methods for valuing capital assets. The historical cost of capital assets often has very little use for future oriented decisions. Historical cost helps achieve the matching principle because the cost of a capital asset represents the economic sacrifice given up to obtain the asset. However, historical cost is required for tax purposes, so there is an important reason for using cost.

    - Net Realizable Value – the amount that would be received from the sale of an asset after the selling costs are deducted. Many real estate transactions involve appraisal fees, legal fees, land transfer taxes, etc. and the vendor of the property is often surprised to receive much less cash than expected when the property has been sold.
    - Replacement Cost – the amount that would have to be spent to replace a capital asset. Replacement cost is more subjective than historical cost. This measurement basis is commonly used by property and casualty insurance companies to determine levels of insurance coverage for entities.
    - Value-in-use – the net present value of the net cash flows that the asset will generate over its life, or the net present value of the cash flow that the asset would allow the entity to avoid paying—is a very useful measure of a capital asset, but is problematic because individual assets are rarely responsible for generating cash on their own, and estimating the future cash flows that an asset will generate is usually difficult. This alternative to

historical cost accounting requires many assumptions and estimates that can make the value-in-use estimate very unreliable.

What is Cost?

- Betterments make a capital asset more valuable to the entity, perhaps by increasing the asset's useful life, or by improving its efficiency or effectiveness. Betterments result in an increased cost of the capital asset since these costs are capitalized. Repairs or maintenance are expenditures that allow an asset to operate as intended and should be expensed when incurred—they do not improve the asset. It is not always obvious whether an expenditure is a betterment or a repair/maintenance.

  - Betterments such as the restaurant renovations (Strawberries Inc.) in Chapter #3 should be capitalized. In that example, the renovations contributed to the restaurant's ambiance, and by improving the ambiance, the owner's should expect an increase in its customer base eventually leading to more revenue for the firm.
  - When an entity purchases a bundle of assets (such as land and a building) for a single price, management needs to allocate the purchase price to the individual assets in the bundle. The purchase price should be allocated in proportion to the market values of the assets in the bundle. The market value of individual assets will often only be estimates and any amount within a reasonable range would be acceptable. As a result, managers have some flexibility and can address their reporting objectives.
  - How the cost is allocated among the assets in the bundle is important because it can have tax and financial reporting consequences. The *CICA Handbook* and GAAP do not provide much specific guidance about how assets should be amortized. Preparers have flexibility and will make the allocation based on their objectives as long as the allocation is reasonable. Since land is not amortized, a preparer would prefer to allocate a greater proportion to the building since CCA could be utilized to minimize taxes.
  - Since the relationship between an asset and revenue is usually not clear, what is systematic and rational is a matter of judgement. As a result, different ways of amortizing are acceptable under GAAP and by and large the choice of the method is up to the managers. Also, useful life and residual value must be estimated; therefore, a range of possible acceptable estimates exist.

Amortization

- Assets are consumed for two reasons: physical use and obsolescence. Amortization is not intended to reflect the change in a capital asset's market value, and the book value of an asset is not intended to be an estimate of its market value. Land is not amortized since the economic value of land is not considered to decrease in value over time.

  - The choice of amortization method has no effect on cash flow, except for secondary effects caused by payouts that are based on financial statement measures (such as bonus payments).
  - The choice of amortization method "matters" if there are outcomes that are based on financial statement numbers. In the beginning years of the life of an asset, accelerated amortization decreases net income (higher amortization expense) as well as retained earnings and will result in lower income than straight-line amortization. This situation reverses itself in the later years of the asset.
  - The number of years in an asset's useful life is determined by management. This estimate is used in the amortization calculation. Residual value is another estimate determined by management. Changes in either variable will alter the reported amortization expense. The ability of management to establish useful life and residual

value allows for potential manipulation of reported income through the amortization expense.

- For example, a high estimate for residual value will lower the yearly amortization expense and a high estimate for the asset's useful life will lower the yearly amortization expense. In general, the faster the amortization schedule, the higher the amortization expense so the lower the income reported on the income statement. The difficulty is that the relationship between individual capital assets and revenue generation is not obvious, thus, assumptions have to be made regarding how to amortize these assets. Due to the arbitrary nature of the estimations required, figures on the income statement may be subject to a great deal of manipulation. This flexibility often serves the self-interests of preparers.
- Amortization policies do not affect an entity's objectives of financial reporting. An entity can choose accounting policies to satisfy any objective of financial reporting while still minimizing taxes.

Amortization and Taxes

- The half-year rule allows an entity to deduct for tax purposes in the year an asset is purchased, only one-half the amount of CCA that would otherwise be allowable.

  - The half-year rule tries to lessen the incentive for entities to purchase capital assets late in a fiscal year. While this rule may have valid fiscal policy purposes, it is not consistent with the purpose of amortization for financial reporting purposes (matching).
  - The concept of CCA is intriguing when considering that an entity may use this deduction for a 150 year old building it has purchased. This point further illustrates that CCA has no relationship to an asset's market value.
  - An entity that does not have to follow GAAP could use CCA rules as the basis of amortization in its financial statements to eliminate the need to adjust when determining taxable income.

Intangible Assets

- Generally, intangible assets are reported on the balance sheet only if purchased. Otherwise the costs associated with these assets are expensed as incurred.

  - The rationale for this approach has some appeal. When an entity spends money developing its brand name or doing primary research or investing in human capital, it is difficult to know whether these investments will generate revenues and profits in the future. As a result, the conservative thing to do is expense as incurred. In other words, there is often much more uncertainty about the future benefit of an intangible asset than a tangible one.

  - This approach was satisfactory when most of an entity's capital assets were tangible (equipment, buildings, furniture and fixtures). In the 21st century, the Canadian economy has become increasingly dependent on knowledge-based industries—industries that depend on research and development, human capital, brand names and trademarks for their success. For entities in these industries, many or most of the economic resources are ignored by traditional accounting.

  - Expensing these costs as incurred can have dramatic effects on the financial statements. First, matching is abandoned since the costs of generating revenues are not being expensed when the associated revenue is being recognized. Second, income measurement is distorted. For uses of accounting information that rely on an association between economic benefits and costs (for example, performance measurement), expensing intangible costs as incurred weakens the usefulness of net income as a proxy for economic performance. The treatment also affects many traditional financial analysis measurements, such as gross margin, profit margin, return on assets and equity, and debt-to-equity ratios.

- Compounding the problem is that when intangible assets are purchased, they usually can be reported on the balance sheet. This can create some dramatic differences in valuations and make comparisons among different entities difficult. However, this situation applies to all assets in that valuation is affected by when an asset is acquired. The conservative thing to do is expense as incurred.
- Under successful efforts accounting (for oil and gas exploration costs) only the costs associated with successful projects are capitalized. Using this approach, the company would record higher expenses, lower income, and therefore be more conservative.
- Under full cost accounting a company capitalizes all costs incurred to find new sources of oil and gas. Using this approach, the company would record lower expenses, higher income and therefore be more aggressive. In addition, by capitalizing all costs, not only does the profit increase on the income statement, but assets may be overvalued on the balance sheet.
- If an asset has lost its revenue generating ability it may be written down. A write-down has significant effects on the financial statements of an entity. A decision to write down a capital asset is never reversed. In the period it is recognized, the write-down causes a decrease in income and a decrease in retained earnings and associated assets. Keep in mind that a write-down is an accounting entry and does not affect the entity's cash flow or gross margins.
- In future periods the write-down causes higher net income (due to lower value of assets and subsequent lower amortization expenses) and higher return on assets (ROA). Since management has considerable flexibility in recognizing write-downs, this presents an opportunity by management to achieve its reporting objectives. Write-downs will also increase debt-equity ratios because of the decrease in retained earnings which decreases equity.
- While write-downs are often classified as unusual in financial statements, many entities report write-downs and other so called unusual items on a recurring basis. In these cases write-downs might be thought of as ordinary operating costs rather than unusual.

Accounting Changes – Policies and Estimates

- Changes in accounting policies can arise due to changes in inventory methods, amortization schedules, etc. Such changes may occur as a result of changes in GAAP or may result from management's decision.

  - The following information must be disclosed in the event of an accounting change:
    - nature of the change
    - justification for the change
    - the effect of the change on net income
  - Accounting choices do not affect the amount of cash that enters and leaves an entity, but the choices can affect the classification of cash flows.
  - If a company decides to change an accounting policy the change is applied retroactively. That means previous years financial statements are restated as if the new accounting method had always been used.

Capital Assets and the Cash Flow Statement

- If an expenditure is capitalized, the outlay appears on the cash flow statement as an investing activity. If that same expenditure is expensed when incurred, the expenditure is included in cash from operations (CFO). There may be secondary cash flow effect of accounting choices such as the amount of cash that is paid as a bonus to a manager.

  - After-tax interest expense is added back to net income in the numerator of the calculation to make the measure of return on assets independent of how the assets were financed. If this adjustment were not made return on assets would be greater if the company financed its assets with equity instead of debt.

Financial Statement Analysis Issues

- ROA is also affected by the accounting choices made by the managers (amortization method, useful life estimates, capitalized costs and big baths).

Study Problems

Study Problem 1 (Preparing amortization schedules) In July 2005 The Black Dog Press Limited (Black Dog) purchased new equipment for $500,000. Black Dog's Chief Financial Officer, Marcia Ferguson estimates that the equipment's useful life will be 5 years and that its residual value will be $100,000.

a. Prepare an amortization schedule for each year of the equipment's life using:
   i. straight-line amortization
   ii. declining balance amortization (20%)
   iii. units-of-production method

   Your amortization schedule should show the amortization expense for each year, the net book value (NBV) of the equipment, and the accumulated amortization at the end of each year. For the units-of-production method, assume that 15% of the production was produced in both 2006 and 2007, 20% was produced in 2008 and 2009, and 30% was produced in 2010.

b. Which method do you think Marcia would prefer if she had a bonus based on the company's net income? Explain.

Study Problem 2 (Interpreting a write-down) Fairfield Ltd. (Fairfield) is a public company that is located in southern Alberta. In fiscal 2005, Fairfield had a considerable increase in sales and their net income was going to exceed shareholders' expectations by more than 15% or $37,000,000. Fairfield's Chief Executive Officer (CEO) Andrew McCulloch recognized that the high earnings during the year was a result of events that were not considered part of Fairfield's normal business activities, and that this increased level of earnings was not sustainable in the foreseeable future.

Before finalizing its financial statements, Andrew evaluated the company's assets and determined that several were overvalued. As a result, Fairfield's assets were written down by a total of $25,000,000 so that the assets would not be reported on its books at more than market value. All of the assets written down were being amortized, and their remaining useful lives ranged between 10 and 12 years.

a. Explain the effects on the current year's financial statements, as well as the implications for future years' financial statements, of the write-down.
b. Describe how users of the financial statements would be affected by the write-down and how the financial statements should be interpreted as a result of recording the write-down.
c. Why do you think Fairfield opted to write down the assets?
d. Is it relevant that Fairfield wrote down these assets? Explain.

Study Problem 3 (Effect of capitalizing versus expensing research and development costs)
Duck Hook Inc. (Duck Hook) is a golf technology company located in eastern Ontario. Duck Hook has successfully marketed a product that promises to help golfers improve their scores by hitting the golf ball straighter down the fairway. Duck Hook operates in a highly competitive industry as many competitors have surfaced in recent years looking to capitalize on an aging population (in Canada) looking for more recreational activities. To remain competitive, companies in this sector should invest heavily in research and development to ensure that they continuously have new products to bring to market. However, Duck Hook has slowed its investment in research and development in the last few years.

Duck Hook prepares its financial statements in accordance with GAAP, so it expenses all research costs and any development costs that do not meet the criteria for capitalization. To date, none of Duck Hook's development costs have met the criteria for capitalization. The following information has been summarized from Duck Hook's financial statements:

Duck Hook Inc.
Extracts from Financial Statements
HookH

	2006	**2005**	**2004**	**2003**	**2002**
Summarized from the Income statement					
Revenues	3,480,000	2,350,000	1,780,000	1,150,000	850,000
Other Expenses	1,780,000	1,375,000	870,000	685,000	200,000
R&D Expenses	900,000	1,236,000	1,455,000	975,000	450,000
Net Income / (Loss)	800,000	(261,000)	(545,000)	(510,000)	(200,000)
Summarized from the Balance sheet					
Total assets	5,150,000	2,875,000	1,450,000	770,000	500,000
Total liabilities	1,896,000	1,104,000	1,050,000	395,000	175,000
Total shareholders' equity	3,254,000	1,771,000	400,000	375,000	325,000
Summarized from the Cash flow statement					
Cash from operations	375,000	250,000	(470,000)	(1,250,000)	(900,000)
Cash from investing activities	(1,450,000)	(1,350,000)	(950,000)	(925,000)	(350,000)

a. Recalculate net income for 2004 through 2006, assuming that research and development costs were capitalized and expensed over three years.
b. What would total assets be at the end of 2004 through 2006 if research and development costs were capitalized and expensed over three years?
c. What would shareholder's equity be at the end of 2004 through 2006 if research and development costs were capitalized and expensed over three years?
d. What would cash from operations and cash expended on investing activities be for 2004 through 2006 if research and development costs were capitalized and expensed over three years?
e. What would the following ratios be, assuming (1) research and development costs were expensed as incurred and (2) research and development costs were capitalized and expensed over three years?

    i. return on assets
    ii. debt-to-equity ratio
    iii. profit margin percentage

f. How would your interpretation of Duck Hook differ depending on how research and development costs are accounted for? Which accounting approach do you think is more appropriate? Explain. Your answer should consider the objectives of the users and preparers of accounting information, as well as GAAP.

Study Problem 4 (Effect of recording an error on the financial statements) In 2002 Nolan Ltd. (Nolan) purchased machinery for $126,000. In error, Nolan's bookkeeper Colin Argyle recorded the purchase as an expense rather than capitalizing the cost and recording it on the balance sheet as an asset. The error went unnoticed until late 2005, when the machinery was sold for $25,000 and no record can be found of it in the accounts.

a. Show the entry that Colin made to record the purchase of the machinery. Show the entry that Colin should have made.
b. Nolan uses the straight-line method for amortizing its machinery and the useful life assigned similar machinery in the past has been six years. What would be the effect of the error on net income and total assets (amount and direction of the error) in 2002, 2003, and 2004?
c. What would be the effect of the error on net income and total assets (amount and direction of the error) in 2005, the year the machinery was sold?
d. What would be the effect of the error on the cash flow statement in each of years 2002 through 2005?
e. Assuming the error is material, what would the implications of this error be for users of the financial statements? Explain.

Study Problem 5 (Accounting changes – policies and estimates) On November 1, 2002, Summerfield Waste Management Inc. (Summerfield) purchased a bulldozer for $525,000. Summerfield's management estimated that the bulldozer would be useful for nine years, at which time the machine could be sold for $75,000. Summerfield uses straight-line amortization on all its capital assets. In October 2006 management realized that due to a problem with insurance coverage, the bulldozer would not likely be useful beyond fiscal 2007. Therefore, Summerfield decided to shorten its estimate of the machine's useful life to five years and the estimate of the residual value to zero. Independent's year end is October 31.

a. Is the change being made by Summerfield considered a change in accounting policy or a change in accounting estimate? Explain. How would the change be accounted for?

b. What amortization expense would Summerfield have originally reported in fiscal 2003, 2004 and 2005 for the bulldozer?
c. What amortization expense would Summerfield have reported in fiscal 2004, 2005 and 2006 for the bulldozer after the accounting change had been made?
d. What amortization expense will Summerfield report for the year ended October 31, 2006?
e. What are the implications of this change to users of the financial statements? Explain.
f. Do you think this type of change can be objectively made? Explain. What possible motivations could Summerfield's managers have for making the change? Explain.

Solutions to Study Problems

Solution to Study Problem 1

Note: the following response assumes that the fiscal year ends June 30.

a.

i. Straight line - Annual amortization expense = ($500,000-$100,000)/5 =$80,000

Year	Cost	Accumulated Amortization Dec. 31	NBV Dec. 31	Amortization Expense
2006	500,000	80,000	420,000	80,000
2007	500,000	160,000	340,000	80,000
2008	500,000	240,000	260,000	80,000
2009	500,000	320,000	180,000	80,000
2010	500,000	400,000	100,000	80,000
Total				400,000

ii. Declining balance

Year	Cost	Accumulated Amortization Dec. 31	NBV Dec. 31	Amortization Expense
2006	500,000	100,000	400,000	100,000
2007	500,000	180,000	320,000	80,000
2008	500,000	244,000	256,000	64,000
2009	500,000	295,200	204,800	51,200
2010	500,000	336,160	163,840	40,960
Total				336,160

iii. Units of production

Year	Cost	Accumulated Amortization Dec. 31	NBV Dec. 31	Amortization Expense	% UOP
2006	500,000	60,000	440,000	60,000	15%
2007	500,000	120,000	380,000	60,000	15%
2008	500,000	200,000	300,000	80,000	20%
2009	500,000	280,000	220,000	80,000	20%
2010	500,000	400,000	100,000	120,000	30%
Total				400,000	

b. For a bonus based on net income, Marcia would prefer the units of production method in the early years, since the lower expense results in higher income. Of course, over the life of the asset, the effect on income would be the same but with units-of-production method Marcia gets her bonus earlier, which she would prefer when considering the time value of money.

Solution to Study Problem 2

a. The $25,000,000 write-down reduces income in the current year because of the loss and increases the income in future years because the amortization expense will now be lower. As a result, Fairfield only exceeded shareholders' expectations by $12,000,000, instead of by $37,000,000.

b. Assuming that the users accepted the write-down at face value, their perceptions of the future profitability of the firm would be reduced substantially. The financial statements of the current year should be interpreted with the understanding that the total write-down reduced current earnings and is a one-time occurrence. Most users would see the effect of the one-time write-down in 2005. What would be less obvious is the improvement in earnings after 2005 as a result of the lower amortization charge. The effect of the write-down after 2006 would not be explicitly stated or reported separately. The effect on amortization expense would be reflected in ordinary operations. As a result, some stakeholders could have a more positive sense of the performance of the company than is merited.

c. The motive for the amount and timing of the write-down appears to be to avoid the prospect of dealing with shareholders' expectations of profits that were not sustainable. Andrew may have been trying to show a stable income trend rather than having an unusually good year followed by a poorer year, which may not have been well received by the market. By initiating the write-off, Andrew may have been trying to dampen shareholders' expectations for future profits. Another explanation is that the assets were actually overstated on the balance sheet and a write-down was suitable. This highlights the problem for users. It will rarely be clear what the motivation of the managers is so it is more difficult to understand the financial statements.

d. It may not matter in the sense of shareholders being misled if they understand exactly what was done. However, those who receive the financial statements of the company in the next few years may not be aware of the write-down and believe that the firm is more profitable than would have been the case in the absence of the write-down. The write-down could also have an effect on contracts that are based on financial statement numbers.

Solution to Study Problem 3

a. to e.

	2006	2005	2004	2003	2002
Revenues	3,480,000	2,350,000	1,780,000	1,150,000	850,000
Other Expenses	1,780,000	1,375,000	870,000	685,000	200,000
R&D					
From 2002			150,000	150,000	150,000
From 2003		325,000	325,000	325,000	
From 2004	485,000	485,000	485,000		
From 2005	412,000	412,000			
From 2006	300,000				
Total amortization	1,197,000	1,222,000	960,000	475,000	150,000
Total expenses	2,977,000	2,597,000	1,830,000	1,160,000	350,000
Income (capitalize R&D)	503,000	(247,000)	(50,000)	(10,000)	500,000
Total assets (before)	5,150,000	2,875,000	1,450,000	770,000	500,000
Add R&D capitalized	900,000	1,236,000	1,455,000	975,000	450,000
Less accumulated amortization	4,004,000	2,807,000	1,585,000	625,000	150,000
Adjusted total assets	2,046,000	1,304,000	1,320,000	1,120,000	800,000
Less liabilities	1,896,000	1,104,000	1,050,000	395,000	175,000
Shareholders' equity	150,000	200,000	270,000	725,000	625,000
Cash from operations (before)	375,000	250,000	(470,000)	(1,250,000)	(900,000)
Add back R&D expenditures	900,000	1,236,000	1,455,000	975,000	450,000
Adjusted cash from operations	1,275,000	1,486,000	985,000	(275,000)	(450,000)
Cash from investing (before)	(1,450,000)	(1,350,000)	(950,000)	(925,000)	(350,000)
Less R&D expenditures	900,000	1,236,000	1,455,000	975,000	450,000
Adjusted cash from investing	(2,350,000)	(2,586,000)	(2,405,000)	(1,900,000)	(800,000)
Income as reported	800,000	(261,000)	(545,000)	(510,000)	(200,000)
ROA (expense R&D)	20.0%	-12.1%	-49.1%	-80.3%	
ROA (capitalize R&D)	30.0%	-18.9%	-4.1%	-1.0%	
Debt/equity (expense R&D)	.58	.62	2.63	1.05	.54
Debt/equity(capitalize R&D)	12.64	5.52	3.89	.54	.28
Profit margin(expense R&D)	.23	-.11	-.31	-.44	-.24
Profit margin(capitalize R&D)	.15	-.11	-.03	-.01	.59

f. In the first few years, Duck Hook appears to be more profitable and less levered with the R&D costs capitalized. However, that relationship eventually reverses when the growth in R&D investment slowed. Given the uncertainty of future benefits from the R&D, expensing would seem more appropriate. The value of the asset cannot be reliably estimated so expensing is consistent with conservatism, although the predictive value of net income is certainly sacrificed as is the usefulness of net income as a measure of management performance. On the other hand, not capitalizing research costs ignores what is clearly a valuable asset in general and undermines matching. Expensing also removes any information value of the accounting treatment for research because management does not have to assess the future usefulness of the expenditure (if management had to decide whether to capitalize or not, it would be making a statement about its assessment of the usefulness of the research). However, research can be very hard to assess, which would open the door for management having more opportunity to pursue self-interests. The preparers of the financial statements would likely prefer to report higher income in the earlier years and would prefer to show more equity on the balance sheet. Very likely, many users would dismiss the capitalization of these costs in their own analysis of the financial statements.

Solution to Study Problem 4

a.

The entry that was made:

Dr.	Maintenance expense (expense +)	126,000	
	Cr. Cash (asset -)		126,000

The entry that should have been made:

Dr.	Machine (asset +)	126,000	
	Cr. Cash (asset -)		126,000

b. Assuming the machinery was purchased January 1, 2002, and assuming no salvage value, the annual amortization expense would be $21,000. As a result of the error, net income would have been understated in 2002 by $105,000 ($126,000 - $21,000). In 2003 and 2004, income would be overstated by $21,000, the amount of amortization that was not expensed because of the error.

As a result of the error, total assets would have been understated in 2002 by $105,000 ($126,000 - $21,000). In 2003 and 2004, total assets would be understated by $84,000 ($126,000 - $42,000) and $63,000 ($126,000 - $63,000) respectively.

c. Assuming the machinery was sold at the end of the year (2005), the amortization expense would be understated by $21,000 because no amortization expense would have been recorded. The accumulated amortization at the time of the sale should have been 4 x $21,000 = $84,000 and the net book value would have been $42,000. As a result, there should have been a loss of $17,000. However, because the machinery was expensed in 2002, there was no asset recorded on the books so there is a gain on disposal of $25,000. Had the machinery been accounted for properly, there would have been a net effect on the income statement of -$38,000 (-$17,000 - $21,000). Instead there is a gain of $25,000, for a net difference of $63,000.

d. There would be no overall effect on cash flow because of the error (assuming no tax or other secondary effects). However, there would be classification differences. In 2002, CFO would have been understated by $126,000 (because the machinery was expensed) and cash from investing activities would have been overstated by $126,000 because the machinery should have been classified as an investing cash outflow. There would be no effect on the other years because no cash was exchanged in the other years until 2005, when $25,000 was received for the sale of the machinery. This should be reported as an investing cash inflow.

e. The error could be very misleading for users. The income statement, balance sheet, and cash flow statement would all have material errors. As a result some stakeholders could make bad decisions. For example, as a result of the error a shareholder might have sold his or her shares because of the seemingly poor performance when in fact actual performance would have been better. There is virtually no chance that an external user of the financial statements would be aware of the error.

Solution to Study Problem 5

a. The change is a change in accounting estimate because Summerfield will continue to use the same straight-line accounting method, but will apply the method with different estimates of the bulldozer's useful life and residual value. The change should be accounted for prospectively, meaning that the amortization expense would be calculated from the current year going forward using the new estimated useful life and residual value.

b. Annual amortization expense = ($525,000-75,000)/9 = $50,000.

c. The change in accounting estimate would be implemented prospectively, so the amortization expense in 2003 to 2005 would not change.

d. The accumulated amortization at the end of fiscal 2005 will be 3 x $50,000 = $150,000 so the net book value will be $375,000. Given a zero residual value, the amortization expense over the remaining 2 years, including 2006, will be $187,500.

e. The users of the financial statements will see a reduction in income from the increased amortization expense as well as lower book values of the asset over the remaining useful life. There may be some information in the revised useful life because it says something about the need for capital expenditures sooner than expected. Whether a user could infer this from the change would depend on if and how the information was disclosed. In any case, there will be an increase in the amount of amortization for the next two years.

f. The change in estimate may be objective under some circumstances although in most cases there will be a fair bit of discretion as to the amount and timing of the change in estimate. The way that this change is described indicates that management intends to replace the bulldozer at the end of fiscal 2007. A change of estimate that reflects a clear intent can probably be considered objective. However, management does not always have to be completely forthright with its intentions. There are alternative motivations for the same change, such as reducing income to lower expectations that investors may have of future earnings or maybe trying to reduce income for some reason (perhaps to reduce income-based payouts to previous owners or to aid in securing government support). Note that income tax effects could not be a consideration.

Chapter 10
Liabilities

Chapter Overview

Chapter 10 may be the most challenging chapter in the text. Liabilities comprise a number of very complex accounting topics including bonds, leases, pensions, and future income taxes. The purpose of the coverage is to allow you to be conversant about the accounting for these very common accounting topics. The coverage of these topics is extensive however if you take the time to work through the material in the study guide you will have a good understanding of the issues.

The material in many of the sections in the chapter is based on GAAP rules. Accounting for bonds, leases, pensions, and future income taxes, as well as commitments, contingencies, and subsequent events, are covered mainly from the perspective of GAAP. However, it is important to remember that not all organizations are constrained by GAAP. For example, a private company using its statements mainly for tax purposes might choose to not follow the rules for leases, pensions, and future income taxes and simply do what's required by the tax act. Since disclosure has no relevance for taxes, commitments, contingencies, and subsequent events would likely also be ignored. Even private entities whose audience may be broader than CCRA might prefer not to follow some of the GAAP rules for simplicity and cost savings.

In Chapter 10 you will learn about the nature of liabilities and how they are valued. This chapter also provides an in-depth discussion of accounting for bonds and other forms of long-term debt. The chapter ends with a discussion of disclosure issues surrounding contingencies, commitments, and subsequent events.

Summary of Key Points

♦ Liabilities can be obligations to pay money to suppliers, lenders, employees, shareholders, etc., or to provide goods or services to customers.

  ➢ Some liabilities, such as accounts payable, can be measured precisely for financial reporting purposes. However, in some cases, the liability may be uncertain and may need to be estimated by the entity.
  ➢ According to GAAP, liabilities have three characteristics:
    - They require the sacrifice of resources.
    - They are unavoidable.
    - They are the result of past transactions or economic events.

♦ Current liabilities are usually not discounted to their present value.

♦ Current liabilities discussed are:
  - Bank and other current loans
  - Accounts payable
  - Collections on behalf of third parties
  - Income taxes payable
  - Dividends payable
  - Accrued liabilities
  - Unearned revenue

- Accounting for bonds—the basic recording of the issuance of a bond issued at face value is not very difficult. When bonds are issued at discounts and premiums the calculations are a little more complex. Bonds are issued at discounts when the coupon rate (the rate paid by the issuer) is lower than the effective rate (the market rate of interest). Bonds are issued at premiums when the coupon rate is higher than the effective rate.

  - The price of a bond is equal to the present value of the cash flows that will be paid to the investor, discounted at the effective interest rate. The effective interest rate is determined by market forces and depends on the risk of the bond. A riskier bond has a higher effective interest rate.

- A lease is a contractual arrangement where an entity (the lessee) agrees to pay another entity (the lessor) a fee in exchange for use of an asset. Most of the attention provided for lease accounting is presented from the lessee's perspective. How leases are accounted for can significantly effect the financial statements.

- There are two types of pension plans: defined-benefit and defined-contribution plans. In a defined contribution plan, the employer makes a fixed contribution to the plan, but the actual benefit that the employee receives after retirement depends on the investment performance of the pension fund. Accounting for a defined contribution pension plan is simple: the pension expense is debited and cash is credited as the company makes its pension contributions.

  - Companies that have defined benefit pension plans have a great deal of flexibility in estimating their contribution and this can lead to an over or under-funded pension fund.

- Future income tax assets and liabilities arise because the accounting methods used to prepare the general purpose financial statements are sometimes different from the methods used to calculate taxable income. Future income taxes have nothing to do with the amount of tax an entity has to pay.

- A contingency is a possible liability or asset whose existence and amount depend on some future event. For financial reporting purposes a contingency could be accrued, disclosed, or ignored. Each alternative brings problems. Accrue or disclose something that ultimately doesn't occur and users get an overstatement of the risks and costs facing the entity. Ignore a contingency and the risks and cost might be understated.

- A commitment is a contractual agreement to enter into a transaction in the future. Commitments are executory contracts and are not recorded until an exchange occurs. If it is assumed that the commitment is binding on both parties an argument can be made that the GAAP treatment for commitments gives rise to unrecorded liabilities in the sense that the entities have obligations to pay for (or deliver) goods and services.

- Subsequent events are economic events that occur after an entity's year end, but before the financial statements are released to users. The *CICA Handbook* identifies two types of subsequent events: 1) Events that provide additional information about circumstances that existed at the year end—the financial statements should be adjusted to reflect the new information. 2) Events that happened after the balance sheet date—only disclosed in the notes to the financial statements.

- Two financial ratios that are useful for credit and risk analysis: the debt-to-equity ratio (previously discussed in the book) and the interest coverage ratio. Financial risk amplifies the business risk of the firm. This risk arises due to the fixed financial obligations of the firm and is measured by the debt-to-equity ratio.

  - Analysts primarily use cash flow ratios (or debt service ratios) such as the interest coverage ratio to see if a firm can service their debts. Credit analysts use them to test a firm's solvency.
  - It is difficult to create general rules for ratios—norms vary with circumstances.
  - The interest coverage ratio can be generalized to measure the ability of an entity to meet any or all of its fixed financing charges. This involves changing the interest expense in the numerator by other or all fixed costs. The larger the ratio, the better able the entity is to meet its interest payments.

Study Points and Study Tips

What are liabilities?

- In general, liabilities should be valued at their present value, although there are many exceptions in practice. For example, future income taxes and current liabilities are not discounted using the time value of money.

  - ***Payables*** – short-term obligations created by obtaining goods and services. These include accounts payable, interest payable and taxes payable. Notes payable are payables in the form of written promissory notes.
  - ***Unearned Revenue*** – cash collected in advance of performing a service. Instead of cash, a future service is due to the consumer. You are required to pay tuition in advance of attending university courses. The university collects your money before providing you any education. The money received (by the university) would be recorded as unearned (deferred) revenue in the university financial statements.
  - All users need to scrutinize an entity's liabilities. An entity that has too many obligations may be in danger of going bankrupt.
  - An economic event can be recorded as a liability only if the entity is obligated to provide it in the future. Although there are uncertainties regarding some liabilities due to:

    - unspecified amounts, i.e. for the end of period utility bills, the entity may have to estimate the liability before it has received the actual invoice
    - unspecified payment date, i.e. for unearned revenue and warranties, the date on which the liability occurs is difficult to estimate accurately

  - As noted in Chapter 2, a liability does not have to be a legal obligation. For example, a warranty is a guarantee given by the entity to replace or compensate customers if its products stop working or break down. The value of such compensation cannot be known exactly. However, the entity must estimate the future expense due to the warranty based on experience and report it in the same period as the revenue due to the matching principle.

Bonds and Other Forms of Long-Term Debt

- The U.S. Bond market is the world's largest securities market. In its basic form, a bond is a loan. There are many different types and terms of debt instruments. Bonds are issued by public corporations and governments and are owned by insurance companies, mutual funds, pension funds, banks, etc. For this reason accounting for bonds is important because bonds affect all of our lives in some manner.

- Debt is more risky to issuers (because interest and principal must be repaid on schedule). Debt is less expensive than equity since interest is tax deductible to the issuer (and dividends are not). The cost of servicing the debt is recorded as an expense before taxes on the income statement. This cost is calculated using yield instead rather than the coupon rate.
- The proceeds of a debt issue increase the cash flows from financing activities and the redemption of the debt at maturity decreases the cash flow from financing activities.
- Accruing Interest on Long-Term Debt—the accumulation of interest to a loan (debt) amount. This material was covered in Chapter 3's discussion of adjusting entry.
- There are two methods for amortizing the discount/premium using the straight-line and effective interest methods. The straight-line method allocates an equal amount of the discount to interest expense each period, thus it is easy to understand. The effective interest method is more complicated and requires more skill to analyze.
- Mortgages are loans where the borrower pays interest and principal throughout the life of the loan. Mortgages usually consist of long-term debt secured by property.

    - Mortgages are usually paid in the form of fixed monthly installments that combine principal and interest (blended payments). Each monthly mortgage payment results in a debit (decrease) to mortgage payable, a debit to mortgage interest expense, and a credit (decrease) to cash.

- Early Retirement of Debt—if the overall level of interest rates decreases companies have an incentive to retire existing high-interest-rate debt and issue new debt at lower interest rates. A company can issue callable bonds in order to take advantage of situations when interest rates decline. Although, in order to attract bondholders, companies must issue callable bonds at higher interest rates due to the added risk (of the bonds being called) assumed by the bondholder.
- Callable bonds are similar to redeemable preferred shares. Between 2002 and 2004 the majority of investors experienced the lowest interest rates in 50 years in Canada and have had their bonds called by the issuer.

Leases

- There are two types of leases: 1) Capital leases and 2) Operating leases. The key concept for whether a lease should be classified as capital or operating lease is whether the benefits and risks of ownership are transferred to the lessee.

    - Operating leases are relatively straightforward. The lease payments are treated as operating expenses (on the income statement and cash flows from operation). In many annual reports, operating leases are reported in the same section as commitments.

- For a lessee, a lease should be classified as a capital lease if any of the following three criteria are met:

    - It is likely that the lessee will take title of the asset;
    - The lease term is long enough that the lessee receives most of the economic benefits available from the asset (usually defined as 75% or more of the leased asset's life); or

- ➢ The lessor is assured of recovering its investment in the leased asset and earning a return on the investment (usually defined as the present value of the lease payments being greater than or equal to 90% of the asset's fair value).

- For a lessor, a lease is considered a capital lease if:
  - ➢ Any of the three criteria described for the lessee is met;
  - ➢ The credit risk of the lessee is normal; and
  - ➢ The lessor is able to estimate any un-reimbursable costs the lessor must incur as part of the lease agreement.

- There are two types of capital leases from the lessor's perspective: 1) sales-type lease 2) direct financing type lease.
  - ➢ With a sales-type lease the lessor records the sale of the leased asset when the lease comes into effect, and recognizes interest revenue over the term of the lease.
  - ➢ A direct financing lease is a straight financing arrangement where the lessor purchases assets on behalf of the lessee and leases them to the lessee.
  - ➢ Companies that lease assets to others are much less common than companies that lease assets from lessors. Accounting by lessors is not covered in detail in Chapter 10 and would be more appropriate in an intermediate accounting course.
  - ➢ The more general issue of this discussion of leases is off-balance sheet financing. Leasing was the first big off-balance sheet financing issue to confront accounting. Of course the most current of the off-balance sheet issue was the Special Purpose Entities that Enron utilized, which have been in wide use by many entities, usually legitimately.
  - ➢ The capitalization of a lease results in higher assets and liabilities, lower net income in earlier years, higher cash flows from operation and lower cash flows from financing. Most of a firm's financial ratios look worse if they treat a lease as a capital lease rather than an operating lease. So management often prefers operating leases particularly if their compensation is linked to the company's ratios or the firm's debt covenants place limits on these ratios.
  - ➢ Profitability ratios (ROE, ROA) are lower for capital leases due to lower net income and higher assets. Leverage ratios (Debt-to-equity) are higher for capital leases due to the recognition of the lease liability. Liquidity ratios (Current ratio, working capital) are lower for capital leases. Asset turnover is lower for capital leases due to the recognition of the lease asset.
  - ➢ Accounting tries to reflect the underlying economic activity of an entity. How leases are accounted for doesn't change the entity's economic situation but can dramatically affect how that economic situation is reported. There can be secondary economic effects of accounting choices, such as payouts pertaining to contracts and adherence to covenants.
  - ➢ When a company sells capital assets to a purchaser and immediately leases the property back, the transaction is known as a sale-leaseback arrangement. When assets are sold in sale-leaseback transactions, GAAP do not allow gains or losses to be fully recognized on the income statement in the year of the sale. Instead, the gains or losses must be deferred and recorded on the balance sheet.

Pensions and Other Post-Retirement Benefits

- Currently there is considerable controversy about the assumptions that are used to determine an entity's pension expense.

- For a defined-contribution plan, the pension expense for the year is the contribution that the employer is required to make to the plan according to the agreement with the employees. A pension liability is reported on an employer's balance sheet if the full contribution to the plan has not been made by the end of the period.
- For a defined-benefit pension plan it is necessary to determine the annual pension expense and the amount of money the employer must contribute to the plan each year. The pension expense in a year does not have to be the same as the amount of cash that the employer contributes to the plan. In recent years, regulators have pressed Air Canada to come up with a strategy to revive its under-funded defined benefit pension plan. In 2004 Air Canada had a pension deficit of $1.3 billion.
- The pension asset or liability does not provide information about the actual condition of the pension plan. It is the difference between the accounting measure of the pension expense and the amount funded. The pension asset or liability informs users of the extent to which funding has exceeded recognition in the accounting records (pension asset) or recognition in the accounting records has exceeded funding (pension liability).
- The rules in the *CICA Handbook* are designed to allow preparers to smooth income. The full economic impact of events that could cause significant fluctuations in the annual pension expense are not reflected when they occur, but instead are often amortized, thereby smoothing out their effects.
- Because of the complexity of the assumptions that must be made to calculate the pension expense, preparers must exercise considerable judgment. These judgments can significantly affect the numbers that are reported in the financial statements, and as a result, preparers have some flexibility with which to achieve their reporting objectives. For example, a higher discount rate lowers all pension obligations (from an accounting standpoint). However, plan assets remain unaffected, thus resulting in a lower net pension liability. The reduced liability shows a falsely strong financial position for the entity (overstatement of earnings and a stronger balance sheet).
- Companies often provide postretirement benefits such as healthcare and life insurance to their employees and dependants after retirement. These benefits are estimates from the nature of the plans that the firm offers its employees and assumptions regarding their retirement age, mortality rates, and future trends in health care costs. The expected postretirement liability is then the discounted value of the estimated postretirement benefits. Many large firms are considerably under-funded. In hindsight, this should not come as a surprise given the declining stock markets, interest rates at 50-year lows, and an aging workforce in North America.
- Companies like General Motors Corporation currently have post retirement benefit liabilities that are under-funded by billions of dollars. Under-funded liabilities have a significant affect on the core operations of these companies as cash is diverted away form day-to-day activities.

Future Income Taxes

- Temporary differences give rise to future income taxes, permanent differences do not. Permanent differences are differences between the income tax expense and taxes payable that will never reverse themselves.

  - The income tax expense component of the journal entry is a plug. The amount of tax owing and the future income tax debit or credit is calculated.
  - The future income tax balance on the balance sheet reflects temporary differences between the accounting value of assets and liabilities, and the tax value of assets and liabilities on the balance sheet date, multiplied by the entity's tax rate (actually the tax rate when the future tax amounts are expected to reverse). The debit or credit to future

income taxes in the journal entry is the amount required to adjust the opening balance in the future income tax account to the required closing balance.

- Temporary differences arising from liabilities are not covered, except in passing, in the book.
- The taxes payable method is offered as an alternative to the future income tax accounting. This approach might be used by companies not constrained by GAAP.
- Future income tax balances reported on many companies' balance sheets are significant. The calculations should not be your main focus but rather to understand where the numbers come from so you can interpret financial statements effectively.

Contingencies

- The accounting difficulty with contingencies is that there is often significant uncertainty regarding the outcome of the contingency and/or the amount. CBC Radio Canada (the Corporation) deals with various claims and legal proceedings throughout its fiscal year. Some of these claims are significant in size and could result in substantial expenditures. The Corporation realizes that they may have to settle some of these claims. Therefore provisions for these expenditures are recorded based on management's best estimate.

  - Managers must exercise judgement in deciding how to report (if at all) a contingency. The terms used to guide how the accounting for contingencies should be done are quite subjective and require interpretation—likely or unlikely and reasonably measurable.
  - The *CICA Handbook* requires contingent losses that are likely (to occur) and that are reasonably measurable to be accrued. Contingent losses that are likely to occur but cannot be reasonably measured should be disclosed in the notes but do not have to be accrued.
  - Contingent gains are never accrued under GAAP. This follows the principle of Conservatism.

Commitments

- Under GAAP, the existence of commitments must be disclosed in the financial statements if it (a) involves an unusual degree of risk, (b) commits the entity to significant expenditures; or (c) commits the entity to issue shares. Except for (c), managers have flexibility in deciding whether to disclose the existence of commitments. The amount of detail provided about a commitment varies across entities.

  - Some entities tend to not report all commitments for fear of an adverse reaction from the capital markets. One of the dilemmas is that GAAP's definition of future liabilities is quite flexible and leaves significant room for interpretation.
  - CBC Radio Canada has commitments for sports rights, procured programs, film rights etc. This information is found in the Notes to Financial Statements. It is encouraging to see this high level of disclosure for a federally funded entity. Although, in this case, solid disclosure should not come as a surprise considering the Auditor's Report is signed by Sheila Fraser, the Auditor General of Canada.

Subsequent Events

- When accurately using historical cost accounting, users may not have potentially useful information of an important economic event that happens after the end of an entity's fiscal year.

  - What should be disclosed as a subsequent event is not well defined. The *CICA Handbook* states that events that will have a significant effect on the entity in a subsequent period should be disclosed.

Financial Statement Analysis Issues

- Debt-to-equity ratio – a measure of the amount of debt relative to the amount of equity an entity uses for financing. Analysis of this measure requires an understanding of many factors such as the industry in which the entity competes.

  - Onex Corporation has a staggering debt-to-equity ratio of over 15. Users need to be cautious since Onex is an investor corporation with many subsidiaries (i.e. Loews Cineplex Group) and Onex does not guarantee the debt of any of its operating (investee) companies.
  - Research in Motion (RIM) on the other hand has a debt-to-equity ratio of 0. This simply means that debt has not been used in any of its financing. Debt makes an entity more risky since more fixed interest charges must be paid.

- Interest coverage ratio – a measure of the ability of an entity to meet its fixed financing charges. The larger the ratio, the better able the entity is to meet its interest payments.

  - Magna International Inc. has relatively high interest coverage of approximately 43. Although Magna shows a strong net income its debt-to-equity ratio is under .15. A high net income can be beneficial for this measure but also a low amount of interest expense will reduce the denominator, thus increasing the ratio.
  - Unfortunately, the interest coverage ratio can sometime provide a ridiculous calculation for users. For example, Open Text Corporation has interest coverage of over 500. Since Open Text has a debt-to-equity of 0 the interest coverage ratio is not very useful.

- Issues such as off-balance sheet financing (e.g. operating leases), assumptions (e.g. pensions), and "funny" liabilities (e.g. future income taxes) can dramatically affect the amount of liabilities an entity will report. It is important to understand the necessity of looking behind ratios to understand where they come from before they can conclude what they mean.

  - Off balance sheet items refer to contractual obligations not recognized as liabilities on the balance sheet. The motivation behind all such off-balance sheet activities is to reduce an entity's reported liabilities. The effect of such activities is to reduce the reported liability without reducing the economic liability faced by the entity.
  - In 2002, the Kellogg Company (the world's leading producer of cereal) reported over $300 million of off-balance-sheet arrangements related to operating leases in the Management's Discussion and Analysis. The key here is that Kellogg has provided the user with appropriate disclosure. However, not all companies make their financial reports that user friendly.

- Given a choice, most entities prefer to report higher revenues, higher earnings, more assets and fewer liabilities in their financial statements. Motivation for these objectives is driven by management bonuses linked to the entity's financial performance or the desire to influence the price of the common shares. An entity is most likely to misrepresent liabilities by:

  I. non-disclosure of commitments and contingencies
  II. altering accounting assumptions to reduce liabilities
  III. improper release of reserves to boost income
  IV. recognizing revenue before satisfying obligations

Study Problems

Study Problem 1 (Determine the proceeds from a bond) Management at Gorilla Inc. (Gorilla) are looking to raise capital to purchase a new office building. However, they do not want to give up control of their organization in exchange for the raised capital. After meeting with their investment bankers, the management team has decided to issue bonds to the public. On June 23, 2005, Gorilla will make a $5,000,000 bond issue. The bond matures in 7 years on June 22, 2012, has a coupon rate of 4%, and pays interest annually on June 22. Indicate how much Gorilla will receive in proceeds from its bond if the effective interest rate when the bond issued is:

a. 3%
b. 4%
c. 5%

Study Problem 2 (Valuing liabilities) On October 31, 2005, Doug Dutchie purchased kitchen equipment from one of Canada's fastest growing coffee and baked goods chains for $300,000. Doug received a two-year, $300,000, interest-free loan for the purchase price. The terms of the loan require Doug to pay $150,000 on October 31 of each of the next two years, beginning on October 31, 2006.

a. What alternatives exist for reporting the liability? What are the problems and benefits of the alternative approaches?
b. Prepare the journal entry that Doug should make to record the purchase of the equipment (assume a 6% discount rate). Explain the amount you recorded for the equipment on the balance sheet.
c. Prepare the journal entries that Doug should make on October 31, 2006 and October 31, 2007 to record payments on the loan.
d. How much should Doug report as a liability for the loan on its balance sheet on December 31, 2005 through 2007?

Study Problem 3 (Accounting for leases) On April 1, 2005 Coyle Inc. (Coyle) signed a 10-year lease to purchase some high-end digital imaging equipment. The equipment was necessary to secure a multi-million dollar contract to print user manuals for one of the largest manufacturing companies in Canada. According to the terms of the lease, Coyle must make annual lease payments of $50,000 on March 31, commencing in 2006. The interest rate that applies to the lease is 6%.

a. If Coyle's lease were accounted for as an operating lease, what amount would be recorded as an asset for the leased digital imaging equipment on April 1, 2005?
b. If the lease were accounted for as an operating lease, prepare the journal entries that would have to be made in fiscal 2006 and fiscal 2008 to account for the lease.
c. If Coyle's lease were accounted for as a capital lease, what amount would be recorded as an asset for the leased digital imaging equipment on April 1, 2005?
d. If the lease were accounted for as a capital lease, what journal entry would be required on April 1, 2005?
e. If the lease were accounted for as a capital lease, what journal entries would be required on March 31, 2006 to record the lease payment?
f. If the lease were accounted for as a capital lease, what journal entry would be required on March 31, 2006 to record amortization of the equipment?
g. What would the NBV of the leased equipment and the lease liability on Coyle's March 31, 2006 balance sheet?

Study Problem 4 (Future income taxes) For the fiscal year ended June 30, 2005 Cold Call Canada Ltd. (Cold Call) had income before taxes of $9,000,000. Cold Call's tax return shows taxable income of $9,900,000 for that year. The tax basis of Cold Call's assets exceeded the accounting basis by $1,600,000 on June 30, 2005, and the balance in the future income tax account on June 30, 2004 was a credit of $600,000. Cold Call has a tax rate of 30%.

a. Prepare the journal entry that Cold Call should make to record its income tax expense for fiscal 2004.
b. What is Cold Call's net income for fiscal 2004?
c. What would Cold Call's net income be if it used the taxes payable method?
d. Explain the difference between (b) and (c).

Study Problem 5 (Effect of transactions and economic events on ratios) The CFO of Bayswater Ltd. (Bayswater) wants to know the effect that a number of transactions and economic events will have on several financial measures for the company's fiscal year ended August 31, 2005. Complete the following table by indicating whether the listed transactions or economic events would increase, decrease or have no effect on the financial measures listed. Explain your reasoning and state any assumptions made.

	Ratio/amount before taking the transaction/economic event into effect.	**Debt / Equity Ratio**	**Current Ratio**	**Interest Coverage**	**Cash from Operations**	**Return on Assets**
		0.88:1	**1.045**	**5.73**	**$2,475,000**	**7.81%**
a.	Bayswater signed a contract to purchase merchandise beginning in 2008 at an agreed-to price.					
b.	Bayswater paid amounts owed to suppliers for goods purchased on credit in the previous fiscal year.					
c.	Bayswater made a contribution to its defined-contribution pension plan.					
d.	A tornado destroyed a delivery vehicle owned by Bayswater on September 3, 2005					
e.	Bayswater had a decrease in its future income taxes.					
f.	Bayswater arranged a new operating lease.					
g.	Bayswater paid $760,000 to resolve an environmental matter that was launched two years ago.					

Study Problem 6 (Classifying transactions and economic events) Classify the following transactions and economic events that Bekkem Ltd. (Bekkem), a professional soccer franchise, was involved with as commitments, subsequent events, or contingencies. Some may fit more than one classification. Bekkem does not want to *bend* any accounting rules. Assume that the year end is June 30, 2007. Indicate how each should be reflected in the financial statements and explain your reasoning. In responding, consider the usefulness of the information to different users of the financial statements.

a. On July 11, 2007 Bekkem's top scorer David Edgar signed a five-year contract to play for the team. The contract is the largest ever agreed to by Bekkem.

June 30 07

b. In May 2007 a travel agency that Bekkem was suing for damages for breaching a contract made an offer of $400,000 to settle the case. As of the year end Bekkem had not decided whether to accept the offer or go to court. The offer is far below what Bekkem is suing for.
c. On July 12, 2007 Bekkem signed a two-year lease with Posh Stadium. The annual lease payments will be $500,000 per year.
d. On July 10 the company lost a lawsuit launched by a disgruntled former goalkeeper. Bekkem is required to pay the former goalie $70,000 in damages.
e. In January 2007 Bekkem guaranteed a $250,000 bank loan made to a minor league team Bekkem owns in Nova Scotia. Bekkem is responsible for paying principal and any outstanding interest in the event that the minor league team is unable to make its payments.

Solutions to Study Problems

Solution to Study Problem 1

a. Effective interest rate = 3%

PV of principal repayment = $5,000,000 x .81309 = $4,065,450

PV of interest payments = $200,000 x 6.23028 = $1,246,056

Proceeds of bond issue = $5,311,506

b. Effective interest rate = 4%

PV of principal repayment = $5,000,000 x .75992 = $3,799,600

PV of interest payments = $200,000 x 6.00205 = $1,200,410

Proceeds of bond issue = $5,000,010 (not equal to $5,000,000 because of rounding)

c. Effective interest rate = 5%

PV of principal repayment = $5,000,000 x .71068 = $3,553,400

PV of interest payments = $200,000 x 5.78637 = $1,157,268

Proceeds of bond issue = $4,710,668

Solution to Study Problem 2

a. The liability could be reported at $300,000 (the total of the payments), or at the present value of those payments. The present value method requires that a discount rate be determined, while the nominal approach overstates the cost of the asset.

b. Note that this problem initially does not provide the discount rate (interest-free loan) so you have to consider the need to choose it. Some discount rate must be chosen. The following response assumes a 6% rate. The present value of a series of two payments of $150,000 discounted at 6% = 1.83339 x $150,000 = $275,009

The allocation of the payment between interest and reduction of principal is shown in the table below:

		Interest expense	Principal reduction
2006	275,009	16,501	133,499
2007	141,510	8,490	141,510

Dr.	Kitchen Equipment (asset +)	275,009	
	Cr. Loan payable (liability +)		275,009

c. The journal entry on October 31, 2006

Dr.	Interest expense	16,501	
	Loan payable	133,499	
	Cr. Cash		150,000

The journal entry on October 31, 2007

Dr.	Interest expense	8,490	
	Loan payable	141,510	
	Cr. Cash		150,000

d. At December 31, 2005, the total liability is the remaining principal of $275,009 plus 2 months accrued interest ($2,750) for a total of $277,759.

At December 31, 2006, the total liability is the remaining principal of $141,510 plus 2 months accrued interest ($1,415) for a total of $142,925.

No balance is owed at December 31, 2007.

Solution to Study Problem 3

a. If the lease is treated as an operating lease, no leased asset is reported on the balance sheet.

b.
The same entry will be made each year.

Dr.	Rent expense	50,000	
	Cr. Cash		50,000

c. The present value of the lease payments is $50,000 x 7.36009 = $368,005

d.

Dr.	Asset under capital lease	368,005	
	Cr. Lease liability		368,005

e.

Dr.	Interest expense (6% of 368,005)	22,080	
	Lease liability	27,920	
	Cr. Cash		50,000

f.
Assuming straight-line amortization:

Dr.	Amortization expense (368,005/10)	36,801	
	Cr. Accumulated amortization		36,801

g.
The net book value of the equipment would be $368,005 – 36,801 = $331,204.
The net book value of the lease liability would be $368,005 – 27,920 = $340,085.

Solution to Study Problem 4

a.

Dr.	Income tax expense	1,890,000	
	Future income taxes*	1,080,000	
	Cr. Income taxes payable (30% of $9,900,000)		2,970,000

*The opening balance in the future income tax account was a credit of $600,000. The ending balance needs to be a debit of $480,000 (Tax basis > accounting basis by $1,600,000, therefore 30% * $1,600,000). To obtain a debit balance of $480,000, a debit to future income taxes of $1,080,000 ($600,000 + $480,000) is required.

b. The company's net income was $9,000,000 - $1,890,000 = $7,110,000.

c. If the taxes payable method were used, the income tax expense would be equal to taxes payable, or $2,970,000 and net income would be $6,030,000 ($9,000,000 - $2,970,000).

d. The amounts differ because one method requires that the income tax expense be based on the methods used for financial reporting purposes, while the other method simply sets the income tax expense at the amount paid for income taxes in the current period, which is based on methods required by the *Income Tax Act*.

Solution to Study Problem 5

		Debt/Equity Ratio	**Current Ratio**	**Interest Coverage**	**Cash from Operations**	**Return on Assets**
a.	Sign commitment (assume not recognized in the financial statements	No effect	No effect	No effect	No effect	No effect
b.	Paid amount for goods previously purchased— Accounts payable decreases, equity increases	Decrease	Increase	Increase	No effect	Increases
c.	Pension plan contribution (assume non-current future income tax liability, Dr. Pension Expense, Cr. Cash)	Increases	Decreases	Decreases	Decreases	Decreases

d.	Tornado loss (subsequent event)	No effect	No effect	No effect	No effect	No effect
e.	Decrease in future income taxes (assume a decrease in a non-current future tax asset) (ignores the effect of cash payment and tax expense)	No effect	No effect	No effect	No effect	Increase
f.	Arrange operating lease (assume effect considered at inception of lease)	No effect	No effect	No effect	No effect	No effect
g.	Environmental loss (assume the loss was not recorded until the cash was paid)	Increases (less equity)	Decreases	Decreases	Decreases	Decreases

Solution to Study Problem 6

a. The contract is a subsequent event that must be disclosed in the notes to the financial statements so that the users of the financial statements are made aware of the contract. The contract occurred after the end of the year, is significant, and is a completely new contract. Full disclosure requires that information that could influence a user's decision be provided in the notes to the financial statements. The arrangement is also a major commitment that Bekkem is making and should be disclosed for the same reasons as provided above.
b. This is a contingent gain. At June 30, 2007, the gain does seem probable and a minimum amount does seem reasonably measurable. However GAAP does not permit the accrual of contingent gains. Given that Bekkem may go to court, the outcome may be that nothing is received and court costs are incurred for no benefit, or it may be that a much larger amount than $400,000 is awarded. Conservatism typically drives accounting treatment of contingent gains. If the primary users are the bank or other creditors, conservatism may be appropriate. Current and potential investors in the equity of the firm may be better served by full disclosure, as they can form their own conclusions regarding the appropriate response.
c. This is a subsequent event. The lease is clearly not a capital lease, since the term is a small fraction of the expected useful life of the stadium. The lease payments should be disclosed, so that users of the financial statements have the opportunity to assess the impact of those payments on the likely ability of the company to meet its financial obligations as they become due.
d. This is a subsequent event because the lawsuit was resolved after the year end. The settlement clarifies a situation that existed on June 30, 2007 and so the amount that is owed to the former goalkeeper must be recognized and the liability reported on the balance sheet. In this case, the financial statements themselves should be adjusted to reflect the new information.
e. The arrangement is a contingency, which involves a risk that the guarantee could become a liability if the minor league team is unable to make the payments. There is no liability at the present moment but full disclosure requires that the users of the financial statements be aware of the arrangement as it substantially affects the risks faced by Bekkem. Preferably, users would be informed, at least in general terms, of the current status of the other firm's financial health and provided with some assessment of the probability, given current information, that the commitment will be honoured.

Chapter 11
Owner's Equity

Chapter Overview

For the most part Chapter 11 is straightforward. There a few twists and turns, such as repurchases of a corporation's own stock and property dividends. The section on leverage provides important insights into how the financing of an entity affects some performance indicators such as net income, return on equity, and earnings per share.

While not crucial to the chapter, the section on employee stock options provides coverage of an interesting, current, and evolving accounting issue. This section provides you with an opportunity to discuss why accounting standards can be controversial and why accounting is political. This section ties in with the economic consequences, which are discussed explicitly in the chapter and are a theme throughout the book. The treatment of employee stock options was continuing to evolve. Accounting standard setters in Canada and the US, along with the International Accounting Standards Board, have moved toward tightening the reporting requirements for stock options such that managers would have to expense the fair value of options; they would not be able to choose only to disclose the cost in the notes. Also, Microsoft Corporation had announced that it was going to replace its stock option program with a restricted stock program. Microsoft also announced that it was going to retroactively expense its stock options. Because of these ongoing changes you should be aware that some coverage in the book may be outdated. Such accounting policy changes illustrate that accounting is not a static discipline.

The introduction presents a slightly different way of thinking about the right-hand side of the accounting equation: that liabilities and equity represent the two ways that an entity's assets can be financed. The equity portion of the accounting equation is also presented to show equity as the residual interest in assets after the liabilities have been satisfied.

In this chapter you will examine different types of entities (corporations, partnerships, proprietorships) and differences in their financial reporting. Many of you may either own a small business, or upon graduation will become an entrepreneur or professional. Careful consideration of the advantages and disadvantages of different types of accounting entities is crucial in the early stages of forming any organization. In addition, many of you will enjoy a career in a large multinational corporation that issues publicly traded securities. In this chapter you have an opportunity to learn about the characteristics of equity and equity securities and discuss transactions that affect equity.

This chapter describes the use and impact of leverage. Different stakeholder groups may view the use of leverage as either a positive or negative strategy. Current creditors may not appreciate the added liabilities on the balance sheet however, common shareholders may benefit with added profitability generated by the debt proceeds.

Summary of Key Points

♦ Owner's Equity is the investment that the owners of an entity have made in the entity. Equivalent terms you may see in a financial statement include:
  - Shareholders' equity – owner's equity of a corporation.
  - Partners' equity – owner's equity of a partnership.
  - Owner's or Proprietor's equity – owner's equity of a proprietorship.

- Owners' investments in corporations can be direct or indirect:
  Direct – reported in the Capital Stock account. Capital Stock represents the amount of money that shareholders have contributed to the corporation for shares in the corporation.
  Indirect – reported in the Retained Earnings account. Retained Earnings is the sum of all the net incomes a corporation has earned since it began operations, less the dividends paid to shareholders.
- There are two types of partners in a limited liability partnership (LLP):
  - Limited Partners – same limited liability as a shareholder of a corporation.
  - General Partners – liable for all debts and obligations of the partnership.
- The two main features of corporations are limited liability and the classification of a corporation's equity on the balance sheet.
- Partnerships and proprietorships are not incorporated and do not provide limited liability, although limited liability partnerships provide limited liability protection to some of the partners (limited partners).
- Partnerships and proprietorships are not constrained by GAAP. Unlike public corporations, which have a statutory requirement to follow GAAP (according to the corporations acts), that can be waived in certain situations; there is no such statutory requirement for partnerships and proprietorships.
- Not-for-profit organizations (NFPO) are economic entities whose objective is to provide services and not make a profit. An NFPO does not have owners or ownership shares that can be traded or sold.
- Since there are no owners, an NFPO will not have an owners' or shareholders' equity section in its financial statements. However, the difference between assets and liabilities must be referred to somehow. Different NFPOs use different terms such as *net assets* or *resources* instead of equity.

♦ Common shares
- Different classes of common shares
- Par value
- Contributed surplus

♦ Preferred share features
- Cumulative
- Convertible
- Redeemable
- Retractable
- Participating

♦ Transactions affecting Retained Earnings
- Net income or loss
- Dividends
- Correction of errors
- Retroactive applications of a change in accounting policy
- Share retirement

♦ Types of dividends:
- Cash dividends
- Property dividends
- Stock dividends

- Entities looking to increase return earned on equity investments may issue debt and use the proceeds to earn profits. The section on leverage uses an example to explain the nature of leverage and to demonstrate the benefits and risks of using leverage in the capital structure of an entity.

- An employee stock option gives an employee the right to purchase a specified number of shares of the employer's stock at a specified price over a specified period of time. Employees, particularly senior executives, often derive a higher percentage of their earnings from stock options rather than salary. However, stock options are also perishable and may be worthless if the entity experiences poor performance.

- How an entity reports will affect the distributions of wealth among the various stakeholders of an entity. The decisions and outcomes that are affected by accounting information have economic consequences for both the entity and the stakeholders.

- Financial statement analysis of equity highlights two common measures of performance: earnings per share and return on equity. Some discussion of the difference between the book value of equity and the market value of equity is also provided. The section also re-emphasizes the importance of accounting information for valuation purposes, especially for private entities where no market valuation is readily available.

Study Points and Study Tips

Corporations, Partnerships, and Proprietorships

- A corporation is a separate legal and taxable entity. The owners of a corporation are its shareholders. There are essentially two types of corporations: private and public. A private corporation may have as few as one shareholder.

  - Private corporations are not necessarily small companies. For example, The Jim Pattison Group, located in Western Canada, has over 26,000 employees, sales of $5.5 billion and assets of 3.4 billion. One major difference for Mr. Pattison is that he is not required to disclose his financial statements to the public.
  - A NFPO is not organized to earn a profit so it is not appropriate to use the term net income when discussing a NFPO. Usually the "bottom line" on a NFPO's statement of operations (the term sometimes used for a NFPOs "income statement") is called the excess of revenues over expenses. Any "net income" earned by the NFPO is reinvested in the organization. NFPO's are an important component of the Canadian economy.
  - Dalhousie University is an example of an NFPO. A close look at Dalhousie's Balance Sheet reveals that the term equity is substituted with *Net Assets*. Accounts listed under *net assets* for Dalhousie include endowment principal and restricted funds). Try taking a look at your university's financial statements to get a better idea.

Characterisitics of Equity

- Common shares represent the residual ownership in an entity. Common shareholders are entitled to whatever earnings and assets are left over after obligations to creditors (debt holders) and preferred shareholders have been satisfied. In 1999, Laidlaw Inc. (Laidlaw) reported over $2.2 billion of common shares in the equity section of its annual report. In June 2001 Laidlaw filed for Chapter 11 (bankruptcy) under the Companies Creditors' Arrangement Act in Canada. As approved under the plan the equity ownership of the common shareholders was wiped out with no consideration. This meant that if you owned common shares of Laidlaw your shares were rendered worthless.

- Common shares usually carry voting rights and the common shareholders elect the directors of the corporation. The billionaire Barclay brothers are currently battling Conrad Black to buy Britain's Telegraph newspaper owned by Hollinger International (Hollinger). Even though Lord Black owns only 30% of the common shares he controls 72% of the voting rights of Hollinger.
- Preferred shares offer its owners: 1) a preference to dividends over common shares and 2) returns in the form of dividends which are taxed at a much lower level than interest income on debt. In recent years, Nortel Networks Ltd. has continued to pay dividends on their preferred shares having long since eliminated the dividends payable to common shareholders.
- Share repurchases—when shares are repurchased the common stock account is reduced by the average price paid by investors for the common shares. If the shares are repurchased for more than the average price the excess is debited to retained earnings. If less than the average price is paid the shortfall is credited to the contributed surplus account. Share repurchases can strongly express management's belief that shares are undervalued without revealing information that may be sensitive to competition. Vivendi Universal bought 21 million of its own shares in the wake of the September 11, 2001, attacks in a bid to support the company's stock price and intervene on behalf of the small shareholders.

Retained Earnings, Dividends, and Stock Splits

- Property dividends—recorded at the market value of the property distributed on the date the dividend is declared. If the book value of the property is different from the market value a gain or loss is recorded on the income statement

  - A stock split is a division of an entity's shares into a larger number of units, each with a smaller value. No journal entries are required to record a stock split. A stock split has no real economic significance. Some shareholders view a stock split as a win-fall however research has proven that the shareholder is no further ahead after the split.
  - In March 2000 shares of Research In Motion (RIM) were trading around $250 per share ($Cdn). Since most common shares are purchased in lots of 100 units, an investor would have needed $25,000 for a minimum investment into RIM. The Board of Directors of many companies often approve stock splits in order to attract a broader cross-section of shareholders.

Leverage

- In the context of the discussion of leverage uncertainty is introduced as a probability distribution of possible future outcomes. You should not think of the outcome of an uncertain future event as random. For business opportunities, management allocates probabilities to different outcomes (say optimistic, pessimistic, and most likely).

  - The example on page 678 shows net income and return on equity under three different financing arrangements—100% equity, 50% debt/50% equity, and 90% debt. (While not shown, EPS will also be affected.)

    - Leverage serves to increase the variance of possible outcomes. With more debt in the capital structure, the entity can earn a larger ROE but it can also earn a smaller ROE. The effect depends on the return earned on the debt versus the cost of the debt.

- As explained in Chapter 10 the trouble with debt is that interest must be paid regardless of whether the outcome is good or bad. In 2004, Bombardier Inc. reported over $8 billion in long-term debt (the long-term debt has doubled since 1999). With air travel declining in recent years, and with a significant debt-load, many financial analysts have downgraded Bombardier's debt to 'junk' status which signals high risk to investors.
- You might be confused in the example by the fact that ROE increases while net income decreases. The reason is that while net income decreases the amount of equity investment decreases along with the net income.
- Note that the example ignores tax implications, which can have significant implications on the attractiveness of different alternatives. Interest payments are a tax-deductible expense which lowers the cost of borrowing.
- While using large amounts of debt may seem attractive, lenders will demand higher and higher interest on the loans as the amount of debt in the capital structure increases. The increased interest rate is compensation for the increasing risk that lenders face with increasing debt. When Laidlaw's debt-to-equity ratio began to appear too high, bondholders were not willing to increase the company's leverage any more so the company issued more common equity. Strangely, this strategy actually decreased the debt-to-equity ratio.

Economic Consequences

- ♦ Management compensation – lower short-term expenses translate into higher short-term net income and thus more optimistic news reported to the public.

  - ➢ Compliance with debt covenants that are based on accounting measurements – Creditors prefer more conservative accounting since they do not benefit from an increase in corporate profit or an increase in risk in the company's business strategy.
  - ➢ The selling price of an entity when the price is based on net income or other accounting measurements – Deferring expenses may benefit the seller by presenting the entity as having a deceptively inflated income.
  - ➢ The amount of tax an entity pays – Even though CCRA are not fooled easily, tax avoidance is not illegal. Almost every entity will have an objective of minimizing taxes through acceptable accounting practices.
  - ➢ Rate changes for regulated companies when the rate is based on accounting measurements – for example, companies enjoying monopolies may have an incentive to present lower net-incomes to contravene regulatory policies.
  - ➢ The ability of an entity to raise capital (some entities have argued that their ability to raise capital has been adversely affected by certain accounting standards)

Financial Statement Analysis Issues

- ♦ Book value of equity is usually not a good indicator of market value. Reasons for the difference include that assets are not restated to their market values, many assets are not reflected in GAAP financial statements, and future-oriented information is not captured by GAAP accounting. Recent research by Baruch Lev reports that the magnitude of the difference between book and market values has increased in recent years because (he argues) of the increased significance of knowledge-based assets that are not captured by GAAP accounting.

- Two forms of EPS are discussed—basic EPS (which gets most of the attention) and fully diluted EPS (which is discussed briefly).
    - EPS is calculated using the weighted-average number of shares outstanding during the period. Figure 11-3 shows you how to calculate the weighted-average number of shares outstanding.
    - Despite the attention it receives Earnings Per Share (EPS) has a number of significant limitations:
        - Like any ratio, EPS has no absolute meaning. It must be considered in relation to some benchmark. JDS Uniphase Corp. is a fibre optics manufacturer that was once a prominent employer in Ottawa, Ontario. The company has endured a significant downturn in the telecommunications sector but still has a negative EPS since the company literally has no earnings. When a company has a net loss this complicates other ratios such as the Price-to-earnings ratio since again there are no earnings.
        - EPS depends on the accounting policies and estimates reflected in the financial statements.
        - EPS may be affected by changes in the number of shares outstanding during a period. For example, if an entity repurchases some of its shares, EPS will increase.
        - EPS does not indicate the ability or willingness of an entity to pay dividends.
        - It can be very difficult to compare the EPS figures of different entities, not only because of different accounting choices, but because EPS is also affected by how an entity is financed.

- Return on equity – a measure of return earned by resources invested only by the common shareholders. ROE is discussed further in Chapter 13.
    - Alliance Atlantis Communications Inc. the producer of the successful series *CSI: Crime Scene Investigation,* had a -54% return on equity for the nine months ended December 31, 2003. This number does not provide the user with very much information since most of the losses were incurred as a result of severance payments and office closures from the closure of their Entertainment Group division.
    - On the other hand Rothman's Inc., a producer and seller of tobacco products consistently reports an ROE of over 40. Higher ROE's mean an investment is more attractive, but risk must be considered as well when evaluating investments. However, American tobacco companies have recently been battling class-action lawsuits and have, on some occasions, had to settle multi-million dollar claims.
    - Limitations of traditional accounting are again discussed here. It would be easy for you, in light of all these limitations, to conclude that accounting information is not very useful. This conclusion is far from true and could disastrously lead to not using accounting information effectively. The approach taken in this text is to make you aware of the strengths and weaknesses of accounting so that you can be more effective users and preparers of the information.

Study Problems

Study Problem 1 (Equity Transactions) The shareholders' equity section of Douro Ltd.'s balance sheet is shown below:

Douro Ltd.
Extracts from the December 31, 2005 Balance Sheet

Shareholders' Equity	
Preferred Stock (Authorized 500,000, Outstanding 125,000)	$ 3,125,000
Common Stock (Authorized 5,000,000, Outstanding 2,500,000)	4,500,000
Retained Earnings	17,200,000
Total Shareholders' Equity	**$ 24,825,000**

During fiscal 2006, the following occurred:

i. On February 28, 500,000 common shares were issued for $500,000.
ii. On August 31, 375,000 common shares were issued for $875,000.
iii. Dividends on preferred stock of $250,000 were declared and paid.
iv. Dividends on common stock of $1,000,000 were declared and paid.
v. Net income for fiscal 2006 was $4,875,000.

Required:

a. Calculate the weighted-average number of common shares outstanding during the year.
b. Calculate basic earnings per share for the year ended December 31, 2006.
c. Calculate the return on shareholders' equity for the year ended December 31, 2006.
d. Prepare the shareholders' equity section for Douro Ltd.'s December 31, 2006 balance sheet.

Study Problem 2 (Repurchase of shares) For the following two transactions, prepare the required journal entries:

a. On September 9, 2006 Durham Inc. (Durham) announced that it would be repurchasing up to 1,700,000 of its common shares on the open market. On September 16, 2006 Durham repurchased 1,360,000 shares for $17,000,000. On the date of the repurchase Durham had 34,000,000 shares outstanding and the amount in the Common Stock account was $68,000,000.
b. On November 20, 2006 Taunton Ltd. (Taunton) announced that it would be repurchasing up to 725,000 of its common shares on the open market. On November 25, 2006 Taunton repurchased 652,500 shares for $4,350,000. On the date of the repurchase Taunton had 7,250,000 shares outstanding and the amount in the Common Stock Account was $36,250,000.

Study Problem 3 (Accounting for equity transactions) During the year ended September 30, 2006 Chucky's Chicken Schwarma Corp. (Chucky) had the following equity related transactions and economic events. On September 30, 2005 the balance in Chucky's common stock account was $400,000 with 50,000 shares outstanding, the balance in its Preferred Stock account was $0 with no shares outstanding, and Retained Earnings was $237,500.

i. On October 7 Chucky issued 10,000 common shares for $100,000.
ii. On November 25 Chucky issued 2,500 preferred shares for $125,000
iii. On March 31 Chucky paid a dividend of $0.005 per common share.
iv. On June 30 Chucky declared a reverse stock split whereby the number of shares outstanding was reduced by half. A shareholder that had 50 shares before the reverse stock split would have 25 after the split.
v. On September 30 Chucky paid dividends to preferred shareholders of $.10 per share.

vi. On September 30 Chucky paid a dividend of $0.005 per common share.
vii. Net income for 2006 was $115,000.

Required:

a. Prepare the journal entries required to record items (i) through (vi).
b. Prepare the equity section of Chucky's balance sheet on September 30, 2006 and provide comparative information for September 30, 2005.
c. Show the equity section of Chucky's balance sheet as it would have been reported in the September 30, 2005 financial statements. Explain the difference between the equity section for 2005 as reported in the 2006 annual report versus the 2005 annual report.
d. Calculate earnings per share and return on shareholders' equity for the year ended September 30, 2006. If earnings per share for 2005 had been reported as $1.75 per share, what amount would be reported for the year ended September 30, 2005 in the 2006 annual report?
e. How did the reverse stock split affect the performance of Chucky?

Study Problem 4 (Calculating earnings per share) For the year ended December 31, 2005 Widdis Inc (Widdis) reported net income of $1,875,000. On December 31, 2004 Widdis had the following capital stock outstanding:

Preferred stock, no par, $4 annual dividend, cumulative, authorized 30,000 shares outstanding	$ 250,000
Common stock, no par, authorized 400,000 issued and outstanding	2,500,000

On April 22, 2005 Widdis issued 15,000 common shares for $120,000 and on July 31, 2005 it issued 20,000 common shares for $200,000.

Required:

a. Calculate Widdis' basic earnings per share for the year ended December 31, 2005.
b. How much of a dividend should Widdis's shareholders expect to receive in 2005?

Study Problem 5 (Analyzing the effects of different financing alternatives) Madill Ltd. (Madill) is in need of $1,500,000 to finance expansion of its operations. Management is considering three financing alternatives:

i. Issue 200,000 common shares to a group of private investors for $15 per share. In recent years dividends of $.60 have been paid on the common shares.
ii. Issue 80,000 cumulative preferred shares with an annual dividend of $3 per share. The preferred shares are redeemable after 5 years for $27 per share.
iii. Issue a $1,500,000 bond with a coupon rate of 7% per year and maturity in 20 years.

It is now late August 2006. Madill's year end is August 31. Madill plans to raise the needed money at the beginning of its 2007 fiscal year, but management wants to know the financial statement effects and implications of each of the alternatives. Madill's accounting department has provided a projection of the right-hand side of the balance sheet as of August 31, 2007 and a summarized projected income statement for the year ended August 31, 2007. The projected statements do not reflect any of the proposed financing alternatives. If the current expansion plan is successful, Madill anticipates the need to raise additional in the near future. One of Madill's loans has a covenant that requires the debt-to-equity ratio be below 1.0. Madill has a tax rate of 35%.

Madill Ltd.
Summarized Projected Income Statement as of August 31, 2007

Revenue	$	2,850,000
Expenses		2,100,000
Income tax expense		262,500
Net income	**$**	**487,500**

Madill Ltd.
Summarized Projected Liabilities and Shareholders' Equity as of August 31, 2007

Liabilities	$	1,125,000
Shareholders' equity:		
Preferred Stock (400,000 shares authorized, 0 issued)		0
Common Stock (unlimited number of shares authorized, 400,000 outstanding)		1,425,000
Retained Earnings		1,200,000
Total Liabilities and shareholders' equity	**$**	**3,750,000**

Required:

a. Calculate net income for Madill under the three financing alternatives.
b. Calculate basic earnings per share and return on shareholders' equity.
c. Prepare a report to Madill's management explaining the effect of each of the financing alternatives on the financial statements. Include in your report a discussion of the pros and cons of each financing alternative. Also, make a recommendation as to which alternative it should choose. Support your recommendation.

Solutions to Study Problems

Solution to Study Problem 1

a.

Months	Percentage	Number of shares	Weighted average
Jan – Dec	100.0%	2,500,000	2,500,000
Mar – Dec	83.0%	500,000	415,000
Sept – Dec	33.3%	375,000	124,875
Total			**3,039,875**

b.

Net income	$4,875,000
Preferred share dividends	250,000
Income available to common shareholders	$4,625,000

Basic EPS = $4,625,000/3,039,875 = $1.52

c.

Beginning common stock	$ 4,500,000
New issue for cash	500,000
New issue for cash	875,000
Total	$5,875,000

Beginning retained earnings	$17,200,000
Less cash dividend on common	1,000,000
Less cash dividend on preferred	250,000
Plus net income	4,875,000
Ending retained earnings	$20,825,000

Preferred stock	3,125,000
Common stock	5,875,000
Retained earnings	20,825,000
Total shareholders' equity	$29,825,000

Average shareholders' equity:
= ($24,825,000 + $29,825,000)/2 = $27,325,000.

Return on shareholders' equity =

($4,875,000 – 250,000) / 27,325,000 = 16.9%

d.

Preferred stock (authorized 500,000, outstanding 125,000)	$ 3,125,000
Common stock (authorized 5,000,000, outstanding 3,375,000)	5,875,000
Retained earnings	20,825,000
Total shareholders' equity	$29,825,000

Solution to Study Problem 2

a.

Dr. Common stock	2,720,000	
Retained earnings	14,280,000	
Cr. Cash		17,000,000

b.

Dr. Common stock	3,262,500	
Retained earnings	1,087,500	
Cr. Cash		4,350,000

Solution to Study Problem 3

a.

i.

Dr. Cash	100,000	
Cr. Common stock		100,000

ii.

Dr. Cash	125,000	
Cr. Preferred stock		125,000

iii.

Dr. Retained earnings	300	
Cr. Cash		300

iv.
No entry is required.

v.

Dr.	Retained earnings	250	
	Cr. Cash		250

vi.

Dr.	Retained earnings	150	
	Cr. Cash		150

b.

	2005	**2006**
Preferred stock (outstanding 0, 2,500)	$0	$ 125,000
Common stock (outstanding 25,000, 30,000)	400,000	500,000
Retained earnings	237,500	351,800
Total shareholders' equity	$637,500	$976,800

Ending retained earnings = $237,500 – 300 – 250 – 150 + 115,000 = $351,800.

c.

	2005
Common stock (outstanding 50,000)	400,000
Retained earnings	237,500
Total shareholders' equity	$637,500

The shareholders' equity section of the September 30, 2005 balance sheet indicates that 50,000 common shares were outstanding while the comparative information at September 30, 2006 shows that 25,000 shares were outstanding. The reason is the effect of the reverse split during 2006.

d.

Months	Percentage	Number of shares	Weighted average
Oct – Sept	100%	25,000	25,000
Oct - Sept	100%	5,000	5,000
Total			30,000

Net income	$115,000
Preferred share dividends	5,000
Income available to common shareholders	$110,000

Basic EPS = $110,000/30,000 = $3.67

Return on shareholders' equity:

Average shareholders' equity = ($637,500 + $976,800)/2 = $807,150

ROE = $110,000/$807,150 = 13.7%

Since the number of shares from the previous year was halved as a result of the reverse stock split, EPS for 2005 would be reported as $3.50 in the 2006 annual report.

e. There is no reason to expect the reverse stock split to affect the operating results of the company. The motivations for stock splits usually relate to financing considerations, not operating benefits. The reverse split would affect reported EPS but the change in the measurement does not affect the actual performance.

Solution to Study Problem 4

a.

400,000 shares outstanding for 12 months	400,000
15,000 shares outstanding for 8 months	10,000
20,000 shares outstanding for 5 months	8,333
Weighted average shares outstanding	418,333

Net income	$1,875,000
Preferred share dividends	120,000
(Assumes the preferred dividend was paid)	
Income available to common shareholders	$1,755,000

Basic EPS = $1,755,000/418,333 = $4.20

b. No dividends have been declared, but the preferred shareholders are entitled to $4 per share in 2005 for a total of $120,000. Net income does not give a strong clue about the amount of dividends investors should expect. In 2005, no dividends were paid and this might be the best indicator. The ability to pay dividends depends on the availability of cash. The willingness to pay dividends depends on the investment opportunities available and the need for cash of the entity.

Solution to Study Problem 5

a., b.

	Common shares	Preferred shares	Bonds
Revenue	$2,850,000	$2,850,000	$2,850,000
Expenses	2,100,000	2,100,000	2,100,000
Income before interest and taxes	750,000	750,000	750,000
Interest expense	0	0	105,000
Income before tax	750,000	750,000	645,000
Income taxes (35%)	262,500	262,500	225,750
Net income	$487,500	$487,500	419,250
Less preferred dividends	0	240,000	0
Income available to common shareholders	487,500	247,500	419,250
Weighted average common shares outstanding	600,000	400,000	400,000
Basic EPS	$.81	$.62	$1.05
Preferred stock		1,500,000	
Common stock	2,925,000	1,425,000	1,425,000
Retained earnings	1,327,500	1,207,500	1,379,250
Shareholders' equity	$4,252,500	$4,132,500	$2,804,250

Ending common shareholders' equity	$4,252,500	$2,632,500	$2,804,250
Beginning common shareholders' equity	$2,625,000	$2,625,000	$2,625,000
Average common shareholders; equity	$3,438,750	$2,628,750	$2,714,625
Net income less preferred dividends	487,500	247,500	419,250
Return on equity	14.2%	9.4%	15.4%
Liabilities	1,125,000	1,125,000	2,625,000
Debt/equity ratio	0.265	0.272	0.940

Note that because the financing was arranged at the beginning of the year, it would also be reasonable to include the effects of the financing in the beginning shareholders' equity.

c. To the management:

The financing alternatives have significant implications for the future of your firm. If more common shares are issued, the percentage of the voting shares owned by the current shareholders will be significantly diluted, although they will still control the firm. Depending on the distribution of the existing ownership, the new shareholders may represent a very significant voting block. A very important cash flow advantage of common shares is that there is no commitment to make payments of dividends or redeem the shares. The probably that the firm will fail should the investment not pay off as quickly as expected is much lower. If preferred shares are issued, there will be no dilution of control, but the investors in those shares will expect dividends. The $240,000 each year in dividends could create cash flow problems if the firm experiences financial difficulty. While the dividends on the preferred do not have to be paid, failure to do so will make it necessary to not pay dividends on common shares until the preferred dividends are paid up in full. A benefit of preferred shares, however, is that it is a way to raise equity temporarily without sharing fully in the success of the business. The debt alternative has the benefit of tax deductibility but there is a very definite commitment to annual interest payments and the need to refinance the debt in 20 years.

Given the expectation that the firm will continue to expand over the next few years, the long-term plan must include some mix of debt and equity. The question then becomes one of the optimal sequence of issuing each. The debt option raises the risk of violating the 1.0 limit of the debt-to-equity ratio, although if profitability is expected in the near future, retained earnings will grow and shareholders' equity will increase over time. It will likely be advantageous to wait to issue common shares until there is more evidence to support management's predictions of future profits. In that case, fewer shares will need to be issued to raise a given amount of cash and less dilution of control will result. Debt is desirable if future profits and cash flows are fairly certain so that the company can meet its obligations. Debt is preferred since with debt there is no need to share profits. However, the greater the uncertainty about future profits and cash flows (both in timing and amount) the less attractive debt becomes.

Chapter 12
Investments in Other Companies

Chapter Overview

With the development of the global economy and capital markets, many of the organizations in today's world have more than one business entity. These entities could be subsidiaries, joint ventures or partnerships. The primary motivation for covering accounting for investments in other companies was to support your understanding of consolidated financial statements. Investments by one company in another company are very complex and you may feel that the topic goes beyond the scope of an introductory course in accounting. On the other hand, this material is important. The majority of the financial statements that most people come across, the financial statements of public companies are consolidated. If you are to fully understand financial statements you need to understand what consolidated financial statements represent.

When reading this chapter you should cover the main issues in consolidation accounting without getting too much into the mechanics. The emphasis on consolidation accounting is because users of financial statements come in contact with that topic most. One very important section of the chapter is "Are Consolidated Financial Statements Useful?" that begins on page 734. It addresses the benefits and limitations of consolidated financial statements and should be one specific area for your focus.

There are several means for one entity to invest in another entity. For example, common stock carries the advantage of voting rights. With more voting control the parent company may have the ability to influence the subsidiary depending on the degree of control. Debt securities are another means for one entity to invest in another. However, control is not the motive for investing in debt since bonds and other debt securities do not offer the investor voting rights.

The material in this chapter is heavily GAAP based. However, the choices the standard setters made are not the only possible approaches, and alternative approaches could have dramatic effects on the financial statements. For example, non-controlling interest appears on GAAP balance sheets because 100% of a subsidiary's book value of net assets is reported on the balance sheet. If only the parent's share of the net assets were included there would not be any non-controlling interest. Or, if 100% of the fair values of net assets were reported, the amount of non-controlling interest would be different. It is important that you recognize that the GAAP are not the only possible way to conduct accounting practices.

Summary of Key Points

- Some of the reasons why one company will invest in another include:
  - Put idle cash to work.
  - Strategic reasons—to influence or control another entity.
  - Expansion.
  - Ensure markets for their products by buying customers.
  - Ensure the availability of needed inputs.
  - Diversification.

- Control—consolidation accounting. If a parent company controls a subsidiary the parent can make all of the important decisions of the subsidiary.

- Significant influence—equity accounting. If an investor corporation does not control an investee, but can affect its important decisions, the investor corporation is said to have significant influence.

- Passive investment (no influence)—cost method. If the investor corporation (parent) has no influence over the decision making of the investee or at least no more influence than any other small investor, the investment is called a passive investment and it is accounted for using the cost method of accounting.

- Consolidation accounting – most of the financial statements stakeholders analyze are those of public companies, which are usually consolidated.

  - Accordingly, having some understanding of what goes into consolidated financial is necessary for understanding most of the financial statements you will encounter (goodwill, inter-company transactions, non-controlling / minority interest).
  - Control means the investor is able to make the important decisions of the investee and determine its strategic operating, financing, and investing policies on an ongoing basis, without the support of other shareholders.

- Goodwill – the amount a parent pays for a subsidiary over and above the fair value of the subsidiary. Goodwill arises as a residual value in an acquisition. It is a premium paid for the investee's reputation, brand names or other qualities that enable it to earn an excess return on investment, justifying the higher price.

  - The existence of economic goodwill is not the same as accounting goodwill. Accounting goodwill is merely a function of accounting standards.

- The Consolidated Balance Sheet on the Date the Subsidiary is Purchased - key adjustments are:

  - The market values of the subsidiary's net assets are reflected in the consolidated balance sheet;
  - The goodwill purchased is reported in the consolidated financial statements;
  - The Investment in Subsidiary reported on the parent's (not consolidated parent's) balance sheet is eliminated to avoid double counting; and
  - The subsidiary's shareholders' equity is eliminated to avoid double counting.
  - The example in Table 12-2 shows the transition from the individual balance sheets of the parent and subsidiary into the consolidated balance sheet. The example shows and explains the adjustments that must be made to prepare the consolidated balance sheet.

- The Consolidated Balance Sheet in Periods After a Subsidiary is Purchased - key adjustments that are required whenever consolidated balance sheets are prepared:

  - The adjustments that were made on the date a subsidiary was acquired must be made each time (see the above section).
  - Amortization of fair value adjustments;
  - Possible write-down of goodwill;
  - Elimination of the effects of inter-company transactions. Consolidated financial statements are affected by inter-company transactions.

- Non-Controlling (Minority) Interest - represents the equity that non-controlling shareholders of subsidiaries have in the net assets of the subsidiaries. Non-controlling interest arises because 100% of book value of subsidiaries' net assets is reported on the consolidated balance sheet even though the parent does not own 100%.

- Equity accounting is used when the investor has significant influence over the investee. Significant influence means the investor can influence but not control the investee. The *CICA Handbook* suggests that between 20% and 50% of the votes of an investee corporation is an indication of significant influence, but judgment must be used to determine whether significant influence exists in any given situation.

- Passive investments are investments for which the investor corporation cannot influence the strategic decision making of the investee corporation.

Study Points and Study Tips

Control: Accounting for Subsidiaries

- **Current Assets**-current assets of the combined entity in its consolidated balance sheet are the sum of their pre-acquisition current assets less cash used in the investment. This is because the cash used in the investment by the investor to acquire the investee will reduce the current assets of the investor.
- **Non-Controlling Interest**- non-controlling interest accounts are reported in the consolidated financial statements of the parent company. Non-controlling interest appears just above shareholder's equity on the balance sheet. This represents the assets of the investee that are not owned by the investor. Non-controlling interest is not exactly a liability. It should be treated as a credit balance.

  - The *CICA Handbook* also requires that the consolidated income statement report 100% of the revenues and expenses of a subsidiary.

- **Capital Stock**-the capital stock values of the two companies are not added together on the consolidated balance sheet. It is only the capital stock value of the investor that should appear. The share capital of the investor did not change as a result of the acquisition.
- **Retained Earnings**- Retained earnings of the investee are not added to that of the investor.
- **Income Statement**-the revenues and expenses of the investor and investee are combined and then the earnings attributable to the non-controlling shareholders are subtracted.

- Control – the consolidation method should not be applied if:

1) The parent company (investor) has only temporary control over the subsidiary (investee).
2) The subsidiary is not considered to be controlled (despite greater than 50% holding) due to government action, bankruptcy or reorganization of the subsidiary.

- Shell Canada Ltd. (Shell), based in Calgary, is 78% owned by the Royal Dutch Shell group, one of the world's biggest oil companies headquartered in London (England) and the Netherlands. However, Shell Canada Ltd. has no conventional oil production in Canada. In this example, controlling Shell is attractive to the parent company because of its national gasoline station network.

- Significant influence - the actual market value of the investee company plays no role in the reporting of investments under the equity method. However, for financial analysis, market value of the investee company is a better indicator of value.

  - AT & T Wireless Services Inc. is a large investor corporation which holds 20% - 50% ownership in the majority of its investments. For example, AT & Wireless Corp. owns 34% of Rogers Wireless Communications Inc. (Rogers). Recently, AT & T Wireless had attempted to negotiate an agreement whereby they would divest this position however the two entities could not reach an agreement. In essence, divesting is simply the opposite of investing. In this case, Rogers could benefit from the decreased stake of AT & T Wireless since Rogers would gain more control (influence) over its own future direction.

- Passive investment (no influence) – companies have a few different objectives when investing in securities that are publicly traded. Clearly, one objective of investing in another company is control. Return on excess capital is another objective of investing in another company.

  - The *CICA Handbook* provides guidance as to what constitutes a passive investment. Less than 20% of the voting shares is evidence of a passive investment, but judgment is needed to evaluate the specific circumstances. In the business media there is an interesting story about voting shares (control) almost every day.
  - Non-voting securities are always accounted for as passive investments because without voting power it is not possible to have influence.
  - There are two classifications of passive investments:

    - Temporary investments—can be converted to cash reasonably easily and management intends to sell them within a year. Temporary investments are classified as current assets and are subject to the lower of cost and market rule. A temporary purchase of debt or equity securities may be for an entity to capture dividends, interest or capital gains.
    - Portfolio investments—cannot be readily converted to cash within a year or management does not intend to convert them to cash within a year. Portfolio investments are classified as non-current assets. Portfolio investments are written down only if a decline in value is expected to be permanent.

  - The classification of passive investments requires consideration of management intentions so management will be able to pursue its reporting objectives. In these cases management can, for example, increase the entity's reported liquidity by classifying an investment as temporary. A particular classification is not a commitment to sell or not sell an investment. The strategic goal of passive investments may include scientific partnerships, risk-sharing and synergy.
  - It is difficult to see the rationale for reporting publicly traded securities at their cost when market values are readily and objectively available. Also, one has to wonder about conservatism in that temporary investments are written down but not up. Many managers probably prefer that passive investments not be recorded at their market value even if they are publicly traded because the need to write the value of the shares up or down each year would add uncontrollable fluctuation in net income.
  - Both Bell Globemedia (15% investment) and TD Capital Group (14% investment) have a passive investment in Maple Leaf Sports and Entertainment Limited (MLSEL). A couple of hundred million dollars may seem like it could buy these two stakeholders some clout

at the boardroom table. However, the Ontario Teachers' Pension Plan (58% investment) controls the future of the Toronto Maple Leafs, the Toronto Raptors and the Air Canada Centre in Toronto.

- ➢ The procedural material presented is designed to help you understand financial statement information. It is not intended to have you understand the procedures themselves. It is important to focus on the bigger picture of analysis.

- ♦ Exhibit 12-1 provides an extract from the financial statements of Onex Corporation that shows Onex's holdings of companies it controls. Notice how the ownership percentage is often insignificant but the voting control is often dominant. This brings forth the issue of multiple voting shares. Canada has had a long tradition of dual-class shares where the investor corporation has an iron grip on the company. Historically, issuing two classes of shares was a way of raising equity in outside markets while retaining control of the company in Canadian hands.

- ♦ Other prominent Canadian companies having dual-class shares are Shaw Communications Inc., Telus Corp., and CanWest Global Communications Corp. The NYSE has not allowed U.S. companies to introduce dual-class shares since 1994.

Goodwill

- ♦ Goodwill - you may get confused about the fair valuing of assets and liabilities that takes place when a subsidiary is acquired. It is important to emphasize that fair valuing only takes place when the subsidiary is acquired, not each year when consolidated financial statements are prepared.

  - ▸ The story of the changes to the accounting for goodwill is another example of the political nature of accounting. The change is related to the elimination of pooling-of-interests as a method of accounting for acquisitions in the US.
  - ▸ Corporate America was opposed to the elimination of pooling-of-interests accounting, but as part of the compromise that came with the new standard the requirement to amortize goodwill was eliminated. Goodwill did not arise under pooling-of-interests so there were less expense and higher income on the consolidated income statement.
  - ▸ You will find the story behind the change in accounting for goodwill interesting and it emphasizes the complex environment in which accounting operates.

- ➢ While goodwill is attributed to a variety of intangible assets, it is important to emphasize that it is not possible to know what goodwill really is because it is a residual. Also, another explanation for some or the entire amount paid in excess of the fair value of the subsidiaries net assets is that the parent paid too much.
- ➢ Non-controlling interest arises because of how accounting standard setters have chosen to report the net assets of a subsidiary in consolidated financial statements. If a different approach was used the amount of non-controlling interest would be different or wouldn't exist at all. For example, if only the parent's share of a subsidiary's assets and liabilities were included in consolidated statements there would be no need for a non-controlling interest. If 100% of the fair values of assets and liabilities (including the non-controlling shareholders' share of the fair value increases) the amount of non-controlling interest would be different.
- ➢ Hundreds of companies have used off-balance-sheet financing to increase their operations. Investor corporations often increase liabilities associated with operations in which the investor corporation has a non-controlling interest. The fact that the *CICA*

Handbook requires that the consolidated balance sheet include 100% of the subsidiary's liabilities, even though the parent may own less than 100% of those liabilities, is a good thing for stakeholders since it provides more disclosure for decision-making.

Are Consolidated Financial Statements Useful?

- It is important to understand the strengths and limitations of consolidated financial statements and the types of decisions they are or are not relevant for. Consolidated financial statements are very limiting for many users of the financial statements.

  - Private companies might choose not to prepare consolidated financial statements, depending on their circumstances. Consolidated financial statements are not useful for tax purposes and lenders will be most interested in the financial statements that they are actually lending money to. Because a consolidated entity is not a legal entity, it is not actually loaned money.
  - In many private companies, the shareholders will have access to the financial statements of the separate individual corporations with consolidated statements not providing much additional value to them.
  - Aside from public and private corporations, many not-for-profit organizations prepare consolidated financial statements. For example, The Corporation of the City of Peterborough, Ontario (the "City") prepares audited annual consolidated financial statements which are readily available to all (taxpayers) stakeholders for review.
  - These consolidated financial statements reflect the assets, liabilities, sources of financing and expenditures of current funds, reserve funds, and the capital fund of the City. The reporting entity is comprised of all organizations, committees and local boards accountable for the administration of their financial affairs and resources to the City and which are owned or controlled by the City. The City's financial statements include the following fully consolidated local entities such as:

    1) Peterborough Public Library Board
    2) Peterborough Utilities Commission
    3) Peterborough Housing Corporation

  - In addition, another corporate layer exists. The shares of many subsidiaries of the City are owned by The City of Peterborough Holdings Inc. (a holding company created in 1999). In turn, the holding company is wholly owned by the Corporation of the City of Peterborough.
  - The importance of this point is to illustrate that government business entities are now focused on providing greater transparency to stakeholders. The idea of consolidated financial statements is to provide financial information of an entire economic entity, not just about the parent corporation alone. While you may not have a direct 'stake' in Microsoft or Wal-Mart, you are a stakeholder of the community in which you live. For this reason, you should take some time to analyze where your tax dollars are spent (or will be spent).

Study Problems

Study Problem 1 (Calculation of goodwill) On June 30, 2006 Prehistoric Antiques Inc. (Prehistoric) purchased 100% of the common shares of Dinosaur Ltd. (Dinosaur) for $610,000. At the time of the purchase, Prehistoric's management made the following estimates of the fair values of Dinosaur's assets and liabilities:

Assets	$750,000
Liabilities	225,000

Required:

Calculate the amount of goodwill that Prehistoric would report on its June 30, 2006 consolidated balance sheet as a result of its purchase of Dinosaur. How much goodwill would Prehistoric report on its unconsolidated balance sheet on June 30, 2006 as a result of the purchase? Explain.

Study Problem 2 (Comparison of equity and cost methods of accounting) On April 1, 2006 White Hat Inc. (White) purchased 150,000 common shares of Cornwallis Ltd. (Cornwallis) for $675,000. The investment represents a 49% interest in Cornwallis and gives White significant influence over Cornwallis. During fiscal 2006 Cornwallis reported net income of $87,500 and paid dividends of $0.05 per share. No adjustments to Cornwallis's net income for fair value adjustments, inter-company transactions, or goodwill are required. Both companies have March 31 year ends.

Required:

a. Prepare the journal entry that White would make to record its investment in Cornwallis.
b. What amount would be reported on White's March 31, 2007 balance sheet for its investment in Cornwallis? How much would White report on its March 31, 2007 income statement from its investment in Cornwallis?
c. Suppose White used the cost method to account for its investment in Cornwallis. What amounts would be reported on its March 31, 2007 balance sheet and income statement?

Study Problem 3 (Investments with significant influence) On October 1, 2006 Kawartha Spacecraft Inc. (Kawartha) purchased 35% of the voting shares of Bondar Ltd. (Bondar) for $25,000,000 cash. As a result of the purchase, Kawartha has significant influence over Bondar because it can appoint two members of Bondar's board of directors. For the year ended September 30, 2006, Bondar reported net income of $17,500,000. On the date that Kawartha purchased Bondar, the fair value of Bondar's net assets exceeded the book value by $2,500,000. The difference is being amortized over five years. In addition, Kawartha's share of profit on inter-company transactions included in Bondar's net income was $275,000. During fiscal 2006 Kawartha received $325,000 in dividends from Bondar. Kawartha also has a September 30, year end.

Required:

a. Prepare the entry that would be made to record Kawartha' investment in Bondar.
b. What amount would be reported on Bondar's September 30, 2006 income statement as income from its equity investment in Bondar?
c. What amount would be reported on Kawartha's September 30, 2006 balance sheet for investment in Bondar?
d. Why is the amount reported on Kawartha's income statement as income from its equity investment in Bondar not simply Bondar's reported net income multiplied by Kawartha' ownership interest.

Study Problem 4 (Consolidated income statement) Explain how the following items would affect the consolidated net income of Granville Corp. (Granville) in the year the subsidiary Uptown 17 Limited (Uptown) is purchased and the year after it is purchased:

a. Impairment of the value of goodwill.
b. Land with a book value of $34,000,000 on the Uptown's balance sheet on the date the Uptown was purchased has a fair value of $85,000,000 on that date.
c. Machinery with a book value of $17,000,000 on the Uptown's balance sheet on the date the Uptown was purchased has a fair value of $25,500,000 on that date. The machinery has a remaining useful life of six years.
d. Inventory with a book value of $3,400,000 on the Uptown's balance sheet on the date the Uptown was purchased has a fair value of $3,910,000 on that date.
e. Dividends paid by the Uptown to Granville.
f. Services sold at a profit by the Uptown to the Granville.
g. Uptown is 80% owned by Granville.

Study Problem 5 (Inter-company transactions) Port Royal Inc. (Royal) is a 100% owned subsidiary of Crusty Supper Ltd. (Crusty). During the year ended August 31, 2006, Royal sold, on credit, merchandise costing $35,000 to Crusty for $60,000. During fiscal 2006 Crusty sold, on credit, the merchandise it had purchased from Royal to third parties for $100,000. These were the only transactions that Crusty and Royal entered into during 2006 (with each other or with third parties) and there were no other costs incurred.

Required:

a. Prepare an income statement for Royal for the year ended August 31, 2006.
b. What amount of accounts receivable would Royal report on its August 31, 2006 balance sheet?
c. What amount of inventory and accounts payable would Crusty report on its August 31, 2006 balance sheet? Assume that no other inventory existed (other than what has been mentioned in this problem).
d. Prepare Crusty's August 31, 2006 consolidated income statement assuming that inter-company transactions are not eliminated. How much would be reported for accounts receivable, inventory, and accounts payable on the August 31, 2006 consolidated balance sheet?
e. Prepare Crusty's August 31, 2006 consolidated income statement assuming that inter-company transactions are eliminated. How much would be reported for accounts receivable, inventory, and accounts payable on the August 31, 2006 consolidated balance sheet?
f. Discuss the differences in the information you prepared in parts (d) and (e). Which information is more useful to stakeholders? Explain.

Study Problem 6 (Selecting the method for accounting) Otonabee Inc. (Otonabee) owns 35% of the issued share capital of Cavan Ltd. (Cavan). While the directors of Otonabee attend board meetings of Cavan, Cavan is managed independently. Cavan merely informs Otonabee about its activities through board meetings and management reports.

Required:

When Otonabee prepares its financial statements, which reporting method should be used to present its investment in Cavan? Explain.

Study Problem 7 (Consolidated balance sheet) Annapolis Inc. (Annapolis) owns 80% of Crab Cake Corp. (Crab). Cash paid for the investment is $100,000. Since acquisition, Crab shares fell in value by 20%, causing Annapolis's investment in Crab to be $80,000 in market value terms. Net income of Crab was $50,000. Given below are the accounts prepared before acquisition.

Pre-acquisition Balance Sheet	**Annapolis**	**Crab**
Current Assets	$600,000	$200,000
Other Assets	400,000	100,000
Total	1,000,000	300,000
Current Liabilities	500,000	175,000
Common Stock	350,000	75,000
Retained Earnings	150,000	50,000
Total	1,000,000	300,000

Required:

Please prepare the post-acquisition balance sheet using the consolidation method.

Case Study

Slippery Pickerel Securities Ltd. (Slippery) is a public corporation; a regional investment adviser registered with the Investment Advisers Association of Canada (IAA). Financial statements are used to determine bonuses for partners, directors and senior officers, file tax returns, and to satisfy the local credit union (lender). Sales in 2005 were $10,500,000 mostly from commissions and fees charged to clients. You are the president of your university's Business Students' Association and have summer employment with a mid-sized national accounting firm. You have been asked by Slippery's CEO, Frank Fillet (Fillet), to review accounting policy for the investments Slippery has accumulated over the last 5 years.

Icy Insurance Services Ltd. (Icy)

Slippery bought 10,000 shares of Icy, a life insurance company, three years ago for $50 per share. Icy has 200,000 shares outstanding. The investment has been reported as a passive investment. No dividends have been declared on the shares. Last year, the market values were in the $20 - $25 range. Slippery now reports the investment as long-term and Fillet has stated that Slippery would never sell the investment unless market values return to $50. Fillet is confident that this will be the case in five to 10 years.

Machiavellian Mortgage Services Ltd. (Machiavellian)

Slippery owns 40% of the shares of the outstanding shares of Machiavellian and has 8 of 20 members on the board of directors. The remaining 60% of the shares are widely held (no more than 2% of the voting shares are held by any one individual or entity.) The remaining directors are not a unified group and, because of this, Slippery's representatives are very involved in the decision-making process. Machiavellian is a company that provides high ratio mortgage financing for first time homebuyers. Machiavellian is in a weak financial position due to several bad loans and rising interest rates. Slippery owns convertible preferred shares issued by Machiavellian. If converted, Slippery could exchange their preferred shares for 15% of Machiavellian's common shares.

Crafty Consulting Services Ltd. (Crafty)

Slippery owns 5,000 (5%) of the voting common shares of Crafty, a financial planning consulting business, and has one seat on Crafty's 15-member board. Crafty has never declared any dividends and earnings are minimal.

Required:

Please prepare a report explaining how Slippery accounts for investments in other corporations and how these investments affect the financial statements.

Solutions to Study Problems

Solution to Study Problem 1

Fair market value of assets	$750,000
Fair market value of liabilities	225,000
Fair market value of net assets	$525,000
Price paid for 100% of common shares	$610,000
Goodwill	$ 85,000

Goodwill is the amount a parent company pays for a subsidiary over and above the fair value of the subsidiary's identifiable assets and liabilities on the date the subsidiary is purchased.

Prehistoric will not report goodwill on its unconsolidated balance sheet since the investment in the subsidiary is represent by the one line on the balance sheet. The goodwill will not be represented on Dinosaur's balance sheet either because goodwill only appears if purchased.

Solution to Study Problem 2

a.

Dr.	Investment in Cornwallis	675,000	
	Cr. Cash		675,000

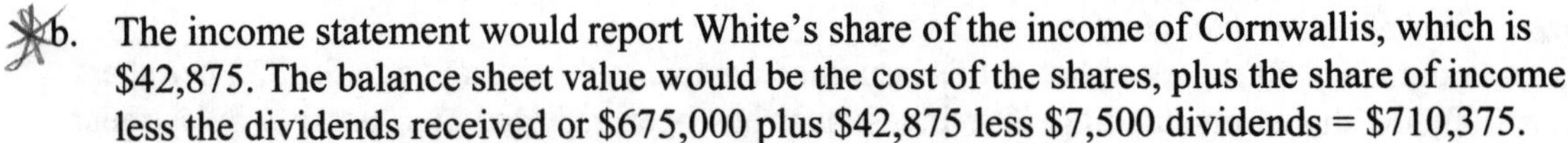

b. The income statement would report White's share of the income of Cornwallis, which is $42,875. The balance sheet value would be the cost of the shares, plus the share of income less the dividends received or $675,000 plus $42,875 less $7,500 dividends = $710,375.

c. With the cost method, the balance sheet would report the $675,000 cost and the income statement would report the $7,500 dividend income.

Solution to Study Problem 3

a.

Dr.	Investment in Bondar	25,000,000	
	Cr. Cash		25,000,000

b.

Share of net income of Bondar (35% of $17,500,000)	$6,125,000
Less amortization of FMV Adjustments ($2,500,000/5)*.35	175,000
Less share of profits on inter-company transactions	275,000
Adjusted income from Bondar	$5,675,000

c. The amount on the balance sheet would be $25,000,000 plus $5,675,000 adjusted net income less the dividends of $325,000 for a net of $30,350,000.

d. The reason is that there is no need for Bondar to make the same adjustments for inter-company transactions or the amortization of the fair market value adjustments. These adjustments are reflective of the value of certain assets on the date the shares were purchased and of the need to eliminate the inter-company transactions.

Solution to Study Problem 4

a. According to the *CICA Handbook* goodwill does not have to be amortized. Management must regularly evaluate the company's goodwill and write it down if its value is somehow impaired. Impairment of goodwill will result in a write-down (expense) and reduce income when it is recognized.

b. Land is a capital asset that is not amortized because it does not wear out and does not become obsolete. Since the fair value adjustments on the land will not be amortized, there will be no effect on net income in any year. An exception to this rule is land that is used for extracting natural resources. In that case the cost of land is expensed as the resource is taken from the land or "used up".

c. The full cost of Uptown's capital assets ($25,500,000) are reported in the consolidated financial statements and must be amortized; not just the portion reported that is reported in Uptown's financial statements ($17,000,000). The amortization of the $8,500,000 fair value increment will decrease income by $1,416,666.67 for each of the six years.

d. The fair value of the inventory on hand when Uptown was purchased was different from the cost of the inventory reported on Uptown's balance sheet. The fair value adjustment on the inventory will reduce Granville's income by $510,000 in the year the inventory is sold.

e. If Granville was short of cash they could have Uptown declare a dividend to help it meet its cash needs. However, consolidated statements eliminate the need for inter-company transactions. Income will not be affected by dividends paid to Granville.

f. Inter-company transactions are eliminated on consolidation so inter-company revenues, expenses, and profits do not affect the consolidated statements. Transactions within a consolidated group do not have any economic significance from the perspective of the parent. Granville could improve its reported economic or financial position by ordering the transaction.

g. The minority interest on the income statement represents the portion of net income of Granville that belongs to the shareholders of Uptown. Minority interest arises in consolidated financial statements when a parent owns less than 100% of the common shares of the subsidiary because GAAP requires that the consolidated statements include 100% of the subsidiary's revenues and expenses. The minority interest in the profits will reduce net income.

Solution to Study Problem 5

a. to e.

	Crusty	Royal	Unadjusted Consolidated	Adjusted Consolidated
Revenue	$100,000	$60,000	$160,000	$100,000
Cost of Sales	60,000	35,000	95,000	35,000
Net income	40,000	25,000	65,000	65,000
Accounts Receivable	$100,000	$60,000	$160,000	$100,000
Accounts Payable	60,000		60,000	0
Inventory	0	0	0	0

f. The information prepared in part e) is much more useful. The consolidated income statement indicates the same income but revenues and cost of sales are distorted when the inter-company transactions are not eliminated. The balance sheet without the eliminations is also misleading because the consolidated entity does not owe any payables and has only $100,000 in accounts receivable.

Solution to Study Problem 6

Even though Otonabee owns more than 20% of Cavan, it is not appropriate to consolidate its accounts with Cavan. Judgement must be used to determine whether significant influence exists in this particular situation. The rationale for the *equity method* is that if Otonabee had significant influence, it could affect the important policies of Cavan such as the timing and amount of dividends. However, the percentages serve as a guide only. In this case, Otonabee should report its investment in Cavan using the *cost method* and not the *equity method.* The *cost method* will treat Otonabee and Cavan as two separate entities. Only the dividends received from Cavan and changes in the market value of Cavan will be recognized by Otonabee under this method.

Even if Otonabee owned over 50% of Cavan, but had no control or influence over Cavan's operations, their accounts should not be consolidated. This is because consolidation will represent Otonabee and Cavan as one organization with unified operations, but in reality they are not.

Solution to Study Problem 7

Post-acquisition Balance Sheet	Consolidated
Current Assets	$700,000
Other Assets	500,000
Total	1,200,000
Current Liabilities	675,000
Non-controlling Interest	25,000
Common Stock	350,000
Retained Earnings	150,000
Total	1,200,000

Amount paid by Annapolis to acquire 80% of Crab is exactly equal to 80% of Crab's net asset value in this case (Note: 80% of Crab net asset value = 80% x (300,000 – 175,000) = $100,000. If the amount paid was more than $100,000, the excess would be treated as goodwill and appear as an intangible asset in the consolidated balance sheet.

Solution – Case Study

Summary

Slippery Pickerel Securities Ltd. (Slippery) is a public corporation; a regional investment adviser registered with the Investment Advisers Association of Canada (IAA). Financial statements are used to determine bonuses for partners, directors and senior officers, file tax returns, and to satisfy the local credit union (lender). Slippery has invested in three other corporations

Icy Insurance Services Ltd.

The cost of this investment is $500,000 (10,000 x $50); market value ranged between $200,000 and $250,000 (at $20 - $25) this year. Slippery intends to keep the investment until market values improve, and seems to have a five to ten year time horizon in mind. The investment is classified as a portfolio investment. LCM write-downs are not made to portfolio investments unless the decline in market value is not temporary. Five to ten years signifies permanence. Since Slippery does not plan to sell the investment in the coming year, it is properly classified as a portfolio investment; since this is the first year for a material decline in market value, no write-down is necessary. This situation is a bit manipulative but within GAAP guidelines. Slippery clearly does not wish to write down the investment and does not have to. Market values are available each day from the stock exchange listings.

Machiavellian Mortgage Services Ltd.

Slippery owns 40% of the shares of Machiavellian, and has 8 of 20 members on the board of directors. Slippery would expect to exert significant influence with this degree of ownership, and thus the equity method would be appropriate. The remaining 60% of the shares are widely held (no more than 2% of the voting shares are held by any one individual or entity). The equity method of accounting is essentially the same as accounting for subsidiaries using the consolidation method. There is evidence of significant influence - the Slippery directors may demonstrate their effective influence over the Machiavellian board. Slippery owns convertible preferred shares (exchangeable for another 15% of the common shares). If Slippery acquired these shares, they would have 55%, and, if represented by a majority on the board, would have control.

Crafty Consulting Services Ltd.

Slippery owns 5% of the voting shares of Crafty and has one seat on the 15-member board. Significant influence does not exist and the cost method should be used. The cost method serves other reporting objectives quite well. Cost and equity might be similar given low earning levels and no dividends.

Chapter 13
Analyzing and Interpreting Financial Statements

Chapter Overview

At this point you should be comfortable picking up a set of financial statements and making sense of the reported figures and not be intimidated by the numbers or by the notes explaining them. You should be able to ask insightful questions about financial statements and understand the power that the managers who prepare the statements have over what's in them. The text has also tried to build a set of analytical tools that provide you with the ability to do some digging into the numbers. Chapter 13 tries to enhance the kit of analytical tools so you can do solid analysis of financial statements. Many of the tools and techniques (in particular the financial ratios) have been presented elsewhere in the book.

This chapter introduces some new concepts, particularly permanent and transitory earnings and quality of earnings. These topics integrate well with some of the major themes of the text. Also consistent with some of the major themes of the text are the limitations and caveats regarding financial statements and financial statement analysis. You are reminded that accounting information does not provide truth or certainty—accounting is an important source of information that must be well understood to be used effectively.

In the chapter the ratios and tools are grouped into four categories:

- Evaluating performance
- Liquidity
- Solvency and leverage
- Other common ratios

These four categories have been discussed elsewhere in the text. In this chapter the coverage has been grouped so that you grasp a more thorough view of the material. In addition, common size financial statements and trend analysis, which have not been covered previously in the text, are introduced.

Chapter 13 begins with a reminder of how Chapter 1 of the text began—that using accounting information requires detective work. You are reminded that accounting information is vital for learning about, and understanding an entity, but that using the information can be challenging, and getting answers to questions is not always straightforward.

Summary of Key Points

- Users analyze financial statements to help them make better decisions. Different decisions require different tools and techniques. The tools and techniques introduced in this chapter will help you solve financial analysis problems. The most valuable skill that you can learn is how to choose the appropriate tool for the task at hand.
- Accounting information is not the only source of information about an entity. Other places where stakeholders can obtain information such as the management discussion and analysis section of public companies' annual reports is discussed.
- Earnings can be viewed as having two elements for purposes of predicting earnings:
    - Permanent earnings: earnings expected to be repeated in the future.
    - Transitory earnings: earnings not expected to be repeated in future periods.

- The *CICA Handbook* requires, or allows, disclosure of information that is helpful for understanding the components of earnings. Three areas discussed are:

  - Extraordinary items
    - not expected to occur frequently
    - not typical of the entity's business
    - not the result of decisions by the managers or owners of the entity
  - Unusual items
    - Revenue, expenses, gains, and losses that do not meet the definition of an extraordinary item but,
    - That is not expected to occur frequently or that is not considered part of the normal business activities of the entity
    - The *CICA Handbook* requires separate disclosure of these items
  - Discontinued operations
    - A business segment that an entity has stopped operating or plans to stop operating
    - The *CICA Handbook* requires separate disclosure in the income statement
    - Separate disclosure occurs when the decision has been made to stop operating the segment

- Earnings quality refers to the usefulness of current earnings for predicting future earnings. There are other definitions used as well, such as its correlation with cash flows. For this text, earnings quality is high if there is a close relationship between current earnings and future earnings. Thus, if an entity's earnings contain a lot of transitory elements, its earnings would be considered to be of low quality.

- Ratios and other analytical tools covered in this section:

Performance measures

- Gross margin percentage
- Profit margin ratio
- Return on assets.
- Return on equity

- Liquidity measures

- Current ratio
- Quick ratio
- Accounts receivable turnover ratio
- Inventory turnover ratio
- Accounts payable turnover ratio
- Average payment period for accounts payable
- Cash lag

- Solvency and leverage measures

- Debt-to-equity ratio
- Debt-to-total assets ratio
- Interest coverage ratio (cash and accrual).

- Other ratios

- Price-to-earnings ratio
- Dividend payout ratio

  - Common size financial statements – the amounts in the balance sheet and income statement are expressed as other elements in the same year's statements.

- Trend analysis – the amounts in the balance sheet and income statement are expressed as a percentage of a base year set of financial statements.

♦ The limitations and caveats discussed in this section are:
- GAAP financial statements are historical.
- Managers prepare financial statements.
- Financial statements are not comprehensive.
- Accounting policy choices and estimates affect ratios.
- Comparing financial statements can be difficult to do.
- Financial statements are not the only source of information.
- Financial analysis is a diagnostic tool.
- Explanations for problems that are identified are not necessarily provided.

Study Points and Study Tips

Why Analyze and Interpret Financial Statements?
Try to think about the different decisions that various stakeholders have to make and how different tools and different information would be appropriate for the decisions each has to make.

This section explains why users analyze and interpret financial statements, and also looks specifically at creditors and equity investors to give some perspective on the different interests that different stakeholder groups bring to the analysis of financial statements.

Know the Entity
♦ Financial statements are only one source of information about an entity.

- The more one knows about an entity, its industry, its economic environment, and so on, the more informative financial statements are.
- The management discussion and analysis is a valuable source of information that is provided in the annual reports of public companies (they are not required by private companies). The MD&A is intended to provide readers with a view of the entity through the eyes of management.

Permanent Earnings and the Quality of Earnings
♦ There is evidence that managers try to manage their financial statements by disclosing bad news events as unusual or in a way that makes them appear transitory, whereas on the other hand, they try to make good news events appear to be permanent.

- Despite this assistance that GAAP provides to distinguish permanent from transitory earnings, GAAP is still a historical-based measurement system. As a result, it can only serve as a baseline for forecasting future earnings. GAAP does not reflect changes that will affect financial statement measurements in future periods.
- Many stakeholders want to use financial statements to predict future earnings. For example, the focus of equity analysts of public companies is the estimation of future earnings. People then compare the actual performance with the estimated performance as a basis for determining success.
- Three categories of disclosures required under GAAP that help users distinguish permanent from transitory earnings:

1) Extraordinary items (EOI) — Exhibit 13-1 provides an example of an EOI from TransAlta Corporations 2000 financial statements. (The example is not an exciting one but EOIs are very rare now.) The designation as extraordinary indicates that an event is transitory. Since extraordinary items are considered to be non-recurring they are reported after income (earnings) from continuing operations.

Extraordinary items are unusual and infrequent gains (losses). Even though most gains (losses) may be either unusual or infrequent, very few gains (losses) are both unusual and infrequent and thus qualify as extraordinary items. Some examples of extraordinary items are:

- expropriations by governments
- gain (loss) from early retirement of debt
- uninsured losses due to natural disasters

2) Unusual items—revenue, expenses, gains, and losses that do not meet the definition of an extraordinary item, but that are not expected to occur frequently, or that are not considered part of the normal business activities of the entity. Unusual items are included in income (earnings) from continuing operations.

Examples of unusual items include:

- impairments and write-offs
- provisions from environmental remediation and litigation
- gain (loss) from sale of investment in a subsidiary
- gain (loss) from a disposal of a business segment and restructuring costs

- ▸ The *CICA Handbook* does not require a transaction or event be designated as unusual, just that it be separately disclosed. As a result, users of the financial statements must carefully evaluate and consider the items reported in the income statement and disclosed in the notes to assess the implications an event may have for future periods.
- ▸ Exhibit 13-2 gives an example of unusual item disclosure from Alliance Forest Products Inc.'s 2000 Annual Report, including extracts for the company's management discussion and analysis; Exhibit 13-3 provides extracts from Rogers Communications Inc.'s 2000 financial statements, which includes a number of items that could be considered unusual.

3) Discontinued operations—a business segment that an entity has stopped operating or plans to stop operating. Exhibit 13-4 provides Cambior Inc.'s discontinued operations disclosures from its 2000 financial statements.

When an entity discontinues a part of its operations, any revenues or expenses, and gains or losses due to disposal of assets are separated from the income (earnings) from continuing operations.

Using Ratios to Analyze Accounting Information

The section examines four analytical themes: evaluating performance, liquidity, solvency, leverage, and other common ratios. The section also introduces common size financial statements and trend analysis.

- At the outset you are advised to keep in mind that:
    - There are no GAAP for ratio analysis or financial statement analysis. A person can modify or create any ratios that he or she feels is appropriate for the intended purpose. What is important is making sure that the right tool is used for the task at hand.
    - While many of the topics, ratios, and tools are presented separately in this section, they cannot be considered independently. The information obtained from different analyses often has to be integrated to obtain the most informed insights.
    - Financial information has to be integrated with information from other sources to get a more complete picture of the entity and its circumstances.
    - Materiality is important. Small changes in some accounts can be very significant and important, whereas large changes in other accounts may be unimportant.
    - Financial statement information cannot be interpreted in a vacuum. The information must be compared to previous years' information from the same entity, the performance of other entities, industry standards, forecasts, and other benchmarks.

Common Size Financial Statements or Vertical Analysis

- Common-size financial statements are an analytical tool in which the amounts in the balance sheet and income statement are expressed as percentages of other elements in the statements.

    - In common-size balance sheets, all figures are expressed as a percentage of total assets.
    - In common-size income statements, all figures are expressed as a percentage of revenue.
    - This technique is very useful to analyze the performance of the firm over time. For example, this technique can be used to study how gross margin of the entity is behaving over time. It is also useful to compare the performance of entities with different sizes. For example, comparing the margins of a small local convenience store with Wal-Mart.

Horizontal Analysis and Trend Statements

- In horizontal analysis all items in the first year (base year) are stated at 100% and in the following years each item is expressed as a percentage of the same item in the base year.

    - Trend statements give a better indication of growth and decline than do common size financial statements because the proportion in the trend data is relative to another year.

Evaluating Performance

- **Gross Margin**-a measure of operating profitability. Gross margin is often stated as a percentage of sales and called gross margin percentage.
- **Return on Investment**-an entity can have a high gross margin, but the amount of investment required to earn those margins might indicate that the performance was not that great.
- **Earnings per Share**-the most commonly used statistic to track an entity's performance. Although the calculation should be simple, the complication arises when there are changes in the number of outstanding shares. The calculation is also problematic when an entity has no earnings.
- **Liquidity Ratios (current ratio, quick ratio, receivables turnover, etc.)**-measure an entity's ability to meet its current obligations. For example, an excessively long receivables collection period may indicate that an entity is having problems collecting payments from its customers.
- **Solvency and Leverage (debt-to-equity, interest coverage, etc.)**-measures of financial risk arising due to the fixed financial obligations of the firm.

Limitations and Caveats about Analyzing Financial Statements
This section explains that while accounting information and financial statement analysis can provide valuable insights about an entity, they are not like magic potions. There are limitations and caveats that you must be aware of before launching into an analysis.

- ♦ GAAP itself is the source of many limitations because of GAAPs assumptions, qualitative characteristics, and measurement characteristics (see Chapter 5). It is important to emphasize that the limitations and caveats do not make financial statements and ratio analysis useless. Do not overreact to limitations and overstate the impact of limitations. You should be reminded that limitations do not render accounting information useless. Rather it is important for accounting information to be used prudently and appropriately.

    - ▪ Earnings management can sometimes lower earnings quality because by moving earnings among periods the relationship between current and future earnings can be distorted.
    - ▪ However, some accounting choices can improve earnings quality by making reported earnings more predictive of future earnings. Some of the accounting choices that are left to management's discretion by GAAP include:
        - choice of inventory method
        - choice of amortization method
        - estimates of economic lives and salvage values of assets
        - recognition of impairment of assets
        - capitalization of expenses
        - choice of method of recording leases
        - classification and timing or non-recurring gains and losses

    - ➢ The section introduces a useful equation for understanding the relation between earnings and cash flow and the impact of accrual accounting choices on earnings over time. The equation is: *Earnings = Cash from operations + Accruals*
    - ➢ The equation shows that by making accounting choices that alter the timing of accrual, earnings changes. The cash flow component can be thought of as being fixed in a given year. Accounting choices don't affect the timing of actual payments and collections. (This is not completely true since payments based on accounting measurements can change with accounting numbers but generally it is true.) Accounting choices by managers affect earnings by changing the amount and timing of accruals.
    - ➢ Financial ratios are only as good as the financial statement figures from which they are compiled.
    - ➢ Many large (global) entities diversify into a number of sectors thus finding comparable entities can be problematic.
    - ➢ Comparing the ratios of entities from different countries presents additional difficulty due to large differences in accounting practices in financial reports.

Indicators of high and low earnings quality
- ♦ Since accounting policies leave some flexibility in their interpretation and some entities are known to have exploited their flexibility to manipulate earnings, users need to be aware of the strategies preparers use to influence reported earnings.

    - ▪ If an entity maintains conservative practices and completely avoids creative accounting it has high quality earnings. In contrast, if a firm adopts aggressive accounting policies and practices, it has a low earnings quality.

Good quality for users (Income Statement):

- conservative revenue recognition
- use of the completed-contract method rather than the percentage-of-completion method
- very few unusual or extraordinary items
- expensing of all operational expenses, interest expenses, etc
- expensing of all restructuring charges

Good quality for users (Balance Sheet):

- use of LIFO for inventory during periods of increasing prices
- sufficient bad debt provisions
- using accelerated amortization instead of straight-line amortization
- short economic lives for assets with low salvage values
- no off-balance-sheet financing such as operating leases
- understandable, dependable and sufficient disclosures
- sufficient provisions for employee benefit plans

▪ Quality of earnings can also be affected by an entity's operating decisions—the timing of its actual transactions.

▪ Cutting back spending on advertising or research that management does not believe is productive makes sense. However, cutting these expenditures just to boost the bottom line can be counter-productive.

➢ Return on assets (ROA) is presented slightly different here than it was in Chapter 9. Here the emphasis is placed on the components of ROA (asset turnover and profit margin) and how ROA is related to ROE. The difference in presentation is that the numerator of the ROA is simply stated as income rather than net income plus the after-tax interest cost. This could result in some confusion as you may use either formula in the end of chapter problems.

Why do managers manipulate financial statements?

1) In order to provide incentive to management, compensation structures are often aligned with corporate profits. When short-term profits increase the investing public gets excited creating demand for the shares of that entity. Since management are usually shareholders (options as well) managers can personally benefit from this type of short-term manipulation.

2) Manipulating financial information is not very difficult. Preparers of accounting information provide the minimum amount of information necessary to comply with reporting requirements. Moreover, managers elect accounting methods from a variety of suitable choices. Much of the advantage the preparer has is due to:
   - the substantial flexibility in interpreting GAAP
   - GAAP is often applied in ways that improve an entity's profits
   - Changes in GAAP take years to occur long after the damage has been done

3) Management is not very likely to get caught. Very few investors that have had personal gains from misleading financial statements have ever complained. Investors only complain when they lose money. Also, until recently, government authorities and self-regulatory bodies have not been aggressive enough in pursuing such manipulation of financial statements. In addition, independent auditors have been reluctant to reveal

financial reporting problems since accounting firms earn millions of dollars in fees from large corporations (and corporations are not required to file audited quarterly financial statements).

Study Problems

Study Problem 1 (Using common size and trend statements to evaluate performance) The income statements of Xaverian Corp. (Xaverian) for the years ended May 31, 2004 through 2006 are shown below:

Xaverian Corp.
Income Statements
For the Years Ended May 31

	2006	2005	2004
Sales	$ 525,000	$ 650,000	$ 780,000
Cost of Sales	315,000	357,500	429,000
Gross Margin	210,000	292,500	351,000
Selling, general, and administrative expenses	75,000	70,000	65,000
Amortization expense	10,000	15,000	20,000
Interest expense	15,000	20,000	25,000
Unusual income	130,000	-	-
Income before taxes	240,000	187,500	241,000
Income tax expense	72,000	56,250	72,300
Net income	**$ 168,000**	**$ 131,250**	**$ 168,700**

Required:

a. Prepare common size and trend financial statements for Xaverian.
b. Use this information from part (a) to evaluate the performance of Xaverian. Explain fully. Your evaluation should include a comparison of Xaverian's performance from year-to-year.
c. How does the unusual income affect your ability to evaluate the performance of Xaverian and to interpret your common size and trend financial statements?

Study Problem 2 (Determining the effects of transactions on ratios) Jane Finch, CFA is a junior financial analyst with Black Creek Asset Management. She has been asked to complete the following table by indicating whether the following transactions or economic events would increase, decrease, or have no effect on the financial ratios listed. She should consider each item independently. State any assumptions she should make. Explain her reasoning.

	Interest Coverage Ratio	Accounts Receivable Turnover	Price-to-earnings Ratio	Return on Assets	Gross Margin Ratio
Ratio before the transactions / economic events	**4.50**	**7.25**	**10.0**	**15%**	**31.5%**
a. Declaration and payment of dividends on common shares.					
b. Write-off of an accounts receivable.					
c. Purchase of advertising costing $17,000.					

d. Sale of land that had a book value of $150,000 when it was sold.					
e. Announcement of a lost contract with a long time customer. The announcement was unexpected by the capital markets.					
f. Write-off of obsolete inventory. The company does this each year.					

Study Problem 3 (Evaluating accounts receivable) Golden Gael Inc. (Golden) is a small accounting firm (partnership) that provides a wide range of tax, audit and consulting services to local individuals and businesses. Individual client's pay cash, while Golden offers its business client's 60 days from the date that the services have been rendered to pay amounts owing. You have been provided with the following information from Golden's accounting records.

	2003	2004	2005	2006
Accounts receivable (on December 31)	$ 13,500	$ 15,000	$ 17,000	$ 18,750
Sales (for the year ended)		190,000	201,250	218,750
Proportion of sales to business clients		60%	70%	80%

Required:

a. Calculate Golden's accounts receivable turnover ratio for 2004, 2005, and 2006.
b. Calculate Golden's average collection period of accounts receivable for 2004, 2005, and 2006.
c. Assess how well Golden is managing its accounts receivable over the three year period.
d. What are some possible explanations for why Golden's collection is less than 60 days? What steps might Golden's management take to reduce the collection period further?
e. Suppose you did not know what the proportion of Golden's sales to business clients' was. How would your calculation of the accounts receivable turnover ratio and the average collection period of accounts receivable be affected? How would your interpretation of the performance of Golden's management be affected?

Study Problem 4 (Understanding return on assets) You are provided with the following information about Pier 21 Corp. (Pier), an integrated tour company in the Maritimes.

	2006	2005	2004	2003	2002
Sales	$375,000	$250,000	$175,000	$125,000	
Net income	115,000	70,000	45,000	30,000	
Total liabilities (at year end)	150,000	145,000	137,500	130,000	115,000
Shareholders' equity (at year end)	120,000	117,500	115,000	110,000	85,000

Required:

a. Calculate Pier's return on assets by determining its profit margin and asset turnover ratio. Assume that profit margin equals net income divided by sales.
b. Calculate Pier's return on equity by using its return on assets and its financial leverage.
c. Explain why it is not possible for an entity's return on assets to be greater than its return on equity.
d. Assess the profitability of Pier. In your response, explain the reasons for any changes in Pier's profitability.

Study Problem 5 (Evaluating performance) Gzowski Ltd. (Gzowski) is an international media company and operates in a highly competitive industry. Price is very important to most customers and it is very difficult for medium sized operators such as Gzowski to differentiate based on product quality. It is possible to differentiate based on service, but most competitors offer reasonably comparable service packages.

The president of Gzowski is reviewing the company's performance in 2005. During 2005, sales increased by 21% to $6,125,000. Average total assets for the year were $1,950,000, net income was $300,000, and interest expense was $90,000. Gzowski's tax rate is 25%.

The president believes that Gzowski can improve its performance in 2006. She would like to see a 20% growth in sales in 2006 and a return on assets of 25%. The president estimates that it will be necessary to increase assets by 15% in 2006. The president does not think that any additional borrowing will be required and, as a result, the interest expense for 2006 will be the same as for 2005.

Required:

a. Calculate Gzowski's profit margin, asset turnover, and return on assets for 2005.
b. What asset turnover ratio is required in 2006 to achieve the president's objectives? What net income is needed to achieve her objectives? What would the profit margin be if the objectives are achieved? For purposes of this question use net income plus the after tax cost of interest.
c. Do you think the president's objectives are reasonable?

Solutions to Study Problems

Solution to Study Problem 1

a.

Xaverian Corp.
Common size income statements
For the years ended May 31

		2006			2005			2004	
Revenue	$	525,000	100.0%	$	650,000	100.0%	$	780,000	100.0%
Cost of sales		315,000	60.0%		357,500	55.0%		429,000	55.0%
Gross margin		210,000	40.0%		292,500	45.0%		351,000	45.0%
SG&A expenses		75,000	14.3%		70,000	10.8%		65,000	8.3%
Amortization expense		10,000	1.9%		15,000	2.3%		20,000	2.6%
Interest expense		15,000	2.9%		20,000	3.1%		25,000	3.2%
Unusual income		130,000	24.8%		-	0%		-	0%
Income before income taxes		240,000	45.7%		187,500	28.9%		241,000	31.9%
Income tax expense		72,000	13.7%		56,250	8.7%		72,300	9.3%
Net income		168,000	32.0%		131,250	20.1%		168,700	21.6%

Xaverian Corp.
Trend income statements
For the years ended May 31

		2006			2005			2004	
Revenue	$	525,000	.67	$	650,000	.83	$	780,000	1.00
Cost of sales		315,000	.73		357,500	.83		429,000	1.00
Gross margin		210,000	.60		292,500	.83		351,000	1.00
SG&A expenses		75,000	1.15		70,000	1.08		65,000	1.00
Amortization expense		10,000	.50		15,000	.75		20,000	1.00
Interest expense		15,000	.60		20,000	.80		25,000	1.00
Unusual income		130,000	-		-	-		-	-
Income before income taxes		240,000	1.00		187,500	.78		241,000	1.00
Income tax expense		72,000	1.00		56,250	.78		72,300	1.00
Net income		168,000	1.00		131,250	.78		168,700	1.00

b. Xaverian Corp. has not performed well over the three year period. Gross margin has decreased over the three-year period, although we cannot tell how that compares to other firms in the industry. From the common-sized financial statements, we observe that the cost of sales was constant in 2004 and 2005, but increased as a percentage of sales by almost 5% in 2006, which suggests that the company has experienced cost increases that it is not able to pass on to customers. Selling, general and administrative costs have been increasing, suggesting that management have not been effective in controlling costs. Decreasing amortization expenses suggest that there has not been significant investment in capital assets, which implies negative prospects for the future. The decreased interest expense in absolute terms could result from costs of financing older assets (where significant loan principal has been paid down) or lower interest rates. The improvement in 2006 is due to the unusual income item and thus the improvement should be interpreted carefully since ongoing costs have increased on a proportional basis over the three years for almost all accounts (except amortization and interest). The trend statements show that some expenses have increased (such as selling, general and administrative) and some expenses have decreased (such as cost of goods sold and amortization), suggesting that some costs are not being well controlled and other costs may be declining due to the company's declining market share or deferral of capital asset purchases. From 2004 to 2005, net income decreased because SG&A increased and sales decreased.

Without more details, it is not possible to arrive at a definite conclusion about the performance of the company. However, all the trends are consistent with a company that is declining and reducing capacity for future growth. The increased selling, general and administrative costs could reflect the costs of hiring additional sales representatives to turnaround sales, perhaps with the expectation that sales will increase while these costs remain relatively constant in future. With the decline of the company (as reflected by the deterioration of recurring revenue), there may be an incentive for management to time the one-time gain listed as unusual income. By visiting the firm and interviewing the owners you may find out key information in order to make better decisions.

c. It would be very misleading to assess the performance of the company without removing the unusual income from the analysis. With the inclusion of that amount in the analysis, the year-to-year comparisons are not meaningful nor are predictions of future profitability appropriate. Fortunately, the adjustment is easy to perform. Without the unusual income, the trend analysis would indicate a 50+% decrease in income before income taxes from 2004 to 2006 rather than the appearance of a turnaround. Similarly, the common size statements show that income before taxes and unusual items was 21% of sales in 2006, which is significantly lower than in the previous two years.

Note: Other "unusual events" may not be isolated. For example, the reduced gross margin in 2006 could have been caused by an unwise purchasing decision that required a significant segment of the inventory being sold at much lower prices than expected.

Solution to Study Problem 2

Note: the following answers assume that the event occurs on the day before the end of the period for which the financial statements are prepared. Also, it is necessary in some cases to make assumptions. You should recognize and make your assumptions explicit.

	Interest coverage	Receivables turnover	Price to earnings	Return on assets	Gross margin
a. Declaration and payment of dividends on common shares.	No effect	No effect	No effect	No effect	No effect
b. Write-off of an accounts receivable.	No effect (i)	No effect (ii)	No effect (iii)	No effect (iv)	No effect
c. Purchase of advertising costing $17,000.	Decrease (v)	No effect	Increase (vi.)	Decrease (vii.)	Increase
d. Sale of land that had a book value of $150,000 when it was sold.	Increase (viii)	No effect	Decrease	Increase (ix.)	No effect
e. Announcement of a lost contract with a long time customer. The announcement was unexpected by the capital markets.	No effect	No effect	Decrease (x.)	No effect	No effect
f. Write-off of obsolete inventory. The company does this each year.	Decrease (xi.)	No effect	Increase	Decrease	No effect

i. Assuming the use of the allowance method, income is not affected. When using the allowance method, management estimates the amount of receivables that will not be collected. When a company writes-off the receivable there is no effect on the net balance of Accounts Receivable (Accounts Receivable – Allowance for Uncollectibles) and also no effect on the income statement.

ii. Assuming that the average receivables amount is determined net of the allowance. However, be aware of the practical difficulties with applying the receivables turnover ratio. Credit sales are not usually disclosed in the financial statements.

iii. Assuming the allowance method, since the write-off does not directly trigger an expense. Since there is no effect on the income statement there is no effect to Earnings per share.

iv. Assets are unaffected, since the net carrying value of accounts receivables is not affected. Thus, the performance and operating efficiency of the company are not affected.

Profits are decreased. Successful advertising may create an asset for the company. Although measuring the value of advertising is extremely difficult. For this reason advertising costs are normally expensed.

vi. Earnings decrease (EPS will be lower) but the price is likely unaffected.

vii. The decrease in earnings is proportionately greater than the decrease in assets.

viii. An assumption is necessary as to whether the disposal generated a gain, loss, or was disposed of at book value. These responses assume a gain. The gain increases earnings.

ix. The gain results in a proportionally greater increase in earnings than in assets. The gain is the difference between the selling price (proceeds) of an asset and its book value.

x. The share price will decrease, since the announcement was not expected.

xi. Earnings will decrease.

Solution to Study Problem 3

a., b.

	2004	2005	2006
Beginning A/R	13,500	15,000	17,000
Ending A/R	15,000	17,000	18,750
Average A/R	14,250	16,000	17,875
Sales	190,000	201,250	218,750
% credit sales	60%	70%	80%
Credit sales	114,000	140,875	175,000
A/R turnover	8.00	8.80	9.79
Collection period	45.6	41.5	37.3

c. The firm appears to be managing its accounts receivable very well as they are, on average, collected more promptly each year.

d. It is not unusual that credit terms for business clients are as much as 60 days. By screening customers with more stringent criteria, receivables may be turned over faster (perhaps some slow paying clients were eliminated or newer, more reliable ones found). The firm may have:

1. Offered a discount to clients who pay their bills off early.
2. Clients may have been checked out with a credit reference agency.
3. Invoices may have been prepared and sent out promptly.
4. Penalties for late payment may have been strict.
5. Is the time limit for payment clearly stated?

To reduce the collection period, Golden can offer higher discounts, refuse to do business with slow-paying clients, require prepayment, or offer superior service levels to clients in exchange for prompt payment. The problem is that in a competitive market such as accounting services, all of the above actions are likely to reduce the profitability of the firm.

e. If the collection period was calculated based on total sales and not credit sales, the partnership's receivables turnover would appear to be deteriorating, so users of the financial statements would be misled. Net income would not be affected by the change in turnover since revenue is recognized on an accrual basis. Faster collection improves liquidity in that more cash is on hand.

Solution to Study Problem 4

a, b.

	2006	**2005**	**2004**	**2003**
asset turnover	1.409	.971	.711	.568
profit margin	.307	.280	.257	.240
return on assets	.433	.272	.183	.136
financial leverage	2.242	2.215	2.189	2.256
return on equity	.968	.602	.400	.308

c. The only way that the return on assets could exceed the return on equity is if equity is negative (so that liabilities would be greater than assets), which is unlikely.

d. The net income of the company has steadily increased over the four-year interval. In addition, profits relative to sales have also increased. The asset turnover has increased, meaning that sales have increased faster than total assets and assets are being used more efficiently to produce sales. Possible explanations include holding off on large capital investments that will benefit future years or fewer receivables. There could also be assets that are efficient or they have effectively managed expenses. The interpretation would differ significantly depending on the actual causes, which would be evident with complete financial statements. The financial leverage ratio decreased for a few years, indicating a decreased proportional use of debt in the capital structure. However, in 2005 the financial leverage started to increase possibly due to the use of more debt financing.

Solution to Study Problem 5

a.

	2005
Sales	$6,125,000
Average total assets	2,925,000
Net income	300,000
Interest expense	90,000
Income tax rate	0.25
After-tax interest cost	67,500

Profit margin = ($300,000 + 67,500)/6,125,000 = 6.00 %

Asset turnover = 6,125,000/2,925,000 = 2.09

Return on assets = .06 * 2.09 = 0.125

b. If average assets increase by 15% to $3,363,750, and sales increase 20% to $7,350,000 the asset turnover ratio will be 2.19. To achieve a return on assets of 25%, with an asset turnover ratio of 2.19, then

0.25 = 2.19 x profit margin

The profit margin = .114

With a profit margin of 11.4%, net income would be $770,400. (($6,125,000*1.20)*11.4% - $67,500)

c. The targets that she has set require an increase in sales of 20% while increasing the profit margin by 5.4% to 11.4%, which seems a rather difficult challenge. To improve ROA the company will have to show an improvement in the asset turnover (perhaps a smaller increase in assets would be required or a larger increase in sales could be achieved) or improve the company's profit margin (perhaps with more stringent cost control).